CISTERCIAN STUDIES SERIES: NUMBER TWO HUNDRED SIXTEEN

Brian E. Colless

The Wisdom of the Pearlers

An Anthology of Syriac Christian Mysticism

CISTERCIAN STUDIES SERIES: NUMBER TWO HUNDRED SIXTEEN

The Wisdom of the Pearlers

An Anthology of Syriac Christian Mysticism

Translated, with an Introduction,
by
Brian E. Colless

Cistercian Publications
Kalamazoo, Michigan

*The work of Cistercian Publications is made possible in part
by support from Western Michigan University
to the Institute of Cistercian Studies.*

Library of Congress: Cataloging-in-Publication Data

The wisdom of the pearlers : an anthology of Syriac christian mysticism /
translated, with an introduction, by Brian E. Colless.

  p.   cm. — (Cistercian studies series ; no. 216)
Includes bibliographical references and index.
ISBN 978-0-87907-316-9
  1. Mysticism—Syrian Church.   I. Colless, Brian.   II. Title.   III. Series.

BX177.15.W57 2007
230'.14—dc22

2007047657

Printed in the United States of America

Dedicated to my mother and father
Irene and Edric Colless
true treasurers of the Pearl

Table of Contents

ORIENTATION

When a book is completed, it is customary for the author to look back over it and produce a preface (a foreword for the reader, an afterword for the writer). In the present case, given the unfamiliarity of the ground to be traversed by the reader, some guidance is needed from the writer at the outset. The one who has found a way through the mazes of the field should try to help others to get their bearings. This is a book about eastern Christianity, more particularly the Syriac churches and their monastic and mystical life; for such an inscrutable oriental subject, orientation is required. Moreover, in all mystical traditions it is emphasized that the novice should not set out along the path without the assistance of a guide or a guru, to point out the landmarks and the pitfalls. Regrettably, the present writer is not that kind of spiritual leader: I have broken the strict ascetic rules, by having a wife, begetting offspring, and owning a house and a gramophone. Nevertheless, I can at least tell you how this book came about, and give you some practice in using its referencing system:

Roman numerals (XCIX) for the excerpts in the *anthology*,

plain Arabic numerals (99) for the paragraphs in the *introduction*,

bold Arabic numerals (**99**) for the items in the *bibliography*.

This tome has taken me several decades to put together, in the midst of many other duties and activities. It all began in 1964, in the course of my studies in Semitic languages and literatures, when I came across Jules Leroy's popularizing book on monks and monasteries of the Near East, translated from French (**19**). He opened my eyes to the amazing missionary expansion of the Syriac and Armenian churches (the Church of the East, the Syrian Orthodox Church, the Armenian Orthodox Church) into the furthest parts of Asia, as documented in a magisterial series of studies by Jean Dauvillier (now collected in a reprint volume). This topic, with particular reference to South-East Asia, was pursued further in my doctor of theology thesis, in the 1970s. Most of this work has been published serially, under the title 'The Traders of the Pearl', in the journal *Abr-Nahrain* (1970–1978).

Secondly, Leroy introduced me to Syriac Christian monasticism and mysticism, and in the late 1960s this became the subject of my doctor of philosophy dissertation, on the eighth-century mystic named John Saba of Dalyatha (**193**). After working for two years on this project, and being assured by everyone that nobody else in the world could possibly be doing the same thesis, I found that Robert Beulay in Paris was in fact editing and translating the same set of discourses by this monk. This led to some serious negotiation, in which I received the better bargain, and Beulay had to change to editing the epistles; but he produced some very useful results (**190, 191, 195, 196, 200, 184, 185**), including a general survey of Syriac Christian mysticism (**195b**), and a detailed study of the mystical theology of John of Dalyatha (**195a**). My contribution to the dissemination of knowledge about this wonderful mystic, whom we shall call John the Venerable in this anthology (LVI–XCV), is gradually being published (**8–12, 197–199, 206**).

The Syriac manuscripts that I used for this purpose were housed in such places as the British Museum and the Vatican Library, but they had originated from some of the monasteries visited and described by Leroy. The most important documents that I had (on microfilm) were from the Greek monastery of Saint Catherine in the wilderness of Sinai, and from the Coptic monastery of the Syrians (Der es-Suriani) in the Egyptian desert (Wadi en-Natrun, the ancient Sketis desert, south of Alexandria), where monasticism flowered, early in the fourth century. In January 1988, I went to both these monasteries as a tourist-pilgrim, with my wife Helen, and other members of a New Zealand university group. We were shown through the Syrian monastery, but did not see the monks' cells or the library, though we were taken to an empty but 'furnished' hermitage out in the desert. There we experienced showers from heaven, even though it 'never' rains in Egypt. It was a Friday when we presented ourselves at the gate of Saint Catherine's in Sinai, the day it is closed to visitors; so we were not able to see inside it, except from above, when we were on Mount Sinai.

The Sinai monastery stands at the foot of the mountain that is traditionally identified as the one where Moses spent forty days and forty nights fasting and communing mystically with God in the cloud of glory (Exodus 24:15-18), and where Moses and the elders of Israel were vouch-safed a divine vision, which was imbued with the colour of sapphire and of the clear sky (24:9-11). These two episodes became models for east-ern Christian mysticism. Moses' experience in 'the cloud of unknowing' is the basis for *The Mystical Theology* of the sixth-century Syrian writer who goes under the pseudonym Dionysios the Areopagite (par. 120 below), and the sapphire-blue vision is central to the spiritual teaching of Evagrios Pontikos, a fourth-century monk in the desert of Egypt (par. 71). These two mystical authors, Dionysios and Evagrios, were influential in the development of Christian mysticism, eastern and western alike.

My personal exposure (with snow on the one and rain on the other) to the mountains of Moses (Mount Sinai and Mount Nebo) was not of the same order of spirituality; and everything seemed to happen in reverse. Climbing Mount Sinai in the winter on an empty stomach was indeed an ascetic exercise, because of the extreme cold in the early morning darkness, though the ascent was not so much exertion as exhilaration, making me plummet to the summit; and watching the unclouded sunrise, a beautiful experience in itself, was not the true beatific vision (even though gazing at the sun is Dante's analogy for it in the *Paradiso*, at the end of *The Divine Comedy*). Conversely, it was on top of Mount Nebo, where Moses viewed the vast vista of the Promised Land (Deuteronomy 34), that I encountered 'the cloud of unknowing': neither the sun nor the scene came into view that day, because the mountain was clouded over. And not a single Syriac mysti-cal manuscript was set before my eyes in any church or monastery I visited, so I experienced no illuminations of any kind. I have only ever handled Syriac manuscripts in the Mingana collection of the Selly Oak Colleges Library in Birmingham. For the rest, it has been discs, microfilms, and photocopies; we live and work in a sanitized, not sanctified, world.

The task of editing and translating the writings of Syriac Christian mystics has been proceeding at a pace, rather than apace (4). Around the turn of the twentieth century, Paul Bedjan edited books by Isaac of Nineveh (153) and Gregory Bar Hebraeus (204), which were subse-quently translated into English by A. J. Wensinck, who provided useful introductions to each, examining the place of Syriac mysticism in religious history (155, 205). E. A. Wallis Budge's labours in this field (he was also working, among many other things, on Egyptian hieroglyphic and Akkadian cuneiform) produced an edition and translation of the spiritual discourses of Philoxenos of Mabbug (**124**), and also of the Syriac versions of books relating to the Egyptian desert monks (**40–42**). J. Gwynn introduced the English-speaking world to the 'demonstrations' of Aphrahat the Persian Sage (**81**), previously edited by J. Parisot (**80**), and also the hymns on faith by Ephrem the Syrian (**88**), later edited by Edmund Beck (**86**).

In 1926 Michael Kmosko presented the Latin-reading world with an edition of the Syriac *Liber Graduum*, The Book of Degrees (**96**), an important example of early mysticism, which he regarded as emanating from the sect known as the Messallians (or Messalians, or Eukhites), a group stressing the power and importance of prayer. In my introduction (paragraphs 171–191) I explore the hypothesis that it was written by Adelphios of Edessa, a prominent Messallian; this could be one reason for its having been transmitted anonymously in Syriac monasteries.

In 1927 F. S. Marsh issued an edition and translation of another somewhat heterodox work, the remarkable Book of Hierotheos (**135**), attributed to the teacher of Dionysios the Areopagite, but actually by Stephen Bar Sudaili, a sixth-century mystic of Edessa.

In the 1930s, more of the treasures hidden in this field were brought to light. Alphonse Mingana published his *Early Christian Mystics* (**2**, 1934), with the Syriac text and English translation of discourses by four previously obscure monks, of the seventh and eighth centuries, namely Simon Taibutheh, Dadisho Qatraya, Joseph (Abdisho) Hazzaya, Abraham Bar Dashandad.

In Sweden, Sven Dedering edited a dialogue on the human soul and its passions, attributed to John of Lykopolis by the Syriac scribes (**106**, 1936). Irénée Hausherr published a French translation of it as being by John the Solitary (**107**, 1939), and he went on to demonstrate that this was the fourth-century Syrian mystic named John of Apamea (**118–119**). In the following decades L.G. Rignell, another Swedish editor, added to this corpus (**108**, 1941; **109**, 1960). Werner Strothmann gave us another collection of John's dialogues and discourses in 1972, with German translation (**110**); and René Lavenant prepared a French translation, which came out in 1984 (**111**). All this Johannine meat is sandwiched between two slices of spiritual bread: Wensinck's publication of a small piece on the spiritual state of the soul (**112**, 1923), and Sebastian Brock's edition of a tract on prayer (**115**, 1979).

Hausherr also produced an edition and Latin version of a book on holy contemplation by Gregorios the Hermit of Cyprus (**143**, 1937), and a number of valuable articles, which have been collected in two volumes (**17–18**). He was interested in the spiritual writings of Philoxenos of Mabbug (**126**, **128**), and he encouraged René Lavenant to publish an edition of the letter to Patriq of Edessa (**127**), in the series *Patrologia Orientalis*.

In the collection known as *Corpus Scriptorum Christianorum Orientalium*, René Draguet has issued the Syriac recensions of the *Asketikon* of Esaias of Sketis (Abba Isaiah) (**62**), and also Syriac commentaries on it by Dadisho Qatraya (**172**) and Joseph Hazzaya (or so it seems to me, **182**). André de Halleux has provided an edition and French translation of The Book of Perfection by Sahdona-Martyrios (**145**). For the same series, Arthur Vööbus has written a history of asceticism in the Syrian Orient (**25–27**).

Joseph Hazzaya (so named in two previous paragraphs, and to be known in this anthology as Joseph the Visionary) wrote numerous epistles and discourses, but for various reasons they were not always transmitted under his own name. Thus, in 1950 Gunnar Olinder published what he believed to be a letter of Philoxenos of Mabbug on the three degrees of the spiritual life (**179**), but this is now known to be a work of Joseph. The search for lost works of Joseph the Visionary is now being conducted with vigour (**180–189**), and in 1982 Gabriel Bunge published a German translation of a goodly number of them (**178**).

Mention may now be made of syriacists I have met personally, who have made a contribution to this area of research. Sebastian Brock and I once had a short encounter at Selly Oak in Birmingham, and I have since plied him with queries. Robert Beulay and I had a long correspondence by mail, but unfortunately he was not among the happy company I met in Paris at the 29th Congress of Orientalists in 1973. François Graffin, who showed me great kindness during my stay, has produced French translations of a number of relevant texts (**87**, **180**, **183**). Antoine Guillaumont asked me some questions that I am still pondering; he gave me offprints of many of his articles, which aided my understanding of The Book of Degrees and its alleged Messallianism (see especially **100**), and his studies on Evagrios and other Egyptian monks are most enlightening (**15**, **54–58**). Paul Harb has shown that Joseph Hazzaya is the real author of the letter on the three degrees attributed to Philoxenos (**181**). Louis Leloir has studied Tatian's *Diatessaron*, and the spirituality of the desert ascetics, and he has elucidated the monastic thought of Ephrem and Sahdona (Martyrios) **(94)**. Bernard Outtier, who studies Armenian translations of Syriac literature, has given me insights into Ephrem's mysticism.

In my doctoral study of Syriac mysticism, from 1966 to 1969 at the University of Melbourne, I was greatly encouraged by my supervisor, John Bowman, then Professor of Middle Eastern Studies, and also by John Arthur Thompson, my first tutor in Hebrew and Aramaic. In 1965 Donald Broadribb introduced me to the Syriac Song of the Pearl, or Hymn of the Soul, which has become the first selection in this anthology (I–XIII). Twenty years later I met Paul-Hubert Poirier, the author of an exhaustive study of the various interpretations proposed for the poem (35). It is surely a parable of the human condition, and since it is allegorical you can read into it whatever you want to find there. A Buddhist might see the Buddha in its hero (like Gautama, a prince who leaves his palace behind), and find the Buddha's enlightenment in the snatching of the pearl from the serpent, and the Buddha's attainment of Nirvana in the prince's homecoming. Manicheans could, and did, interpret it as the life of their prophet Mani. However, while it is quite possible that Buddhism and Manicheism influenced Christian monasticism (par. 164–166, 205–208), and although the poem is generally presumed to be Gnostic, a case can be made for its orthodoxy **(36)**. There is no difficulty in construing it as a symbolic presentation of the Apostles' teaching on the course of the Christian life, constructed along the lines of the parable of the prodigal son (Luke 15:11-31), in combination with the parable of the pearl (Matthew 13:45-46); this approach will be worked out in detail here (par. 11–59). And since Syriac Christian mystics saw themselves as putting the Apostles' teachings into practice, there should be considerable parallelism between the details of the poem and the words of these monks. There may even be echoes of the poem itself in the writings of Abraham Bar Dashandad (par. 271–278), John the Solitary of Apamea (par. 194–198), and the Syrian monk whose spiritual homilies have been preserved in Greek (and also in Syriac translation, **65**) under the pseudonym Makarios the Great (par. 103–116).

A New Zealand monk did his doctoral dissertation on Pseudo-Makarios, at the Pontificia Universitas Gregoriana, and through contact with Syriac scholars (such as Jean Gribomont and Vincent Desprez) he learned to his surprise that there was a syriacist named Brian Colless at

Massey University, not too many miles distant from his own Southern Star Abbey, the Cistercian monastery of New Zealand. I had come from Australia in 1970 to inaugurate religious studies (phenomenology of religion) at Massey University in Palmerston North. When he returned from Rome he made a point of looking me up. This was Anthony Paul Clarkson, Father Benedict, and in the preface to his thesis (**74**) he says that "the *Spiritual Homilies* attributed to Macarius the Egyptian" caught his interest "because of the rich pneumatology contained in them and because John Wesley, the founder of Methodism had been greatly influenced by them". I myself am a Methodist, and we both had an interest "in the history of early monasticism, in ecumenical questions, and in the relationship between dogmatic and spiritual theology", all of which he had brought to his thesis on early Christian spirituality. A few years later I was sitting on the slopes of Mount Egmont (Maori name Taranaki, one of New Zealand's volcanic mountains), listening to the radio and looking at Taranaki's sunny, snowy peak (which had been hiding its glory under a cloud most of the time), when Father Benedict's death was announced on the national news. I was deeply saddened by this loss of a kindred spirit.

In the published part of his dissertation (**74**), Anthony Clarkson considers the innumerable titles and metaphors applied to Christ by Makarios, notably Master, Father, King, Physician, Savior, Redeemer, Pilot, Rider, Charioteer, Farmer, Craftsman, Foundation, Rock, and Pearl. Such role and metaphor theology has an abiding attraction for me. Robert Murray has investigated its manifestations in early Syriac Christian literature, such as the mysterious Odes of Solomon (not considered here), the Acts of Thomas, the Book of Degrees, Aphrahat, and Ephrem (**20**, *Symbols of Church and Kingdom*). In the present anthology, the *pearl* motif has pride of place, and the *treasure* metaphor is also prominent. The index (which also functions as a glossary) will lead the searcher to many others.

When I was wondering where to get a book such as this published, it was Anthony Clarkson who told me about Cistercian Publications in Kalamazoo. He informed the Editorial Director of my existence, and I immediately found myself on her Christmas card list. Rozanne Elder has since shown immense graciousness and forbearance towards me; I have lost count of the Christmas cards she has sent me; to her fellow-workers they serve as gentle reminder or stern rebuke. From Oxford's great Syriac scholar, Sebastian Brock, she has garnered an anthology of *The*

Syriac Fathers on Prayer and the Spiritual Life (1; Cistercian studies series, 101), and mine will be a companion volume to his. Many of the things stated in his introduction have been left unsaid in mine; you might therefore need to read both books at the same time to achieve a full stereoscopic picture. A difference between these two anthologies is that one has complete pieces expounding the same theme (prayer), whereas the other has short excerpts to illustrate the use of the pearl symbol, and also (together with many other extracts in the introduction) to show the typical features of Syriac mysticism. One worrying aspect, to me, is the apparent lack of humour in any of these excerpts. Laughter was, however, not absolutely forbidden to these monks. In his rule for novices, John the Venerable tells them not to show their teeth when laughing. The laughter we encounter in Simon Taibutheh ('Simon of his grace') is derisory and directed at himself (XXVIII), but there must have been some good-humoured chuckling amongst all the deadly seriousness. There was surely wit amid the wisdom.

The book by Jules Leroy (**19**), which started me on this road, was borrowed from a public library in Tasmania. Somewhere along the way I looked at the French original of 1958. Here at the end of the journey I possess my own copy of it, given to me by my colleague Renée Turner, just before her death in 1988. Renée would have asked concerning that book and mine: What about the nuns, Brian? (She had done a thesis on Buddhist nuns). She would also have looked for a counterpart to Sufism's Rabi'a, the eighth-century woman mystic of Basra (**23**, 185–188, 218–225). This book can only offer 'the daughters of the covenant' (par. 132, 164) and Shirin (par. 232). Note, however, that Syriac Christians regard the Holy Spirit as Mother, as well as Paraklete (par. 19). But there are women workers in this field: Margaret Smith (**23**), Margot Schmidt (**22**), Benedicta Ward (**39**), Claire Guillaumont (**57**), and Micheline Albert. To my other colleagues, Enid Bennett, Peter Donovan, Bronwyn Elsmore, I tender my thanks for their listening ears. Sharon Cox, who tastefully typewrote most of the manuscript (over a very long period in which the technology kept changing), can claim the dubious privilege of being the first person to have read this book.

There will be a fair measure of culture shock for those who enter this treasury of pearls and peruse its introductory manual. This is unavoidable; there is no ecstasy without effort, no mystical experience without ascetic labour. One indication that you are moving in a different world will be the personal names: they are not in comfortingly familiar Latinized form (Evagrius Ponticus) but are given in their eastern, Hellenized mode (Evagrios Pontikos), and their Syriac originals (Patriq or Patrikios, not Patricius or Patrick; Sahdona or Martyrios, not Martyrius). However, a few Latinisms and Anglicisms have escaped through the net (Bar Hebraeus, John, Joseph, Simon, Stephen).

This book is dedicated to my mother and father, Irene and Edric Colless, who provided the resources for my secular and spiritual education. They have both passed on, but they firmly and faithfully believe that they are still alive, so it is not a case of *in memoriam*.

Brian Colless

Shalom/Shelama/Salaam/Peace
Palmerston North, Aotearoa/New Zealand, 2007

THE MYSTIC PEARLERS

1   A PEARLER is a pearl fisher or a pearl trader, a person who dives for pearls or deals in pearls. The pearlers we shall meet in this book were early monks of Syria, Mesopotamia, and Persia. They were mystical pearl-divers and pearl-merchants who searched for spiritual pearls. In the words of one of their number, John the Venerable, in the eighth century: 'These precious pearls are gathered and stored among the treasures of his mind by the *merchant* who is occupied with prayer, the strenuous *diver* captivated with desire for the sea that washes him' (LXXVII). His contemporary in the eighth century, Joseph the Visionary, spoke of the ascetic exercises of the solitary monk as 'the labour of the *merchant* up to the time when the *pearl* of great price falls into his hands' (XLVIII). And in the seventh century, Isaac of Nineveh said: 'The *diver* plunges naked into the sea to find a pearl; and the wise monk will go naked through the desert places to find the Pearl, Jesus Christ himself' (XXXIV).

2   Their quest thus led them out into the wilderness, to a state of silent solitude in remote caves and hermitages. In their desert cells these Syriac Christian monks sought to achieve purity of soul, enlightenment of mind, and spiritual union with God by following a typical mystical path of purification, illumination, and unification. We call these Christian monks 'Syriac' because that is the name of the language they spoke: Syriac is a Christian dialect of Aramaic, the mother tongue of Jesus and his disciples, and it became the literary and liturgical language of the churches of ancient Palestine, Syria, Iraq, and Iran.

3   Long confined to their mountain seclusion or desert isolation, many of these mystical pearlers never set eyes on the sea, nor ever watched pearl divers plunging into the ocean, or observed merchants embarking on ships to seek rare treasures on distant shores. Nevertheless, in contrast to the ascetics of the Egyptian monastic tradition

of Saint Antony, Syriac Christian monks were not entirely averse to travelling. Some became missionaries and carried their faith to India and China. Some had been merchants before they put on monastic garb: a seventh-century merchant named Bar Sahdé was miraculously rescued from the clutches of pirates while on a trading voyage to India, and in gratitude to God he entered a monastery on his return home. And the legendary founder of Persian Christian monasticism, Eugenios of Nisibis or Mar Awgin, is portrayed as a pearl fisher from Egypt. The story goes that for twenty-five years he lived on an island in the Suez Gulf, diving for pearls and distributing the proceeds to the poor; after visiting the monks of Sketis in the desert of Egypt, and having been commissioned by Pakhomios (Pachomius), he took seventy followers to Nisibis in Persia. There, on neighbouring Mount Izla (or Izala), he founded a monastery.

4   If this story were true, Eugenios would have been a notable exception to the stay-at-home rule that had long held sway in Egypt. From time immemorial the ancient Egyptians had believed that the valley of the Nile was the only place in which to live and die so as to live anew for eternity. Thus in *The Tale of Sinuhe* an Egyptian of the twentieth century BCE flees to Syria, and there becomes the leader of a nomadic tribe. But he abandons this unstable existence and returns home to serve his pharaoh, who grants him a modest pyramid-tomb to ensure everlasting life for him. The Egyptian ideal was stability: staying in your appointed place in the kingdom of the pharaoh during your lifetime, and abiding in your tomb to serve the god Osiris in the afterlife. This model apparently passed over into Egyptian Christian monasticism: its monks persisted in their cells, expecting to take up eventual residence in a heavenly mansion in the presence of the Lord Jesus Christ.

5   This attitude contrasts with the mentality in the lands of the Tigris and Euphrates rivers, where a peripatetic pattern had been set in *The Epic of Gilgamesh*, dating perhaps from the twentieth century BCE. The hero, Gilgamesh, is stricken with grief at the death of his friend Enkidu. Wrapping himself in an animal skin he roams over the desert and across the ocean in quest of eternal life. His long search brings him to a paradise called Dilmun, where the Mesopotamian counterpart of Noah (here known as Utnapishtim

or Atrakhasis) dwells in everlasting bliss with his wife after having survived the great flood. On the advice of Utnapishtim, Gilgamesh ties some heavy stones to his feet and dives to the bottom of the sea. There he obtains a plant which imparts renewed life to anyone who eats it. Almost immediately Gilgamesh loses the elixir to a snake, which consumes it and gains the power to slough its skin annually. Dilmun is thought to be the Persian Gulf island now known as Bahrain, where men still dive, in the manner of Gilgamesh, to bring pearls up from the sea floor.

6   The teachings of *The Epic of Gilgamesh* are not compatible with Christian doctrines. The admonition of a barmaid named Siduri encapsulates one of its messages:

> Gilgamesh, where are you hurrying to?
> The life you are seeking you will not find.
> When the gods created humankind,
> to humans they allotted death,
> but life they kept in their own hands.
> Gilgamesh, let your belly be filled,
> make merry by day and by night. . . .
> Cherish the little one holding your hand,
> and let your wife enjoy your embrace.

7   This bears a remarkable resemblance to Ecclesiastes 9:7-9, but such exhortations to eat, drink, and be merry were not followed by Christ's apostles. Saint Paul affirmed in this regard that the resurrection of Christ had set a new pattern: 'for as in Adam all die, so in Christ shall all be made alive'; but 'if the dead are not raised then let us eat and drink, for tomorrow we die' (I Cor 15:22, 32, quoting Is 22:13). In saying this, Paul was certainly not advocating debauchery; nor was he suggesting strict asceticism, making the Christian life a continual round of fasting, vigil, and austerity. Yet as early as Tatian in the second century this became the typical Syriac Christian attitude. Known in western church history as a student of Justin Martyr and as the founder of a Christian school in Rome, Tatian was abstemious in the extreme, banning marriage entirely and forbidding the drinking of wine. His ascetic teaching is called Encratism, and his famous *Diatessaron* (harmony of the four

Gospels) emphasizes Encratistic ideals of celibacy, poverty, and homelessness.

8   This pattern of abstinence continued into the fourth century with Julian Saba, who lived in a cave near Edessa, allegedly eating only one meal a week to sustain him in his daily cycle of psalm-singing, meditation, and instruction of disciples. Furthermore, Julian's followers were expected to emulate him as a wanderer. He was constantly on the move, journeying into the desert for periods of prayer, as far as Mount Sinai, where he built a chapel.

9   The Syriac Christian life-style was apparently not derived from the example of Jesus, who is portrayed in the Gospels as homeless and poor, but also as one who 'came eating and drinking' to such an extent that he was stigmatized as 'a man gluttonous and wine-bibbing' (Lk 7:34). Rather, it found a more rigorous model in John the Baptizer, who 'came eating no bread and drinking no wine' (Lk 7:33) but lived on 'locusts and wild honey' in the wilderness (Mk 1:4-6). (Tatian's *Diatessaron* puts John on a vegetarian diet of *milk* and honey.) By the same token the real paragon among the apostles was not Paul, the libertarian hero of the Acts of the Apostles, who said 'all things are lawful' (1 Cor 6:12; 10:23), but Thomas, the austere and abstinent hero of the Syriac world's own hagiographic work, *The Acts of the Apostle Judas Thomas*. No longer a 'doubting Thomas' but someone who accepts Jesus as Lord and God (Jn 20:24-28), Thomas the apostle is sent by Jesus to the East, to the Iranian and Indian realms. The New Testament gives no hint of what Thomas did after making his avowal of the sovereignty and divinity of Christ, but these apocryphal *Acts* purport to fill this gap; and the indigenous churches of India have long maintained the tradition of his martyrdom in their land.

10   The Syriac ascetic ideal is admirably exemplified in the protagonist of the *Acts of Thomas*. He goes about doing good, healing the sick, driving out demons, giving alms to the poor, and imparting instruction; above all it is observed that he engages in frequent fasting and praying, eats only bread and salt, drinks only water, and wears only one garment. At a wedding feast for a princess he refuses to eat or drink, but he preaches that those who follow Christ will receive the food and drink of light and life. The bridal pair are urged

to preserve themselves from the 'filthy intercourse' of their marriage bed, and to prepare themselves for 'the true wedding feast' with the celestial Bridegroom, at which they will be 'numbered with those who enter into the bridal chamber' (cp. John the Venerable, LXXI below). It is not Judas Thomas himself who admonishes the couple here, but 'our Lord in the likeness of Judas', who says to them, 'I am not Judas, but I am the brother of Judas'.

THE SONG OF THE PEARL

11 The idea of being a brother of Christ and being one with him takes us into the mystical realm, as does the image of entering the bridal chamber in which the believer's soul is seen as the beloved of the Bridegroom. The notion of the believer's kinship with the Son of the King of kings is brought out exquisitely in a poem embedded in one Syriac manuscript of the *Acts of Thomas*. This is *The Song of the Pearl*, also known as *The Hymn of the Soul* (I–XIII below).

12 The context of the song is the imprisonment of the apostle Thomas in India. To comfort himself and his fellow-prisoners, Judas Thomas chants this hymn, though its relevance to that situation is not clear. One possibility is that just as the hero of the poem has been sent into Egypt to perform the task of snatching a pearl from the clutches of a sea monster, so the apostle has been sent into the equally benighted land of India to rescue souls from the jaws of death (cp. Ephrem, XVI). Notice in passing that India is in fact mentioned in the poem as a source of rubies (I).

13 A commonly held opinion on *The Song of the Pearl* is that it portrays the Gnostic redeemer myth: the hero-prince is the saviour who himself needs to be saved ('the saved saviour'), but he is able to pass on his saving knowledge (*gnosis*) to those who turn to him.

14 To me it seems more appropriate to take the poem as referring to Everyman, or more particularly everyone who comes to the knowledge of Christ. On this interpretation it is a parable of the Christian way, a 'Pilgrim's Progress' from the City of Destruction to the

Celestial City. A prime difficulty with this theory, however, is that the poem begins with a descent from the heavenly kingdom to the material world, which are symbolized by Persia and Egypt respectively; and while this might fit the career of Christ (Jn 1:1-14), it is not readily applicable to the origin of an ordinary human soul. The preexistence of the soul is not a biblical doctrine, although it gained currency in Christian theology under the influence of Plato and the Alexandrian theologian Origen. Even so, it is not necessary to see a prior existence for the soul in this allegory, any more than in the parable of the prodigal son (Lk 15:11-32); in each case the son leaves his father's home and receives a splendid garment on his return. Given that 'those whom God foreknew he also foreordained to be conformed to the image of his Son' (Rom 8:29), and that 'God chose us in Christ before the foundation of the world' (Eph 1:4), the Christian can in some sense be seen as already in the heavenly kingdom with the Father from the beginning (cp. paragraph 195).

15   On the assumption that *The Song of the Pearl* is an allegory of the Christian's pilgrimage through life, an attempt will be made here to identify its details with doctrines and persons in the Christian Scriptures.

16   The hero of the poem lives as a child in his father's luxurious palace (I). The *kingdom* is clearly the Persian or Parthian empire, established on 'the heights of Hyrcania' (X), and it represents the kingdom of 'our Father in Heaven' (Mt 6:9-10), which is especially concerned with children (Mt 19:14; Lk 18:16).

17   The *father* is 'the King of kings' (VI, XI), the Iranian emperor in his 'homeland the East' (I), ruler over the realm of light (VIII, 'the light of our home, the East'). Likewise God, 'the King of kings and Lord of lords, . . . dwells in unapproachable light' (I Tim 6:16). This idea of God dwelling in a cloud of glory and in unapproachable light will feature prominently in later Syriac mysticism (cp. John the Venerable, LXIII, LXIV, LXXI, LXXII, LXXV, LXXXVIII).

18   The elder *brother* (II) is identifiable as Jesus, 'the firstborn among many brothers' (Rom 8:29; cp. paragraph 104). He is also 'viceroy' (VI) and 'second in rank' to the king (II,VI,VIII), and he is hailed as 'the splendour of my father' (XIII); it is Christ who is seated 'at the right hand of the Majesty on high' as 'the effulgence of his glory' (Heb 1:3; cp. John the Venerable, LIX and LXIII, 'Christ the splen-

dour of the Father'). Jesus Christ also appears as the prince's companion in Egypt (IV), as will be shown below.

19   The *mother* is 'Queen of the East' (VIII) or 'Mistress of the East' (VI), who works with the father on the upbringing of the child (I, II, V, X). In the early Syriac Christian world-view the Divine Mother was the Holy Spirit of God (cp. paragraph 104). This imagery stems from the fact that the Aramaic or Syriac word for 'spirit' (*ruḥ*) is of feminine gender; in the Syriac versions of the Bible, 'the Spirit *herself* bears witness with our spirit that we are sons of God' (Rom 8:17). This femininity of the Holy Spirit (also called the 'Spirit of Holiness' in Syriac) has generated some remarkable images of suckling at divine breasts (LVIII, XCI, John the Venerable; CXXXV, Gregory Bar Hebraeus). In *The Song of the Pearl*, the Spirit also appears in a male guise as the Paraklete, represented by an eagle (VII); on this subject more will be said below.

20   The younger son enjoys the great *wealth* possessed by his parents (I). On the spiritual plane this would refer to the riches of God's grace: 'the God and Father of our Lord Jesus Christ has blessed us with every spiritual blessing in the heavenly regions . . . has destined us to sonship . . . according to the riches of his grace, which he has lavished upon us' (Eph 1:3-8). From his parents' treasury the child is given some of these riches to take with him on his perilous journey (I). These would be spiritual gifts, 'gifts bestowed by God' (1 Cor 2:12). These treasures (gold, silver, rubies, agates) are presumably for his support and strengthening (adamant): 'the Father . . . grant that you be strengthened with power through his Spirit in your being, out of the riches of his glory' (Eph 3:14-17). The girding with adamant is reminiscent of God making the forehead of the prophet Ezekiel 'like adamant, harder than flint' to enable him to confront his adversaries (Ezk 3:9). The equipping of the lad is analogous to putting on 'the whole armour of God, in order to be able to stand against the wiles of the devil' (Eph 6:10-17).

21   The *load* that the child carries is light and easy to bear (I). In fact, the words for 'load' and 'light' here are the same as in Matthew 11:30 in the Syriac New Testament, where Jesus speaks of his yoke being easy and his burden light.

22   The parents make a *covenant* with the lad and write its words on his heart (II), a counterpart to the new covenant with God to

be inscribed on the hearts of the people of God so that they do not forget it (Jer 31:31-34; 2 Cor 3:2-6; Heb 10:15-16). The stipulation of the agreement is that the prince should acquire a pearl in Egypt. The boy is to receive a reward for the performance of this task; thus he will be 'laying up treasure' for himself, not on earth but 'in heaven, where moth and weevil do not spoil' (Mt 6:19-21). The destructive 'moth' is relevant here because the reward is a specially tailored *shining robe* and a *scarlet toga* (II, VI, X, XI, XIII). There is no actual word for 'robe' in the text, merely a single word meaning 'shining thing' (*zahitha*); but it is obviously something worn as a garment. It is a widely attested practice that kings give presents of fine clothing to faithful servants. This is reflected in Isaiah 61, where the Lord declares that he will 'faithfully give their recompense and make an everlasting covenant with them', and he clothes them with 'the robe of righteousness' and 'the garments of salvation' (8,10). Peter tells his readers of 'an inheritance which is imperishable and undefiled and unfading, kept in heaven' for them (1 Pt 1:4). Christian martyrs 'were each given a white robe' (Rev 6:11). Jesus affirms that in the end 'the righteous shall shine forth like the sun in the kingdom of their Father' (Mt 13:43), a picture to be compared with the pearl-hero returning to his father's palace, wearing his glistening robe and his lustrous toga (II, XIII; cp. paragraph 106).

23   The child is required to go down into Egypt. In biblical theology Egypt had been viewed, from the time of the Exodus onwards, as a place of bondage (Ex 2:23,13:3) and death (Ex 12:29-30); and when the child arrives there, he does indeed fall into bondage under an Egyptian king (V, VI) and into a death-like sleep (V). Egypt would represent the world; 'friendship with the world is enmity with God' (Jm 4:4), and one should keep oneself 'untarnished by the world' (Jm 1:27). Speaking of his followers, Jesus says that 'the world has hated them because they are not of the world' (Jn 17:14); the boy in the poem is concerned about being hated by the Egyptians as a stranger and an outsider (IV); the ancient heroes of faith were likewise 'foreigners and exiles on the earth' (Heb 11:13; cp. 1 Pt 2:11).

24   In Egypt the prince is to confront a hissing *serpent* (II, III, VIII); the obvious biblical counterpart is 'the great dragon, that ancient serpent, who is called Devil and Satan' (Rev 12:9). The serpent is 'in the midst of the ocean' (II), and of the many scriptural references

to sea monsters, one seems very pertinent: 'Behold I am against you, Pharaoh, king of Egypt, the great dragon lying in the midst of his streams' (Ezk 29:3).

25   Having established the identity of the King of kings as God the Father, the Queen of the East as the Holy Spirit, the elder son as Jesus Christ, and the younger son as 'Christian' setting out on his pilgrimage-quest, we now need to identify the other characters.

26   The child is accompanied on his journey to Egypt by two *guardians* (III). The concept of 'guardian angels' can be invoked here, as found in the saying of Jesus on not despising 'little ones', for 'in heaven their angels continually behold the face of my heavenly father' (Mt 18:10). Angels are 'ministering spirits' for those 'who are to inherit salvation' (Heb 1:14). In this instance the two guardians might be the two archangels named in the Bible: Gabriel (Dn 9:21, Lk 1:19) and Michael, who fights for the people of God (Dn 10:21, 12:1), 'contending with the Devil' (Jude 9) and 'fighting against the dragon' (Rev 12:7).

27   After the pearl has been won from the serpent, the shining robe is brought by two *treasurers* (X–XI). These seem to be distinguished from the two guardians, as special trustworthy treasurers (X), 'two yet one in likeness, for one sign of the king was marked on both' (XI), who were commissioned to deliver the 'bright ornamented robe'. At the transfiguration of Jesus, when 'his garments became white as light', Moses and Elijah were in attendance (Mt 17:1-8); and they were perhaps 'the two witnesses', who are 'the two olive trees and the two lampstands standing before the Lord of the earth', and who confront the Beast from the abyss (Rev 11). Alternatively, since the term 'treasurer' (*gezabra*) is used by Ephrem as a title for Christ himself and also for bishops, it is possible that the picture here is of the baptized neophyte being welcomed into the church by his Lord and his bishop, or by Christ and the Spirit of Christ (cp. paragraph 141). If we allow that the poem is to be interpreted on more than one level, then various interpretations are applicable here.

28   On arriving in Egypt, the child encounters a free-born person, a fellow-countryman from the East (IV), who is described as 'a *consecrated* person', literally 'a son of unction', from the Syriac root (*m-sh-ḥ*) which produces the word Messiah ('anointed'), translated

into Greek as Christ (Khristos). The Epistle to the Hebrews has some enlightening points here: 'God has anointed you with an anointing of gladness over your fellows' (Heb 1:9, quoting Ps 45:7 [8], with reference to Jesus 'the Son'. Note that the word for 'fellows' in the Syriac version is the same as for 'partner' in the poem). This enigmatic figure would thus be Jesus the Christ, with whom the believer is united: 'a consecrated person, who came and joined me' (IV).

29   In the New Testament, Jesus goes to Egypt as an infant in his birth story (Mt 2:14-15); and here in the poem Christ would be in 'Egypt', the material world, performing his work of salvation for his brethren: 'Here am I, and the children that God has given me' (Heb 2:13, Is 8:18); 'since therefore the children share in flesh and blood, he himself likewise shared the same nature, so that through death he might destroy the one who has the power of death, namely the Devil' (Heb 2:14, and here the Syriac term for 'share' is the same as in 'a partner to share in my pursuits'). Further, 'he had to be made like his brethren in everything, so that he might become a merciful and faithful high priest'; and 'because he himself has suffered and been tempted, he is able to help those who are tempted' (Heb 2:17-18). The mention of 'high priest' reminds us that the same writer compares Jesus with a priest-king named Malkisedeq (Melchizedek, Gen 14:17-20; Heb 7:1-10), who appears mysteriously and then disappears from the scene, as does this enigmatic figure in the poem (IV).

30   The hero gives his companion an *admonition* (or should it be the other way round?) 'against the Egyptians, against joining with the unclean' (IV). Similarly, the Hebrew Christians are warned against 'falling away from the living God' through 'an evil unbelieving heart', for if they are to 'share in Christ', they must 'exhort one another every day' not to be 'hardened by the deceitfulness of sin', as happened to the Israelites who had lived in Egypt (Heb 3:12-18). A typical apostolic exhortation runs: 'Be aware of this, that no immoral or impure person . . . has any inheritance in the kingdom of Christ and of God; . . . do not associate with them' (Eph 5:5-7).

31   If the 'consecrated person' ('son of unction') is the earthly counterpart of the heavenly Christ, elsewhere presented as the second in rank to the king, and as elder brother of the prince (II, VI), then

the younger brother's failure to recognize him is perhaps to be explained by people's inability to recognize Jesus after his resurrection (Jn 20:14, Lk 24:16); or simply by John's assertion that 'the true light that enlightens everyone . . . was in the world . . . and the world did not know him' (Jn 1:9-10).

32　　At this stage of the narrative (IV–V) the young prince certainly becomes a man of 'the world', adopting the *food and dress* of the Egyptians. The Israelites of the Exodus had a hankering for Egyptian foods (Ex 16:3) and customs (Ex 32:1-6), which led them astray. Moreover, Moses warned them that when they were settled in Canaan and had plenty to eat, they might 'forget Yahweh, their God, who had brought them out of the land of Egypt, out of the house of bondage' (Dt 8:12-14). During the apostasy of 'the golden calf', they 'sat down to eat and drink, and then rose up to play' (Ex 32:6, 1 Cor 10:7).

33　　For his part, the pearl prince falls into an oblivious *sleep* and into bondage to a pharaoh (V–VI). He forgets his royal parents, as Israel forgot 'the Rock that begot' him and 'the God who gave birth' to him (Dt 32:18). While people sleep the enemy does his evil work in the dark (Mt 13:25), and the sleeping prince needs the Apostle's exhortations: 'Do not be conformed to this world ('age'), but be transformed, by the renewing of your mind' (Rom 12:2), and 'it is now time for you to wake out of sleep' (13:11).

34　　Everything that happened to the prince was 'perceived' by the king and queen, and they 'grieved' for him (V). The term translated 'grieved' (Syriac *hash*) is used in the New Testament for 'suffered', particularly of the passion of Christ (Heb 2:9,18; 1 Pt 2:23; Lk 22:15). The parents' awareness signifies the omniscience of God: 'God knows everything' (1 Jn 3:20). What is more, 'the Lord knows how to save from tribulation those who revere him' (2 Pt 2:9). The parents drew up a plan and sent their son something to rouse him from his death-like sleep, along these lines: 'Awaken your heart to righteousness and do not sin' (1 Cor 15:34, Syriac version; Greek 'sober up'). 'Awake and rise up from your sleep, and listen to the words of your letter', they say (VI).

35　　The instrument of awakening is a *letter* of reminder from the father, the mother, and the brother (V, VI, VII, IX). Compare the apostle Peter's statement: 'This is now the second letter that I have written to you, beloved, in both of which I have aroused your sincere mind by way of reminder' (2 Pt 3:1); the reminder is of the predictions of the prophets and the commandment of the Lord and Saviour, through the apostles (3:2). In his first epistle Peter speaks of the prophets foretelling the grace that would come to Christians (1 Pt 1:10), and the Gospel coming 'through the Holy Spirit sent from heaven, things that angels desire to look into' (1:12). The prophets, apostles, and angels might be related to 'the kings and princes of Parthia, and all the nobles of the East', who took part in the preparation of the letter for the prince (V). The letter would be the Bible, transmitted by the Holy Spirit (cp. paragraph 114).

36   The coming of the letter as a bird, bringing a reminder of sonship, is reminiscent of the descent of the Spirit of God, 'as a dove', at the baptism of Jesus, and the heavenly voice saying, 'This is my beloved son' (Mt 3:16-17). This possibly implies that we should look for *baptism* as well as the Holy Spirit at this point in the hymn. Accordingly, given that the letter was the prince's awakener (IX), that at the sound of its voice he rose from his sleep (VII), that it awoke him with its voice and led him with its light (IX), then what is believed to be an early baptismal formula (Eph 5:14) offers a baptismal connection for the letter of awakening and illuminating: 'Awake, you sleeper, rise up from the dead, and the Christ will give you light (or: will shine upon you)'. This occurs as a quotation in a context where Christians are described as formerly being 'darkness' but now being 'light in the Lord' and walking as 'children of light' (Eph 5:8), and being 'called to the one hope of your calling: one Lord, one faith, one baptism' (Eph 4:4-6).

37   This idea of *calling* has a counterpart in the *call* to return: the son is commanded to remember his mission and to return to the kingdom of his father (VI). In response he 'snatched up the pearl and turned to go home', not unlike the prodigal son in the parable (Lk 15:17-18). This summons compares with calling 'sinners to repentance' (Lk 4:32): 'Repent, for the kingdom of heaven is near' (Mt 3:2, 4:17); 'Repent and be baptized' (Acts 2:38).

38   Another pointer to baptism is the *invocation* over 'the fearsome hissing serpent' to put him to sleep (VIII). This seems to correspond

to the baptismal formula 'in the name of the Father, and of the Son, and of the Holy Spirit' (Mt 28:19; and also *Acts of Thomas*, paragraphs 27, 49, 121, 132, 157). No other order but Father, Son, and Spirit seems possible or permissible, and that is what is found at this point in the poem: 'the name of my father . . ., and the name of our second in rank, and of my mother the queen of the East' (VIII). Notice, however, that in the letter of awakening, the order is father, mother, brother (VI), which is a more natural sequence. And since the prescribed order of the baptismal formula is found in the invocation over the serpent at the point of awaking and grasping the pearl, it is reasonable to suspect another connection with baptism in this incident. (See also paragraphs 137–138 below.)

39   If the serpent is 'in the midst of the ocean' (II), then it would be necessary to enter the water in order to snatch the pearl (VIII); the *sea* would then represent the waters of baptism. If his body is thus 'washed with pure water' and his heart 'sprinkled clean from an evil conscience', then the prince is in a state of 'full assurance of faith' (Heb 10:22). And if he now desires to return home he must be 'cleansed by the washing of water with the word' (Eph 5:26), for 'unless one is born of water and the Spirit one cannot enter the kingdom of God' (Jn 3:5).

40   Coming out of the waters of baptism signifies being reborn. Hearing the summons of his awakening letter, the hero feels his *freedom* or 'freeborn nature' asserting itself, and he remembers his *royal birth* (VIII). This is Paul's concept of being 'called to freedom' (Gal 5:13; cp. 5:1), 'the glorious freedom of the children of God' (Rom 8:21). Paul also says that 'where the Spirit of the Lord is, there is freedom' (2 Cor 3:17).

41   In the Johannine writings of the New Testament 'the Spirit is there to bear witness, because the Spirit is the truth' (I Jn 5:7), and 'you will know the truth, and the truth will set you free' (Jn 8:32); 'the Spirit of truth will guide you into all truth' (Jn 16:13); 'the Advocate whom I will send to you from the Father, the Spirit of truth' (Jn 15:26), 'will teach you everything and remind you of everything I say to you' (Jn 14:26). This role of *reminding* is likewise the function of the letter: 'remember . . . call to mind . . . be mindful' (VI); 'I remembered . . .' (VIII). The prince finds that the testimony

of the letter tallies with what is written on his own heart; and it is
'the Spirit' that 'bears witness with our spirit that we are children
of God' (Rom 8:16).

42   At the baptism of Jesus the Holy Spirit took the form of a dove
(Mt 3:16), a feminine word in both Greek and Syriac; here it is an
eagle, 'the king of all winged creatures' (VII), a masculine figure.
This may be because the Advocate or Paraklete is deemed to be
masculine in the New Testament, in Greek and Syriac alike. Thus
in the Syriac Bible we see: 'The Paraklete, the Spirit of holiness, *he*
who is being sent by my Father in heaven' (Jn 14:26).

43   The *seal* placed on the letter by the right hand of the king for
protection against Babylonians and demons (VII) may mean the sign
of the cross, or the gift of the Holy Spirit: 'He has put his seal upon
us and given us his Spirit in our hearts as a guarantee' (2 Cor 1:22);
and 'you who have heard the word of truth . . . were sealed with
the promised Holy Spirit, the guarantee of our inheritance' (Eph
1:13-14), 'the Holy Spirit in whom you were sealed for the day of
redemption' (Eph 4:30).

44   The letter is first the prince's awakener and then his *guide*, drawing him on with love (IX). A passage in Galatians 5 has such a role
for the Holy Spirit: 'You were called to freedom' and 'love' (13),
therefore 'walk in the Spirit' (16) and 'be led by the Spirit' (18), for
'the fruit of the Spirit is love, joy, peace' (22), and 'those who belong
to Christ Jesus have crucified the flesh with its passions and desires'
(24). The awakened hero kisses the letter when it arrives, giving it
the Christian 'kiss of love' (1 Pt 5:14). In this regard Evagrios
Pontikos (a fourth-century monk who had an enormous influence
in the Syriac world) may help us to establish the symbolic signifi-
cance of the pearl and the shining robe; Evagrios says that '*faith* is
the beginning of *love*, but the end [or goal] of love is *knowledge* of
God' (see extract LII, where Joseph the Seer has love engendering
faith).

45   The *pearl* certainly symbolizes *faith* in the pearl songs among
Saint Ephrem's *Hymns on Faith*. 'In you', he says to the pearl, 'faith
is depicted in types and symbols' (Hymn 5.2; extract XVII.2 in the
selections below). The contest with the serpent for the precious
pearl (VIII) may therefore be compared with the following injunction: 'Fight the good fight of faith and take hold of eternal life, to

which you were called' (1 Tim 6:12). This refers in Scripture to victory over the passions and the things of the world; in the letters of the apostle John, anyone who 'is born of God overcomes the world, and this is the victory that overcomes the world, our faith' (1 Jn 5:4), in the context of 'the love of God' (5:1-3) and 'the Spirit as the witness' (5:7). The pearl of the poem might thus be not only the 'one very precious pearl' of the parable of the Kingdom (Mt 13:46), but also the 'one faith' of Paul's 'one Lord, one faith, one baptism' (Eph 4:5).

46   The saying of Evagrios on love, faith, and knowledge (cited above, paragraph 44) leads us to suspect that the heavenly robe might represent knowledge of God. In fact the *robe* not only shines but it also grows and has 'impulses of *knowledge* stirring all over it' (XII), perhaps in line with Daniel 12:3-4: 'The wise shall shine like the brightness of the firmament . . . and knowledge shall increase'. The robe also radiates *love* (XII), and the apostle Peter urges Christians to add to their faith a number of virtues, including knowledge and love, and more especially 'the knowledge of the one who called us to [or: by] his own glory and excellence, whereby he has granted us his precious and very great promises, and through these you may escape from the corruption that is in the world because of passion, and become partakers of the divine nature' (2 Pt 1:3-8). The 'precious and very great things promised' (1:4) and the 'abounding' virtues (1:8) might be represented by the precious *stones* and manifold *colours* with which the celestial garment was adorned and embroidered (XI).

47   Taking the *pearl* (VIII) means receiving faith, and accepting the *robe* (XIII) means receiving knowledge; these actions result in the attainment of 'the unity of *faith* and of *knowledge* of the son [or: Son] of God' (Eph 4:13), which constitutes 'perfect manhood', beyond 'childhood' and subjection to people's deceitful wiles (Eph 4:13-14). Similarly, the prince, the son of the king (I, VIII), is no longer a child (I) or the young wayfarer (III) with whom the worldly Egyptians 'dealt deceitfully' (IV).

48   The prince describes his robe as his 'deposit and wealth' (XI). This word *deposit* is used in this way in the New Testament: 'I know in whom I have believed and am persuaded that he is able to preserve my deposit for me for that day' (2 Tim 1:12 and 14).

49   'Their filthy abominable *clothing* I stripped off', says the prince,
after seizing the pearl (VIII). The removal of the Egyptian garb goes
with Paul's admonition: 'Put off your old human nature ['the old
person'], corrupted by deceitful passion . . . and put on your new
nature ['the new person'], created after the likeness of God' (Eph
4:22, 24; cp. paragraph 107). This last phrase leads on to an explanation of another aspect of the robe, namely 'the image of the king
of kings' that it bore (XI).

50   'You have put off the old nature ['person'] with its practices and
have put on the new one, which is being renewed in *knowledge* after
the *image* of its creator', the Apostle affirms (Col 3:9-10), and 'Christ
is all and is in all', he adds (3:11). All this is reminiscent of the *robe*
as a mirror with an image: 'it seemed like a mirror of myself; I beheld
its all in my own all, and I too encountered my own all in it; for
though we were two in distinction we were still one, in one likeness'
(X). Certainly the reference to the new nature 'renewed in knowledge after the image of its creator' (Col 3:10) equates with the
'impulses of knowledge' on the robe (XII) and 'the image of the
king of kings' embroidered over it (XI). Paul also declares; 'Just as
we have borne the image of the man of dust (Adam), we shall also
bear the image of the heavenly one (Christ)' (I Cor 15:49); moreover, 'we all reflect the glory of the Lord as in a mirror and are being
transformed into his image' (2 Cor 3:18). A connection between
a mirror and knowledge of God is made when Paul says, with reference to speaking and thinking like a child because of imperfect
knowledge: 'We now see in a mirror dimly, but eventually face to
face' (I Cor 13:12); this will be the experience of the prince when
he is reunited with his father the king (XIII). The 'mirror' passage
in the Epistle of James is worth noting here: 'If anyone is a hearer
of the word and not a doer, he is like a man who observes his
natural face in a mirror . . . and forgets what he is like; . . . but a
doer of action shall be blessed in his doing' (Jm 1:22-25). This may
throw light on the enigmatic speech of the robe itself: 'I am his who
is diligent in doing . . . and my size has been growing with his labours'
(XII).

51   This *growth* of the robe (XIII) might be connected with the injunction to 'grow in the grace and the knowledge of our Lord and

Saviour' (2 Pt 3:18). The *descent* of the shining garment (XII) may
be compared with a statement of James: 'Every perfect gift is from
above, coming down from the Father of the lights' (of heaven) (Jm
1:17). This gift is sent by the prince's 'parents' from 'the heights'
(X), but also by Christ: 'the splendour of my father . . . had sent
it to me' (XIII; cp. paragraph 141).

52   The original promise to the prince was: 'with your brother . . .
you shall be heir in our kingdom' (II,VI). Throughout the final scene
(XIII) the elder brother appears as the *splendour* of the father, who
welcomes him home. We have illumination on this point from John
the Venerable: he speaks of 'Christ, the splendour of the Father'
(LXIII). In the Epistle to the Hebrews, the 'Son' whom God 'appointed as heir of all things' is 'the *effulgence* of his glory' (1:2-3).
He is 'superior to angels' (1:4), and therefore 'all God's angels worship him' (1:6); these would be the *servants* who sing the praises of
the viceroy, the elder brother (XIII). Jesus Christ is 'the light of the
world' (Jn 1:9, 8:12, 9:5); and 'the light of the knowledge of the glory
of God' is 'in the face of Jesus Christ' (2 Cor 4:6); thus, as 'the
splendour of the father' he provides the shining robe for the prince
(XIII). Another aspect of donning the robe can be seen here: it
means 'putting on the armour of light' (Rom 13:12), which is equivalent to 'putting on the Lord Jesus Christ' (13:14), and also being
'conformed to the image of his son, the first born among many
brothers' (8:29).

53   The King of kings had kept his *promise*: together with the mother
(the Holy Spirit) and the brother (Christ the Son) he had said, 'you
shall be *heir* with your brother in our kingdom' (II,VI), and the young
prince was now 'with him (the splendour of the father) in his
kingdom' and 'would appear with him' before the king (XIII). The
God who is King of kings says: 'He who conquers shall have this
inheritance, and I will be his God and he shall be my son' (Rev 21:8).
To Abraham he had made 'a promise' and 'an oath' (Heb 6:13, 17),
and likewise to 'the *heirs* of the *promise*' (6:17), 'those who through
faith (symbolized by the pearl) and patience inherit the promises'
(6:12), and 'enter into the inner chamber' of the sanctuary, the
dwelling place of God (6:19). Notice that Christ, 'the prince and
perfecter of faith', who has 'endured the cross' and 'taken his seat

at the right hand of the throne of God' (Heb 12:2), is empowered
to bestow the inheritance on his brothers: 'Come, you who are my
Father's blest ones, inherit the kingdom prepared for you from the
foundation of the world' (Mt 25:34), and this is the role played by
him at the end of the poem (XIII).

54   'I had carried out his commands' (literally, 'I had done his commandments'), says the prince (XIII), with reference to his elder
brother, who had been party to the covenant (VI). In the New Testament there are allusions to 'keeping' the commandments of Christ
(Jn 14:21,15:10; 1 Jn 2:4), but also two references to 'doing' his commandments: 'Blessed are they who do his commandments' (Syriac
version; or: 'who wash their robes') so that they may enter into
the city by the gates' (Rev 22:14); and 'Whoever shall do and teach
(them) shall be called great in the kingdom of heaven' (Mt 5:19).

55   The eagle letter had promised that when the prince returned
victorious his name would be read in the *honour roll*, literally 'the
book of the valiant' (VI). This would refer to those who are 'enrolled in heaven' (Heb 12:23) or 'written in the book of life' (Rev
21:27, 20:11-15; Phil 4:3); they alone could enter 'the holy city, the
new Jerusalem' (Rev 21:2, 27).

56   The three *gate* references fit into the familiar oriental picture:
'The king sat in the gate (of Jerusalem) . . . and all the people came
before the king' (2 Sam 19:8). The hero's arrival at an assembly of
princes and nobles and servants would correspond to the following scene in the Letter to the Hebrews: 'You have come to Mount
Sion and to the city of the living God, the heavenly Jerusalem, and
to the myriads of angels, to the festal gathering, and to the assembly of the first-born enrolled in heaven, and to God the Judge of
all, and to the spirits of righteous people made perfect, and to Jesus
the mediator of a new covenant, and to the blood of sprinkling'
(Heb 12:22-24). The celestial city of the King of kings is illuminated
by the glory of God and has the Lamb of God as its Lamp (Rev 21:22);
the city has twelve gates, and each portal is one pearl (21:21).

57   'And with my present and my pearl I would appear with him
before our king', the poem concludes (XIII). The 'present' is presumably the robe and the toga presented to the prince. The Syriac
term for 'present' is *qurbana*, found as 'Corban' in English Bibles
(Mk 7:11). In the Syriac Bible it means 'an offering', either a present

made to the temple and the priests (Mt 5:23, 8:4), or an oblation (Heb 10:10, 14). In the latter case it refers to 'the offering of the body of Jesus Christ' (10:10); and 'when he had offered one sacrifice for sins, he sat down at the right hand of God, . . . for by one offering he has perfected for ever those who are sanctified' (10:12,14). The prince's 'present' may accordingly have a connection with the atoning death of Christ.

58   The *scarlet toga* can be interpreted in this light. Translaters have invariably used the word 'purple' in preference to 'scarlet', possibly because of 'scarlet woman' insinuations in the word. Nevertheless, 'scarlet' and 'purple' are distinguishable in Syriac, notably in the picture of 'a woman sitting on a scarlet beast', she being 'arrayed in purple and scarlet' (Rev 17:3-4), and also 'bedecked with gold and jewels and pearls' (17:4), all of which have good connotations in *The Song of the Pearl* (I, II, XI). The rendering 'scarlet toga' is therefore faithful and appropriate. Although there is a disagreement over whether Jesus in his Passion wore a 'scarlet robe' (Mt 27:28) or a 'purple garment' (Jn 19:2), it is conceivable that Matthew's 'scarlet robe' is the model for the prince's 'scarlet toga' (II), which would then be a symbol of the Passion of Christ and the Atonement, 'an eternal redemption' secured 'once and for all', not with 'the blood of goats and calves but his own blood' (Heb 9:12). This connection is reinforced in the context of the words just quoted, by a reference to 'the covenant', if we bear in mind that in the poem the scarlet toga is bound up with the covenant (II): 'When every *commandment* of the law had been declared to the people by Moses, he took the blood . . . and scarlet wool . . .' (Heb 9:19); and Christ 'is the mediator af a new covenant, so that those who are called may receive the promised eternal inheritance' (9:15). It would appear, therefore, that the 'scarlet toga' is related to the 'scarlet wool' of the old covenant (Lev 14:4; Num 19:6) and the 'scarlet robe' of the new (Mt 27:28), and ultimately the 'blood of the new covenant, shed for many for the remission of sins' (Mt 26:28). These last words come from the institution of the Holy Communion, and if a reference to the Eucharist is sought in the poem, then it may be found in the fact that in the Syriac churches *qurbana* ('offering') signifies the Eucharistic oblation, and *marganitha* ('pearl') means a morsel of the eucharistic bread, as Saint Ephrem indicates (XVII.7 below).

59   The prince's 'present' (XIII) consists of his shining robe and
scarlet toga, the latter representing the 'one offering' of Christ, the
'one sacrifice for sins' (Heb 10:10-14). It is remarkable how the main
themes of the poem converge in this same passage in the Epistle
to the Hebrews (10:10-23, above, 57). Thus, the writer speaks of
'the covenant' written on hearts and minds (10:16), as with the
prince's covenant (II). Further, it is affirmed that the One 'who
promised is faithful' (10:23); and the prince acknowledges that his
royal brother 'had done what he had promised' (XIII). The writer
also declares that 'through the blood of Jesus' the brethren can
'enter with confidence into the sanctuary' (10:19), led by the Priest-
King who is 'over the house of God' (10:21); and the prince is to
be conducted by his elder brother 'to the gate of the king of kings'
and into the presence of the king (XIII). Finally, the author tells the
readers to '*draw near* with a true heart in full assurance of *faith*'
(10:22). The pearl of faith and the gift of redemption (the scarlet
toga) occur together here, since in Syriac the term 'draw near' is
from the same root as *qurbana*, and it has the connotation of bringing an offering to God. The consummation is achieved: the *one
offering* (the sacrificial death of the Redeemer) and the *one pearl*
(the perfected faith of the believer) combine to provide access to
the divine presence, and also to produce a solution to the problem
of the meaning of the poem.

60   The Song of the Pearl is thus 'mystical' in the sense of being
'allegorical', but is it mystical as in 'mysticism'? Whether the author
intended it or not, the structure of the poem is analogous to the
classic mystical framework of three stages (below, paragraph 121:
purgation (I–VIII), illumination (IX–XII), and unification (XIII). On
this view, the protagonist departs for the desert (symbolized by
Egypt) and becomes a solitary (IV), a monk. He undergoes purgation
from corruption and sin, being washed in the sea when he dives
for the pearl (this is implied, not stated). Illumination comes with
the shining robe (X–XI). Unification with God takes place when
the son is reunited with the king (XIII). As in Dante's *Divine Comedy*,
the hero descends to an *Inferno*, the realm of Satan (III–V); from
there he passes through a *Purgatorio* of instruction and catharsis
(VI–VIII); and achieves enlightenment and entry into a *Paradiso*
(IX–XIII) where the beatific vision is attained (XIII). Dante's poem

has four intended levels of meaning: firstly, literal or historical; secondly, allegorical or spiritual; thirdly, tropological or moral; fourthly, anagogical or mystical.

61   On this fourth level, we have already seen some similarities between certain details of *The Song of the Pearl* and teachings of the Syriac mystics. This process of comparison will continue throughout this introduction, without necessarily implying that the various writers are making definite allusions to the poem. The fact that it has survived in only one Syriac manuscript might suggest that it was not widely known in the Syriac churches, but this could be merely accidental. There was also a Greek version of the poem, which was accorded an explanatory paraphrase by Niketas of Thessalonika in the eleventh century (35), and this certainly shows that the pearl poem moved westwards into the Grecian realm, as did the writings of some of the Syriac mystics.

62   Dante put political overtones into his great allegorical trilogy: the question of Church and State, and the role of the Holy Roman Empire. In the Syriac poem it is clearly the Iranian empire that provides the background. It presents an opposite point of view to that found in *The Tale of Sinuhe*, where Egypt is the realm of light and life, and the home to which the hero longed to return (paragraph 4 above). In *The Song of the Pearl* it is Iran in the East that is the desired goal, and Egypt is presented as the place of darkness and death.

THE DESERT ASCETICS

63   Egypt, or its western desert, became a veritable paradise for the practice of asceticism. There spiritual athletes overcame the devil and the demons, and subdued their emotions and passions. The deserts of Sketis, Nitria, and Kellia were places in which monks, nuns, and women disguised as monks could obtain solitude, stillness, silence, mystical visions, and union with God.

64   *The History of the Monks (Historia Monachorum)*, a work dating from about the end of the fourth century and wrongly attributed

to Hieronymus of Dalmatia (Saint Jerome), has this to say on the desert ascetics: 'Some of them possessed divine vision, and others works of ascetic excellence'. Unlike the Syrian monks, they did not expect to receive visionary and ecstatic experiences as a matter of course in reward for their ascetic labours. Johannes Cassianus (John Cassian, 360–435) knew of the extremely severe mortification practised by Eastern monks, but, like the majority of Western ascetics, he tended to suspect that their visionary experiences were produced by demons.

65   Yet the *Apophthegmata Patrum* (Sayings of the Fathers) and the *Lausiakon* (Lausiac History) of Palladios (Palladius, a contemporary of Cassianus) give several examples of western monks going into ecstasy, notably Arsenios, Silvanos, Pakhomios, and Evagrios (48). These men were exalted as paragons by the Syriac mystics. Nevertheless, Greek and Syriac fathers alike issued warnings that visionary experiences must be treated with caution. The criterion offered by Pakhomios was that holy ecstasy is accompanied by a loss of consciousness, whereby only the sanctity of God or the angels is perceived. In visions brought on by evil spirits, Pakhomios points out, the person maintains consciousness and thought, as when a demon appeared (in the form of Christ) to Pakhomios himself.

66   In the next four sections we will meet two western fathers and two Syrian authors whose writings were translated from Greek into Syriac, and who became imposing figures in the history of Syriac mysticism: Evagrios of Pontos (Evagrius Ponticus); Esaias (Isaiah) of Sketis; Dionysios the Areopagite (Pseudo-Dionysius); and Makarios the Egyptian (Pseudo-Macarius). The last-named is accepted in the Eastern Orthodox and Syriac churches as a genuine Egyptian author, but modern scholarship ascribes the Makarios writings to the Syrian or Mesopotamian world.

EVAGRIOS PONTIKOS

67   Evagrios of Pontos (346–399), a disciple of Basil the Great and Gregory the Theologian, was one among the fathers of the Egyptian

desert who advocated mysticism alongside asceticism. After his death his writings were condemned as containing Origenism, teachings stemming from Origenes of Alexandria (Origen), a third-century theologian who believed in the pre-existence of human souls. The book of Evagrios on asceticism, the *Praktikos*, is preserved in Greek; but, significantly, his mystical writings (entitled *Gnostikos*, *Antirrhetikos*, and *Kephalaia Gnostika*) have survived only in Syriac and Armenian. The *Kephalaia Gnostika* (Chapters of Knowledge) consists of esoteric sentences arranged in six 'centuries' (a word denoting one hundred, but actually groups of ninety). About one-seventh are found in Greek, and there are two Syriac versions; one of these attempts to purge the book of its Origenism. Some of his important works, such as the treatises on prayer, on the various evil thoughts, and on the eight spirits of wickedness, are extant under his own name in Syriac, but in their Greek originals they are ascribed to Nilos.

68   No extracts from the writings of Evagrios will be presented in this collection, but his influence will be manifest at many points. Gregory Bar Hebraeus names 'Father Evagrios' as one whose teachings had lifted him 'out of the whirlpool of disintegration and destruction', when he was experiencing grave difficulties in his spiritual life (XCIX).

69   In the mystical theology of Evagrios the purified intellect may have a divine vision at the time of prayer: the intellect sees what is euphemistically termed 'the place of God' or 'the light without form', or 'the light of the intellect', or 'the light of the Holy Trinity'. These Evagrian ideas are echoed, for example, in one of the excerpts from the discourses of John the Venerable (LXXII).

70   The influence of Evagrios is likewise discernible in the readings from Joseph the Visionary. For instance, the fifth sign of the Spirit's operation is, for Joseph, 'the illuminated vision of your mind', which is 'the reception of the light of the Holy Trinity', and which leads successively to 'the vision of the material natures', and 'the revelations and mysteries of Divine Judgement and Providence' (LIII). Here we have the five 'contemplations' of Evagrios, as set down in his *Kephalaia Gnostika* (I, 27): contemplation of the Trinity, of incorporeal beings, of corporeal beings, of Divine Judgement, and of Providence.

71   The mention of 'sapphire' in this same passage of Joseph the Visionary (LIII: 'the illuminated vision of your mind, which is seen in the firmament of your heart like sapphire') can be explained by consulting Evagrios:

> At the time of prayer the intellect will see its state like sapphire or the colour of the sky, which Scripture calls the place of God, which was seen by the elders on Mount Sinai.

Behind this imagery of blueness lies a mystical passage in the Pentateuch (Ex 24:10): Moses and Aaron and the elders of Israel 'saw the God of Israel, and beneath his feet it was like a pavement of sapphire (*or* lapis-lazuli), like the very brightness of the sky'. Evagrios, however, follows the Septuagint, the Greek version, where the idea of a direct vision of God is removed: 'And they saw the place where the God of Israel stood'. This, then, is the origin of the phrase 'the place of God', as used by Evagrios: 'When the intellect is in prayer', he says, 'it is in the light without form, which is called the place of God'. For Evagrios, the illuminated intellect, having attained the passionless state and spiritual contemplation, sees itself as 'the place of God'; and what it sees is itself clothed in the light of God, which is God himself.

72   Other Syriac mystics who were deeply indebted to Evagrios are Stephen Bar Sudaili, Philoxenos of Mabbug, and Isaac of Nineveh.

ESAIAS OF SKETIS

73   Abba Esha'ya or Esaias of Sketis (Isaiah of Skete) was a fifth-century monk who lived among the Egyptian desert fathers in the generation after Evagrios. He may have been the same person as Esaias of Gaza, who died in 491.

74   Sayings of Esaias are included in the *Apophthegmata Patrum* and in his own *Asketikon*, a book of discourses and aphorisms, apparently compiled by a faithful disciple named Petros.

75   Esaias presents the typical teachings of the Egyptian monks: firstly hesychasm, the maintenance of *hesukhia*, the blessed quietude needed for intimacy with God; meditation on the Scriptures; manual labour, such as basket making; combatting evil spirits, thoughts, and passions; discernment or discretion in one's labours to ensure that one is always walking in God's way; humility, which involves casting oneself upon the Lord, entrusting oneself to God's care; renouncing the world, the love of which separates one from the love of God.

76   One idea original with Esaias is that of mounting the cross. Baptism identifies a person with Christ crucified, and so the Christian climbs onto the cross with him and never comes down. The mysticism of Esaias may be summarized thus: the monk's quietude and discernment lead to contemplation (*theoria*) for his purified soul, and union with the Spouse of the soul, the true King, who teaches the soul to pray and to adore him unceasingly, and who gives the soul constant repose while revealing his ineffable glory and grace.

77   The influence of Abba Esha'ya was profound in the Syriac monastic world, mediated through Syriac translations of the *Apophthegmata* and the *Asketikon*. Of the writers included in the present collection, Isaac of Nineveh, Simon Taibutheh, Dadisho Qatraya, Joseph the Visionary (Ḥazzaya) and John the Venerable (Saba) refer and defer to him. His regulations for novices are echoed in the monastic rule of John the Venerable, while Dadisho and Joseph each produced a commentary on the *Asketikon*.

78   In the West, Father Isaiah appears in the Russian Orthodox *Philokalia*. His *Asketikon* was translated into Latin by P.-F. Zino in the sixteenth century, and it became an important text for spiritual study by the Jesuits.

MAKARIOS THE GREAT

79   Abba Makarios the Egyptian, otherwise known as Macarius the Great or the Elder, was a disciple of Antonios (Saint Antony). It was

Antonios who sent him to the remote sandy desert of Sketis. The
life of Makarios seems to have covered the greater part of the
fourth century (*c.*300–*c.*390). His sayings and doings have their place
in the *Apophthegmata* and the *Lausiakon*, and these carried his fame
to the East.

80   A remarkable collection of *Spiritual Homilies* has the name
Makarios attached to it, and these discourses have traditionally
been accepted as the work of Makarios the Egyptian. Modern
scholarship argues, however, that the Makarian corpus of writings
(the homilies and some extra epistles) belongs within the framework of the Messallian movement of the fourth century (75a). The
Messallians (Syriac *mesalleyané*, Greek *messalianoi*) or Eukhites
(from the Greek word for 'prayer') were 'praying' people, who
apparently believed in prayer absolutely. Messallians allegedly set
private mystical experience in opposition to ecclesiastical discipline,
and showed no interest in the sacraments.

81   Messallianism was condemned at the Council of Ephesus in 431,
and its book of instruction, or *Asketikon*, was banned. The Makarian
Spiritual Homilies have been hypothetically identified as this offending
work, and their author is assumed to be Symeon of Mesopotamia,
one of the condemned leaders of Messallianism. Such theories are
rejected by the Eastern Orthodox Churches, which hold the *Homilies*
in high esteem and defend their traditional attribution to Makarios
the Egyptian. The *Lausiakon* of Palladios says of Makarios the Great
that he was constantly in a state of ecstasy, with his mind more
often on God than on the things under heaven. Such a person might
well have been capable of producing the *Spiritual Homilies*, but
neither Palladios nor his contemporaries mention any writings of
Makarios.

82   Even if we reject the Messallian hypothesis, there are in the Greek
text apparent Aramaisms and also such Syriac Christian ideas as
the motherhood of the Holy Spirit, which suggest an Eastern rather
than a Western origin for the Makarian Homilies. Indeed, their
author has been dubbed the first Syriac mystic (Quispel, 37).

83   Certainly, the Syriac world took these spiritual writings to its heart.
Isaac of Nineveh, in speaking of the varying states that the mystic
must go through, ranging 'from peace to perturbation', cites 'the

blessed Makarios', alongside Evagrios, and even sets their testimony over against the opinion of the Messallians.

84   Yausep H̲azzaya (Joseph the Visionary) likewise brings Evagrios and Makarios together. As we have seen (paragraph 70), the *fifth sign* of the Holy Spirit's operation (LIII) is based on the teachings of Evagrios, in particular his 'five contemplations'. The *fourth sign* (LII) is love, and 'from this love there is engendered faith to see hidden things'. This too has an Evagrian ring to it, and we have already noted a saying of Evagrios on the relationship of love, faith, and knowledge (paragraph 44). The first three signs of Joseph, however, are traceable to the Makarian texts.

85   The *first sign* is when the thought of the love of God burns in a person's heart like a fire, producing 'hatred for the world, renunciation, and love for the eremitic and ascetic life, which is the mother and nurse of all virtues' (XLIX). Joseph elsewhere speaks of the coming of the Spirit as 'the fiery impulse', a sensation of fire burning in the soul with such intensity that 'one falls to the ground and eats the dust on it as if it were bread, because of the ardour of divine love and its burning hot blaze'.

86   The same phenomenon is described by Yoh̲annan Saba (John the Venerable), with reference to the coming of the Spirit or Grace in the middle stage of mystical experience: 'Sometimes it stirs up hot fiery impulses in his heart in the love of Christ, and his soul is set on fire, his limbs are paralysed, and he falls on his face. Sometimes it works up a fervent heat in his heart, and his body and soul are enkindled . . .' (LXX).

87   In the Latin West, Bernard of Clairvaux also speaks of a fiery 'sign' (*signum*) associated with God's love. The soul knows that its Lord has come, he writes, when it feels itself inflamed by the divine fire (*Sermones super Cantica Canticorum*, 31.4).

88   In the *Makarian Homilies* we read of the divine and heavenly fire which the Lord came to send upon the earth (Lk 12:49), and those who are aflame with this 'fire of the love of Christ' consider all the things of this world 'contemptible and hateful' (9:9). In another place this Lukan allusion to divine fire is connected with 'the enkindling of the Spirit' (25:9, *purosis tou Pneumatos*). Much of this Homily 25 is found in the Syriac corpus of Makarios, though this

sentence is lacking in the Syriac manuscripts. The author goes on to say that this is the fire that worked in the apostles when they spoke in tongues at Pentecost; this same fire blinded the eyesight of Paul on the road to Damascus, but also enlightened his mind; it appeared to Moses in the burning bush; it caught Elias up from the earth; it warmed the heart of Kleopas and his companion on the road to Emmaus; it imparts its radiance to the ministering spirits (cp. Heb 1:7); it drives away devils and destroys sin; in fact, this divine fire consumes iniquity like thorns or stubble, trying souls like gold in a furnace, and illuminating them (25:9).

89   In the same context (25:5; cp. 39:1, 44:9; 49:3) Makarios refers to Christians being made 'partakers of the divine nature' (2 Pt 1:4). The idea of hating the world and renouncing it, which Joseph the Visionary connects with 'the fiery impulse', is found in another passage from Makarios, which uses the analogy of metal being purified in fire (4:14):

> As iron, lead, gold, or silver, when cast into the fire, are melted and change their natural hardness to softness, and so long as they are in the fire continue to be molten and altered from that hard nature by the hot force of the fire, in like manner also the soul that has renounced the world . . . and has received that heavenly fire of the Godhead and of the love of the Spirit. . . .

Makarios then has the soul 'changed from the natural habit and hardness of sin' and enjoying 'the fervent and ineffable love' of the heavenly Bridegroom (4:14), and 'the ineffable mystical fellowship of the heavenly King' and of 'that heavenly and beloved Spirit', completely 'disengaged from all worldly love' (4:15). Elsewhere it is said that one whose soul has been brought under subjection can be 'deified and made a son of God, receiving the heavenly stamp on his soul' (15:35).

90   With regard to the metal-in-fire simile, in a short discourse by 'John the Visionary', who is presumably but not assuredly the same person as John the Solitary, the dross-purging aspect appears (and the fire consuming iniquity like thorns, 25:9), but the idea of unification becomes paramount:

> As iron when placed in a fire has the fire pass into it to become
> one substance with it, the iron united with the fire assuming its
> likeness and colour, . . . so it is when the love of Christ has come
> into the soul as a living fire which burns away the thorns of sin
> from the soul; it becomes one substance with him and he with
> it . . . and the likeness of its own nature is changed into the
> likeness of God; . . . and it becomes absorbed in love for all
> humankind (XXII).

91   The same analogy is drawn by John the Venerable in a discourse
on the love of God and union with God:

> Consider the fire that unites with the iron in the furnace: the
> appearance of the iron is not perceived there any more, because
> through its union it now has the likeness of the fire. . . . The sons
> of God likewise see themselves in the likeness of their Father;
> thus they all become gods by the grace of their Creator.

92   Incidentally, Bernard of Clairvaux brings together the same ideas
of mystical 'deification' and the union of iron and fire:

> Certainly, being in this state means becoming deified (*deificari*),
> for . . . as a piece of iron, glowing and permeated by the fire,
> divested of its proper original form, resembles the same fire
> perfectly . . . (*De diligendo Deo*, 10).

93   Returning now to the five signs of Joseph the Visionary, and their
relation to Makarios, we find that the *second sign* is the birth of
humility in the soul, 'whereby a person . . . considers himself dust
and ashes (cp. Abraham in Gen 18:27), a worm and no man (Ps 22:6);
all people are considered in his eyes as great and holy, and there
is no difference in his mind between good and bad, righteous and
sinner' (L). And again, 'while ever the solitary experiences this
operation of thoughts, this movement of humility, and these tears,
in his view there is no sinner in creation, but all people are deemed
righteous by him' (XLVIII).

94   Makarios uses the 'dust and ashes' and 'worm' allusions at least
twice (12.3, 26.25). In the first instance (12.3) he is replying to the
question: how can one be 'poor in spirit' after having attained

mystical knowledge? This goes with the point made by Joseph (omitted from the quotation in the previous paragraph) that the person feels humble 'notwithstanding the great and wonderful things done to him by the indwelling Spirit' (L). The answer given by Makarios is that until one reaches this stage, one cannot be poor in spirit, because one has some opinion of oneself until this stage of progress and state of grace has been attained (12,3). Those who wish to be citizens of 'the heavenly city', and be glorified with Abraham ('dust and ashes') and David ('a worm'), two paragons of humility, 'ought to have this humility of mind, and not to think they are anything' (12,4). Makarios then states that Grace works differently in each Christian (12,4).

95   In another place Makarios speaks of grace calming the heart, so that the soul becomes like an innocent child, and the person no longer condemns Greek or Jew, sinner or worldling, but rejoices over the whole world (8.6). This is an important facet of the second sign of Joseph (see XLVIII and L, quoted above).

96   The *third sign* of the Spirit's operation, for Joseph the Visionary, is the mercifulness or *compassion* that arises within the heart, a feeling of universal charity, accompanied by a fountain of tears; 'it is as if all men are dwelling in your heart, and you lovingly embrace them and kiss them, pouring your kindness over them all in your thought', and it becomes impossible to think ill of any person (LI).

97   Makarios has ideas similar to those in Joseph's second and third signs, in his account of 'the dealings of grace in the heart' (18:7), or the various 'operations of the Spirit' (18:10). Sometimes, he says, the children of God are 'as if in weeping and lamentation for the human race' and 'consumed by the love of the Spirit towards humankind'. At other times, 'if it were possible they would take everyone into their own entrails, without distinguishing between bad and good'. And sometimes, he continues, 'they are so humbled beneath all others in the humility of the Spirit, that they think they are the last and least of all' (18:8). Makarios is thus a possible source for the ideas in Joseph's first three signs (186).

98   In a discourse of John the Venerable there is a collocation of various workings of the Spirit, or of grace (LXVII–LXXII), similar to that of Makarios (18:7-11); but it seems to be a case of similarity, not direct dependence, although the idea of such a listing (each

prefixed with 'sometimes') may have been derived from Makarios. In any case, the following statements from John's section on the first stage of the mystic path are relevant to the themes of humility and compassion, discussed in the previous paragraphs: 'Sometimes grace sows *humility* in his heart and makes his thoughts lower than *dust and ashes.* Sometimes it causes him to shed *tears* through the remembrance of his sins. . . . Sometimes it will arouse in his heart pity for the oppressed . . .' (LXIX).

99   Makarios also mentions weeping, and he calls tears 'precious pearls' (25.8), in the context of the 'divine fire' which has already engaged our attention (paragraph 88).

100   Elsewhere Makarios calls the crucified Saviour 'the Pearl': 'He is the Way, the Life, the Truth, the Door, the Pearl, the living heavenly Bread' (17.15). The reference is probably to the pearl of the biblical parable (Mt 13:46), but its position next to the bread also suggests the 'pearl' of sacramental bread offered in the Syriac churches (paragraph 58). Makarios is certainly alluding to the parable of the pearl merchant (Mt 13:45-46) when he says that Christians who have 'the pearl of great price' within them are to be compared with a worn-out pouch, which is lowly and easily despised in its outer form, but inwardly full of pearls (43:2). He also uses the figure of the merchant: 'Christians are like merchants trading for very great gains' (24:1); the merchant commits himself to the sea and the risk of death 'for the sake of gain', whereas the Christian withdraws from the affairs of this life and keeps himself free for 'prayers and supplications', hoping for enlightenment and looking for the Lord to manifest himself (14:1; cp. also 33:2).

101   Makarios also uses the metaphor of *treasure* to represent 'spiritual treasures', quoting Matthew 6:21: 'where your treasure is, there will your heart be also' (11.7, twice; 27.18; and cp. 43.3, 'where your mind is, there also is your treasure'). The 'treasure' in a person's soul is the Holy Spirit (3.3); or 'the heavenly treasure of the Spirit' is 'the Lord himself shining in the heart' (18.1). Christians are like those rare 'pearls and precious stones' which are suitable for a king's diadem; they are 'built up into the crown of Christ', and he 'shines forth and manifests himself' to them (38.2).

102   In the same vein, Makarios mentions the other kind of pearlers; he calls them 'traffickers' (*emporoi*) but he surely means pearl divers;

they 'go down naked into the deep of the sea, into the watery death', seeking pearls fit for a royal crown (cp. XVII). Those who embrace the single life go naked out of the world and down into a sea of evil and darkness 'to bring up precious stones suitable for the crown of Christ, for the heavenly church, for a new world, and a city of light, and a people of angels' (15.51).

103   This is somewhat reminiscent of the climax of The Song of the Pearl, and it might be profitable to compare the allegorical details of the poem with some of the main concepts in the *Spiritual Homilies*. These Makarian writings abound in extended metaphors associated with biblical allusions, and there are some striking correspondences with the Syriac pearl poem, either because the author of the homilies knew the poem, or because both authors were deeply immersed in the metaphors and mystical ideas of Scripture.

104   Like the people of Egypt during the plague of three days of darkness (Ex 10:21-23), the sons of Adam no longer see their relatives and friends under the darkness of sin, as with the pearl prince (V–VI): the relatives (cp. paragraphs 17–19 above) are 'the true *Father* in heaven; the good kind *Mother*, the grace of the Spirit; the sweet and desired *Brother*, the Lord'; and 'the friends and kindred, the holy angels' (28.4). The Christian is a brother of Christ, one of 'a new race, children of the Holy Spirit, shining brethren of Christ' (16.8).

105   The pearl prince was to be heir in the kingdom with his elder brother, when he brought back his pearl (II). Significantly, Makarios says that 'those who possess and wear the pearl, live and reign with Christ forever' (23.1). His illustration is based on a costly royal pearl which only a king can wear on his crown; by the same token, unless one is born of the Spirit of God and made a member of the royal family of heaven, one 'cannot wear the costly pearl of heaven, the image of the inexpressible light, which is the Lord' (23.1).

106   The prince in the pearl poem wears a shining robe (II); Makarios speaks of a 'shining garment' which can be imparted in a mystical experience similar to the transfiguration of Jesus (8.3; cp. Mk 9:2-3). The garment which Christians wear is the Spirit (6.7); their 'divine and heavenly raiment is the power of the Holy Spirit', and anyone who is not 'clad in the raiment of the Spirit' is naked, covered only with 'vile affections' (Rom 1:26); 'God's face is turned away from

souls that are not clothed with the raiment of the Spirit, from people who have not put on the Lord Jesus Christ (Rom 13:14) in power and reality' (20.1). Furthermore (20.3), God clothes us with 'the garment of salvation' (Is 61:10), meaning 'our Lord Jesus Christ, the unspeakable light', and in the resurrection the bodies of faithful souls 'shall also be glorified by the glory of the light', for 'he who raised up Christ from the dead shall give life to your mortal bodies also through his Spirit which is dwelling in you' (Rom 8:1). All this concurs with the interpretation given above (paragraphs 22, 46, 49–52) for the shining robe of the pearl prince.

107   There are other aspects to the shining robe. The prince first adopts the manner of dress of the Egyptians (IV) and serves their king (V, VI), but eventually he strips off the filthy Egyptian garb (VIII) and puts on his new garment (XIII), which has the image of the king of kings on it (XI), and is adorned with glorious colours and jewels (XI). Makarios has 'the evil ruler' of 'the kingdom of darkness' taking humankind captive and clothing their souls 'in the power of darkness' (2.1). He quotes Paul's exhortation, 'Put off the old man' (Col 3:9). This 'old man', 'polluted and unclean', is what the evil one has clothed souls and bodies with (2.2), corresponding to 'the garment of the kingdom of darkness, the garment of blasphemy, unbelief, unconcern, vainglory, pride, avarice, lust', and other 'unclean and abominable' things (2.4). The pearl prince strips off the 'filthy and abominable garb' of Egypt (VIII; cp. paragraph 49). Makarios has 'the sons of light' becoming no longer 'children of the night or of darkness' (1 Thess 5:5) by being 'stripped of the clothing of the kingdom of darkness' and putting on 'the new and heavenly man, Jesus Christ, . . . to be all pure, and wearing the heavenly image' (2.4). This last point might account for the royal image on the prince's robe (XI; cp. paragraph 50), while its colours and jewels (XI), representing virtues (paragraph 46), are explicable thus: 'The Lord has clothed them with the clothing of the kingdom of ineffable light, the clothing of faith, hope, charity, of joy, peace, goodness, kindness . . .' (2.5).

108   The *scarlet toga* of the pearl poem (paragraphs 58–59 above) seems to have no exact counterpart with Makarios, but atonement through the blood of Christ is highlighted in his allegorical interpretation of the Passover and the Exodus (47.1-17). He speaks of

'the lintels of the heart' being 'anointed with his blood, so that the blood of Christ shed upon the cross might be to the soul for life and deliverance, and to the devils of Egypt for woe and death'; it is also 'joy and gladness for the soul' (47.8). Later in the same homily, Makarios presents the children of Israel marching away from Egypt after keeping the Passover; his interpretation is that 'the soul moves onwards, when it has received the life of the Holy Spirit, and has tasted of the Lamb, and been anointed with his blood, and has eaten the true Bread, the living Word' (47.11).

109   Then, in the same way as 'a pillar of fire and a pillar of cloud went before the Israelites, protecting them' (Ex 13:21), the Holy Spirit strengthens the Christian, 'warming and guiding the soul perceptibly (*en aisthesei*)' (47.11). The Syriac version has altered this sentence to read: 'The Spirit of Holiness strengthens us and guides our souls into the harbour of his will (or: desire)'. This would be an allusion to Psalm 107 (106):30, where God saves seafaring merchants (107:23) from a violent storm, 'and he brought them to the harbour they desired'. (In the Syriac the word for 'harbour' or 'haven' is borrowed from Greek *limen*.) Notice here that the pearl prince was led by his eagle-letter (the Paraklete) to Maishan, 'that haven of the traffickers' (IX), and this is where he received his two garments (X). Elsewhere, in *The Acts of Thomas* (where the pearl poem is preserved), the metaphor of 'haven' is used of Christ as the saviour of those who are to be baptized (37 and 156). And in Syriac Christian liturgies baptism is often linked with this harbour idea. This might suggest that the pearl prince received baptism at this point, at Maishan in Iran, rather than when he snatched the pearl from the dragon, in Egypt (paragraph 39).

110   However, the 'haven' motif is also used eschatologically of death and bliss, as is the case with Ephrem, for example. Isaac of Nineveh uses it in this finality sense: he speaks of the monk voyaging across a variable sea 'right to the haven of his decease' (XXXIX). Isaac also has 'the islands of the world to come' (XXX), and 'the dry land' that is attained at the time of death (XXXII). The merchant-like monk 'reaches the haven rejoicing', and 'makes his way to the city of truth', where 'the inhabitants no longer engage in commerce' (XXXIII).

111   The 'death and resurrection' meaning of 'harbour' would be suitable for the 'haven of the traffickers' of the pearl poem (IX), for it is at this point that the royal robes arrive, and majestically clothed in them the prince proceeds to the gate of the city (XIII). It would be reasonable to see death as intervening before the hero enters Paradise, but the giving of baptismal garments, as prefigurations of the celestial robes in the afterlife, is another possible interpretation. Simon Taibutheh (paragraph 237) offers another possibility: he uses the 'haven' metaphor for a stage somewhere between baptism and death.

112   In Homily 43, Makarios expresses ideas similar to those of Isaac of Nineveh on the 'harbour', and his use of this metaphor adds weight to the death interpretation of the 'haven' in the pearl poem (IX, XIII), for they both connect the harbour with the heavenly city. Makarios affirms that 'Christians, when they have been baptized into the Holy Spirit, are without experience of evil', although 'those who have grace, but are still mingled with sin, are subject to fear' (43.3). 'Merchants on a voyage', even with a calm sea and a fair wind, are afraid of storms arising before they reach the harbour (43.4). Likewise, 'Christians, even if they have in themselves a favourable wind of the Holy Spirit blowing' are still subject to the fear that the adversary will 'stir up turbulence and billows for their souls' (43.4). Makarios therefore counsels 'great diligence, so that we arrive at the haven of rest, at the perfect world, at the eternal life and pleasure, at the city of saints, at the heavenly Jerusalem, at the assembly of the firstborn' (Heb 12:23).

113   Among other points of comparison between Makarios and the pearl poem in the *Acts of Thomas*, three may be mentioned briefly. Firstly, the prince endures *bondage* under the king of Egypt: 'I forgot that I was a son of kings, and I served a king of theirs' (V); 'look at your bondage to the one you now serve' (VI). This servitude was brought about by the *guile* of the Egyptians: 'I myself wore their manner of dress. . . . They dealt with me deceitfully' (V). In his allegorical exegesis of the Exodus story, Makarios says in this connection: 'Israel is interpreted as the mind beholding God; he is set free from the *bondage* of darkness, from the Egyptian spirits (47.5). . . . His enemies by *guile* took away his glory, and clothed

him with shame; his light was taken away, and he was clothed in darkness' (47:6).

114   The *letter* that reminds the prince of his royal birth (V–VII) seems to represent the Bible (paragraph 35 above). Makarios lends support here (39.1): 'God the King has sent the Sacred Scriptures as his letters', inviting people to 'ask and receive a heavenly gift of the substance of his Godhead, for it is written, that we should be made partakers of the divine nature' (2 Pt 1:4).

115   The *freedom* that the pearl prince realizes (paragraph 40 above) would be for Makarios 'freedom from passions' (29.7), that is, being 'set at liberty from all mischief of the passions' (4.14); this leads to 'ineffable mystical experience with the celestial King' (4:15). Similarly, 'deliverance from the passions' brings about 'the unspeakable mystical fellowship of the Holy Spirit, in the fulness of grace' (10:2).

116   From all this it clearly emerges that Makarios is a Christian mystic, and his teachings seem to be in accord with Syriac mystical theology. *The Spiritual Homilies* and other Makarian writings, whether their author was Makarios of Egypt or Symeon of Mesopotamia, were of great importance in the Syriac world. Yet, strange to say, most of the parallels we have drawn between Makarios and the Syriac pearlers remain hypothetical because very few of these passages are attested in the Syriac manuscripts of the Makarian corpus. For instance, all the 'pearl' allusions (paragraphs 98–100 above) are lacking in the Syriac collection.

117   Whatever the truth may be in these matters, the world-wide influence of Makarios is beyond doubt. In the Orthodox Churches, Symeon the New Theologian in the eleventh century approved of these writings, and Greek monks still read Makarios before ordination. In western Europe, Pietism's Gottfried Arnold and Methodism's John Wesley were devoted readers of 'Macarius the Great'.

DIONYSIOS THE AREOPAGITE

118 Dionysios the Areopagite was a convert of Paul in Athens (Acts 17:34). Various Greek books appear under his name, but they are

imbued with late Neoplatonism and mystical ideas derived from Gregory of Nyssa. Clearly 'Areopagite' writings are pseudonymous and must have been composed around the beginning of the sixth century. They were accepted by the great Monophysite theologian, Severos of Antioch (d. 538), and a Syriac translation was made by Sergios (Sargis) of Resh'ayna (d. 536).

119   The Dionysian corpus consists of ten epistles addressed to various personages of the first century, and four treatises dedicated to Saint Paul's friend Timothy. The author also mentions a work of his entitled *Outlines of Divinity*. Four 'Areopagite' books have survived: *On the Heavenly Hierarchy* (describing the different classes of angelic beings); *On the Ecclesiastical Hierarchy* (portraying the church as the earthly counterpart of the celestial world); *On the Divine Names* (a study of the names and titles of God in the Bible); and *On Mystical Theology* (a summary of his mysticism).

120   The brief *Mystical Theology* is of chief interest to us here. The theme is 'the ascent of the soul' by 'the negative way'. The soul sets aside the senses and all inward thoughts and reasonings; it then passes into the 'darkness of unknowing' (or 'the cloud of unknowing') to receive enlightenment from 'the ray of divine darkness', which is beyond all light and beyond all being.

121   In the first chapter, Dionysios warns Timothy not to disclose these things to the uninitiated (a common admonition of Syriac mystics); among these he includes philosophers and theologians, who know only by human reason. He outlines the three stages of mysticism, which later became categorized as (1) Purgation, (2) Illumination, (3) Unification. He takes the experience of Moses on the Sinai mountain as his model (1.3).

> *Purification*: Moses purifies himself and separates himself from the impure.
>
> *Illumination*: Moses hears trumpets and sees flashing lights; he goes to the topmost pinnacle of the Divine Ascent, where he beholds the place where the Divinity dwells.
>
> *Union*: the true initiate is plunged into the Darkness of Unknowing, in complete renunciation of self and of reason, and he is united to the Unknowable. By rejecting all knowledge he comes to possess a knowledge that exceeds his understanding.

122   Perfect unification implies deification. This idea has already appeared in Makarios (15.35; cp. paragraph 89), and later writers brought the metaphor of the union of metal and fire into the picture of unification and divinization (paragraphs 90–92). This collocation of ideas also appears in the *Ecclesiastical Hierarchy*. Dionysios says that 'by union with him' God assimilates, 'as by fire, things that have been made one, in proportion to their aptitude for deification'.

123   In a tract purporting to be a commentary on Dionysios, Simon Taibutheh discusses the Godhead and 'the Divinity that is in us', together with a consideration of 'spiritual theory', which may owe something to Evagrios (**2**, Mingana, 163a–167b).

124   Isaac of Nineveh quotes Dionysios by name in a discourse on prayer, to show that names and words are superfluous when the soul becomes the image of the Godhead through unification (**153**, Bedjan, 169). And in a discussion of the classes of heavenly beings (Bedjan, 187) he relies heavily on the *Celestial Hierarchy* (6–7).

125   Gregory Bar 'Ebraya (Bar Hebraeus) makes frequent use of the term 'the cloud' in his *Book of the Dove* (see below, CII, CIV, CVII–CXII), and he sometimes mentions the name of Dionysios. In his chapter 'On the unification of the mind' (*Dove* 3.4, p. 569); and in the *Ethikon* (4.15.8, p. 487) he has 'the great Dionysios the Areopagite, who says, The Divine Cloud is the inaccessible light, wherein God is said to dwell' (1 Tim 6:16; cp. paragraph 17 above). In speaking of the silent solitude of the mystic, he describes it as 'a solitude which makes gods' (*Ethikon* 4.15.11, p. 492). This is the Dionysian (and Makarian) idea of deification; and Gregory continues: 'through it the mind acquires complete unification and perfect mingling with God, and vision and knowledge of him whose glory is exalted above the world, without visible vision and knowable knowledge' (492, Wensinck's translation). Gregory is echoing not only Dionysios here, but also John the Venerable.

126   In one passage in the discourses of John the Venerable (John Saba), grace is said to enlarge the mind of the solitary with visions and revelations until 'the cloud of essential light' is attained (LXVII):

There the mind will look at and shine in the rays of light that
dawn upon it from the Essence. Thereby it ascends and penetrates day by day . . . from glory to glory through the Lord the
Spirit, being transformed into the likeness without likeness, in
union and perfect commingling with God, and the sight and
knowledge of his glory are more sublime than worlds, for they
are seen and known by means of withdrawal of sight and knowledge.

127   In this excerpt we see such cardinal Dionysian doctrines as the
ascent of the mind, union and commingling; and the last phrase
echoes a point made by Dionysios in the *Mystical Theology.*

Unto this Darkness which is beyond Light, we pray that we may
come, and may attain unto vision through the loss of sight and
knowledge, and that in ceasing thus to see or to know we may
learn to know that which is beyond all perception and understanding, for this emptying of our faculties is true sight and
knowledge (2.1).

128   Doubtless because they were attributed to a disciple of Saint
Paul, the writings of Pseudo-Dionysios made a considerable impact
on theological history. In the Syriac world, Joseph the Visionary
(Ḥazzaya) wrote a commentary on them. In the Greek world,
Maximus Confessor and John of Damascus studied them, and Eastern Orthodoxy has never rejected them. In the West, on the basis
of Erigena's Latin translation (858), commentaries were written by
Hugh of Saint Victor, Albertus Magnus, Thomas Aquinas, and Bona-
venture. European mystics were inspired by Dionysios, including
the English author of *The Cloud of Unknowing*, who was also, apparently, the translator of *On Mystical Theology* under the title *Dionise
Hid Divinite.*

129   Having examined four mystical writers (Evagrios, Esaias, Makarios,
Dionysios) whose works were translated from their original Greek
form into Syriac, we now return to the fourth-century Syriac world,
to look at some Syriac contemporaries of Evagrios who were un-
touched by Evagrianism.

130   Aphrahat (Greek *Aphraates*, Persian *Farhad*) was a fourth-century monk and bishop in Persia. During the period 337–345, Aphrahat produced a collection of twenty-three Syriac discourses or 'demonstrations'. These are arranged acrostically: each of the twenty-three homilies begins with a successive letter of the Syriac alphabet (which has twenty-two signs); the twenty-third sermon is an appendix, commencing with the first letter of the alphabet ('alaph).

131   Unaffected by Greek theological ideas, the *Demonstrations* deal with a wide range of Christian beliefs and practices. The most important of them, for our purposes, is the one relating to 'sons of the covenant', because it covers monastic matters. Those pertaining to asceticism and spirituality are: 1. Faith, 2. Love, 3. Fasting, 4. Prayer, 6. Sons of the Covenant, 7. Repentance, 9. Humility, 10. Virginity.

132   Aphrahat addresses his ascetic admonitions to 'virgins' (male or female ascetics who have remained single and chaste), and also to 'saints' (pious men and women who are married but continent). The 'virgins' are the 'sons and daughters of the covenant' (though the Syriac term *qyama* can mean 'resurrection', as well as 'covenant'). Aphrahat reminds 'daughters of the covenant' that they are betrothed to Christ, and so each of them should reject any invitation to be a ministering companion to one of the 'sons of the covenant', because her Betrothed would be angry and divorce her (6.7). Women should live with women, and men should live with men' (6.4) so as to preserve their chastity. Like Tatian (paragraph 7 above) and the author of the *Acts of Thomas* (paragraph 10 above), Aphrahat downgrades marriage; he sees it as virtually a betrayal of God, in that anyone who 'leaves father and mother' (Gen 2:24, Mk 10:7) to enter into wedlock is really deserting 'God his father and the Holy Spirit his mother' (*Demonstration* 18). Here again we see the typical Syriac image of the Spirit as divine mother, as in the Song of the Pearl (I, VI; see paragraph 19 above).

133   Aphrahat's asceticism involves fasting (*Demonstration* 3), and in his discourse on prayer (4) he refers to 'the power of pure fasting'

alongside 'the power of pure prayer' (4.1). Prayer that is 'pure' is associated with 'purity of heart' and 'silence united to a mind that is serene' (4.1). Besides the well-known practice of 'silence' (Greek *hesukhia*) we find here the spiritual terms 'purity' and 'serenity'. The distinction between these two states will play an important part in the more complex mystical theology of such monks as John the Solitary and Joseph the Visionary. 'Serenity' (*shaphyutha*) will be assigned to a higher spiritual plane than 'purity' (moral purity). As an adjective the word *shaphya* has various connotations: applied to solid objects it means 'planed' (wood) or 'plain' (landscape, 'the rough places made plain'), clear of irregularities; referring to liquids it means 'clear' of impurity or disturbance, and thus limpid, transparent, calm; used of the mind (as here) it would mean 'unsullied' and 'serene'.

134   Demonstration 6 (on the sons and daughters of the covenant) begins with the apostolic injunction: 'Let us now awake from our sleep' (Rom 13:11). This is reminiscent of the call to wakefulness in the Song of the Pearl (VI; see paragraph 33–34 above). Then the purification process is announced (6.1): 'Let us purify our heart of iniquity, so that we may see the Lofty One in his glory.' This is surely an allusion to the sixth beatitude (Mt 5:8): 'Blessed are the pure in heart, for they shall see God.'

Other exhortatations in the immediate context (XIV) are certainly based on beatitudes. For example, 'Let there be peace among us, so that we may be called brothers of Christ' stems from 'Blessed are the peacemakers, for they shall be called the children of God' (Mt 5:9; cp. paragraph 18, above, on brothers of Christ). In the same vein Aphrahat says (6.1): Whoever cleanses his heart of deceits, 'his eyes shall behold the King in his beauty' (Is 33:17). Clearly implied in this is the promise that 'the pure in heart . . . shall see God'. This beatitude constitutes the foundation of Syriac Christian mysticism, and this point should be kept constantly in mind as we follow the thread of purity through all the extracts in this book. The purified heart or unsullied mind is where the divine vision is perceived.

135   Aphrahat emphasizes the need for alienation from the world to preserve one's purity: 'We should be strangers to this world, just

as Christ did not belong to this world' (6.1). 'Whoever wishes to be like the angels must alienate himself from people' (6.1). In the Song of the Pearl, the hero is, initially, a stranger to the Egyptians, among whom he lived (IV; see paragraph 23), but he contracts impurity by 'joining with the unclean' (IV) and adopting their food and dress (IV; see paragraph 32). The attainment of purity is stated in his declaration: 'Their filthy abominable clothing I stripped off' (VIII).

136 As we noted earlier (in paragraph 49), the removing of unclean clothing and donning of new robes are to be connected with putting off the old person and putting on the new person (Eph 4:22-24). Aphrahat uses this new-replacing-old pattern in a setting of purifying the body of all uncleanness (6:1):

> Whoever casts off the old person, let him not turn back to his former deeds. Whoever puts on the new person, let him keep himself from all filthiness. Whoever has put on armour from the water (of baptism), let him not put off his armour, so as not to be condemned. Whoever takes up the shield against the evil one, let him keep himself from the darts that he hurls at him.

The clothing to be put on, in this case, is Paul's panoply, 'the whole armour of God' (Eph 6:13-17), and with it 'the shield of faith'. The pearl prince confronts Satan as the sea-serpent, and faith is there signified by the pearl, while baptismal water is implied in his presumed dive into the sea to snatch the pearl from the serpent (VIII; paragraphs 36–39). The pearl might also have overtones of purity: Ephrem sees spotless purity and unsullied clearness in a pearl (XV.3).

137 Aphrahat declares that the Christian's armour comes from the purifying water of baptism. At this point it would be profitable to look at the Baptismal Liturgy of the Syrian Orthodox Church. This liturgy is attributed to Severos of Antiokheia (Severus of Antioch), who lived in the fifth and sixth centuries. The consecration of the water includes the following statements and petitions:

> You have given us the fountain of true *purification*, which purifies from every sin, this water which is consecrated by the *invocation* of you [or: of your Spirit], by means of which we receive the

purification that is given to us through the Holy Spirit. Grant,
O Lord, power to this baptismal water, you who through the
passion of your Christ has granted *purification* from every sin, in
preparation for the *reception* of your Holy Spirit. . . . To you we
offer up glory, Father, Son, and Holy Spirit. . . . You broke the
heads of the *dragons* in the waters. . . . I have *invoked* your great
and wonderful and glorious *name* . . . against the *adversary*. . . .
May the head of the man-slaying *dragon* be broken under the *sign*
of the cross. . . . Send your Holy Spirit on this water and sanctify
it, and make it the water of repose . . . for the forgiveness of
sins, the *illumination* of souls, the washing of *rebirth*, the gift of
adoption, the *garment* of incorruptibility. . . . Grant that those
who are being baptized in this water may strip off the *old person*,
corrupted by the lusts of error, and put on the *new person*, renewed through the *knowledge* of him who created. . . . Through
baptism may they become participants in the resurrection, and,
preserving the gift of the Holy Spirit and increasing the *deposit* of
grace, may they receive crowns of the victory of the *calling* from
on high, and be numbered together with the *firstborn* written in
heaven. . . . Being gloriously renewed and filled with your grace
and strength may they preserve the *deposit* of your *salvation* . . .
and become partakers of the good things of heaven, which you
have *promised* to those who please (or: love) you.' (**6**, Brock)

138   All these words have their origins in the Bible, of course, and
the italicized terms also have counterparts in the Song of the Pearl.
The *invocation* of the divine name consecrates the water and con-
founds 'the adversary'; similarly, invoking the names of the father,
mother, and brother puts the pearl-serpent to sleep (VIII; paragraph
38). The head of the dragon in the water is broken under the *sign*
of the cross, to be compared with the 'enchantments' worked over
the serpent (VIII). The *passion* of Christ, which brings cleansing from
sin, is symbolized by the scarlet toga (II, VI, X, XIII; paragraph 58).
The *reception* of the Holy Spirit is paralleled by the receiving of the
shining robe (XII), here called 'the garment of incorruptibility', and
this also involves stripping off the *old person* (cp VIII; paragraph 49)
and being renewed through *knowledge* (cp XII; paragraphs 46 and
50). The baptismal liturgy speaks of increasing a *deposit of grace* and
preserving a *deposit of salvation*, while the pearl-prince refers to his
robe as his '*deposit* and wealth' (XI; paragraph 48), wealth being

identifiable as riches of *grace* (I; paragraph 20). If the increasing *deposit of grace* corresponds to the richly adorned robe, which says of itself, 'my size has been increasing with his labours' (XII), then the *deposit of salvation* would be equivalent to the scarlet toga (II, XIII). The *calling* from on high goes with the letter (V, VI, VII) from the heights (X) in the land of light (I, VIII). The *promise* of inheritance (cp II, VI, VIII; paragraph 53) is made to the firstborn written in heaven (cp VI; paragraph 55). The *illumination* of souls may be compared with the prince's letter leading him onwards with its light (IX).

139   Illumination of souls is an important aspect of mysticism, and Syriac mysticism basically means claiming this and the other benefits accruing from baptism. For Aphrahat, baptismal new birth produces 'children of light', who are unafraid of the Evil One, 'because the darkness flees from the presence of the light' (6.2). The armour acquired through baptism, according to Aphrahat (as noted earlier), would not only be 'the panoply of God' (Eph 6:13-17) but also 'the armour of light', of which Paul says: 'Let us cast off the works of darkness and put on the armour of light', that is, 'put on the Lord Jesus Christ, and make no provision for gratifying the desires of the flesh' (Rom 13:12,14).

140   On the latter point, Aphrahat (6.2) shows the ways in which the baptized, 'clothed in panoply', 'stand up against the adversary'; 'they, being spiritual, see him when he attacks, and his panoply has no power over their bodies'; 'lust for food': they 'conquer him by fasting'; 'lust of the eyes': 'they lift up their eyes to the height of heaven'; 'sleep': they remain wakeful and vigilant, they sing psalms and pray'; 'possessions': 'they give them to the poor'; 'sweetness': 'they do not taste, knowing that he is bitter'; 'desire of Eve': 'they dwell alone, and not with the daughters of Eve'. At this point Aphrahat cannot resist the temptation to compile a catalogue of women who (in the Scriptures) led men into error or ruin (6.3).

141   With regard to Paul's other injunction, 'Put on the Lord Jesus Christ' (Rom 13:14, cited above), Aphrahat speaks of receiving 'the Spirit of Christ' and of being 'clothed' in it at baptism, thereby suggesting another aspect of the pearl-prince's robe (X–XII; cp Makarios, paragraph 107 above). Aphrahat affirms (6.14):

> From baptism we receive the Spirit of Christ. In that hour when the priests invoke the Spirit, the heavens open and it descends and 'moves upon the waters' (Gen 1:2); and those that are baptized are clothed in it; for the Spirit stays away from all who are born of the flesh, until they come to the new birth by water, and then they receive the Holy Spirit.

Aphrahat then declares that humans are born with an animal soul at their first birth; and at their second birth, through baptism, they receive the Holy Spirit. At death, the animal soul is lifeless and is buried with the body; but the heavenly spirit that they receive goes, according to its nature, to Christ. And if the person has kept 'the Spirit of Christ in purity', this spirit reports to Christ: 'The body into which I went, and which put me on from the water of baptism, has kept me in holiness'. The Spirit will ask Christ to raise that body up in glory at the resurrection; the Spirit will then be joined again to that body so that it may 'rise up in glory'; and the Spirit shall be within for the resurrection of the body, and the glory shall be without for the adornment of the body; and by the power of the Spirit that person shall fly up to meet the King, who will welcome the person with joy, and Christ will 'give thanks for the body that has kept his Spirit in purity' (6.14).

142   All this is reminiscent of the 'bright ornamented robe, adorned with glorious colours' (XI), which spoke as a person ('I am his who is diligent in doing'), which was impatient to be reunited with the body of the prince (XII), and which went with him ('thus clothed in it') when he ascended to the gate of the king (XIII). This perhaps implies that the reception of the robes by the prince takes place (allegorically) after death, which would be represented by the arrival at 'the haven of the traffickers' (IX; cp Makarios, paragraphs 109–112 above).

143   Finally, what use does Aphrahat make of the pearl as a symbol? The figure of the merchant is set in a paradox (6.1): 'Whoever loves fields and merchandise shall be shut out of the city of saints. . . . Whoever desires to become a merchant, let him buy for himself the field and the treasure that is in it (Mt 13:44). . . . Let us sell all our possessions and buy for ourselves the *pearl*, so that we may be

rich (Mt 13:46). Let us lay up our treasures in heaven, so that when
we come we may open them and have pleasure in them' (Mt 6:20).
Christ is the Pearl, the Lamp, the Light; and many other names are
accorded to him (17.1, 17.11; cp Makarios, par.100 above). And
'the Word of God is like a pearl, having a beautiful appearance on
whatever side you turn it' (22.26). A similar analogy is also expressed by Saint Ephrem in his pearl-hymns (XV.3 below).

EPHREM THE SYRIAN

144   Ephrem (Syriac Aprem or Aphrem, Latin Ephraem Syrus) is honoured
      as a saint in the eastern and western churches alike. He was born
      at Nisibis in Persia, early in the fourth century (c. 305). Because of
      persecution he moved from Nisibis to Edessa, and spent the last
      decade of his life there, in a cave. He died in the year 373. A prolific
      writer and revered teacher (he was made a doctor of the church
      by Pope Benedict XV in 1920), Ephrem produced commentaries,
      homilies, and hymns. Selections from his *Hymns on Faith* are pre-
      sented in this anthology (XV–XVII).
145   A story in the biographies of Ephrem has an angel descending
      with a heavenly scroll, which neither Eugenios of Nisibis (the tra-
      ditional founder of Syrian monasticism, paragraph 3) nor Julian of
      Edessa (the early paragon of Syrian asceticism, paragraph 8) were
      worthy to receive; only Ephrem the Syrian of the mountain of
      Edessa was worthy. Ephrem is portrayed as small in stature, bald
      and beardless, solemn of countenance and never giving way to
      laughter. His meagre diet consisted of barley-bread and water, with
      a little pulse and vegetables, and his garments were rags; his flesh
      was dried upon his bones. These details are, however, products of
      late ascetic hagiography. Mortification of the body was part of the
      teaching he gave and the example he set, but with moderation and
      discretion.
146   Celebrated as 'the harp of the Holy Spirit', Ephrem was orator,
      teacher, hymnwriter, choir-leader, and commentator. He is said to
      have conducted a choir of 'daughters of the covenant'. He extolled

the monk's ideals of solitariness and virginity, but he himself was an ascetic, not a solitary. He lived separate from the world, but remained at the service of the Church and the world. He was *in* the world, but not *of* the world, and yet *for* the world. He harmonized theology, poetry, asceticism, and spirituality. He wrote a commentary on Tatian's *Diatessaron* (Harmony of the Four Gospels), but he himself went beyond Tatian's Encratism (paragraph 7 above). Like Aphrahat (paragraph 132) he distinguishes virginity from 'sanctity' (continence within marriage): virginity is superior to 'sanctity', and the 'saintly' form of marriage is superior to a marriage in which the partners follow the Apostle's advice of not denying each other their conjugal rights (1 Cor 7:5). And in his *Diatessaron* commentary, Ephrem points out that according to the Apostle (Heb 13:4) marriage is an honorable estate. In the same work he says of John the Baptizer, one of his models for the monastic life: 'John went away into the wilderness, not to become wild there, but to soften, in the wilderness, the wildness of the inhabited earth'. John, like Elijah, withdrew from the world but did not cease to influence the world. And we may note in passing that Ephrem has an interesting explanation of John's baptizing of Jesus: John was imparting prophethood and priesthood to Jesus. Ephrem presumably had in mind that John was a descendant of Aaron (Lk 1:5).

147   Monks go forth into the desert to do battle with their enemies the demons, and Ephrem says of the anchorite that 'on his going out from the world the power of the Spirit goes out to him, and anoints him as an athlete for combat with the strong one', meaning Satan. All wild and uninhabited places were considered to be the haunts of the Devil and his armies of evil spirits, and in going out to meet Satan the monk was merely following the example of his Lord (Mk 1:12-13, Lk 4:1-2).

148   This confrontation with demonic forces is also depicted in pearl-fishing terms by Ephrem in the pearl section of his *Hymns on Faith*. The divers are 'unclothed men' who are 'symbolic of the poor' (XVII); they 'strip themselves, then put on oil, a symbol of the Anointed Christ', and 'the sea-monster [Leviathan] is crushed' when they grasp the pearl and ascend, 'as Apostles would seize a soul from the ferocious jaws' [of demons] (XVI). Here is a reminiscence of the pearl-prince stripping off the clothing of Egypt (VIII)

and snatching the pearl from the sea-serpent (VIII). For Ephrem the pearl is a multi-faceted symbol: it has 'faces on all sides' (XV); in it 'is depicted *faith*, in types and symbols' (XVII); and 'faith' is probably its main reference in the Song of the Pearl (paragraph 45 above). But he also says, 'in you and in your appearance your Creator is portrayed' (XVII), as well as the Son (XV) and the Kingdom (XV). A typical Syriac Christian use of the term 'pearl' comes out thus: he saw 'in its purity the great mystery, the body of our Lord, which is spotless' (XV), 'the medicine of life' that is placed 'in the hollows of people's hands' (XVII), the morsel of eucharistic bread.

149   As with the pearl-prince and his eagle-letter (IX, and paragraphs 35, 41, 42), Ephrem was led by the Holy Spirit. Palladios says of him (*Lausiakon* XL):

> Ephraim the deacon of the church of Edessa . . . worthily com-
> pleted the journey of the Spirit, without being diverted from the
> straight road, and was counted worthy of the grace of natural
> knowledge and afterwards of the knowledge of God (*theologia*)
> and ultimate blessedness.

In a homily, Ephrem himself declares that monks are such holy temples of the Holy Spirit that they have no need of consecrated buildings; they are their own priests, giving themselves absolution through their tears, 'their fasts being their offerings (*qurban*, eucharist), and their vigils their libations; their prayers being their stewards, and their faith the sanctuary; their minds being the altars, their virginity the perfect sacrifices, their chastity the curtain, and their humility the censer'. Such charismatic independence from the Church smacks of Messallianism (paragraphs 80, 179), but we have already seen that Ephrem himself was firmly attached to the liturgy and the sacraments.

150   Ephrem also speaks of monks being guided by angels; again compare the pearl-prince (III and paragraph 26). Angels impart mystical knowledge to anchorites, Ephrem says, and this may throw some light on the knowledge aspect of the prince's shining robe (X–XI and paragraphs 27, 46, 47). Furthermore, he sees the pearl as a symbol of Christ, the manifested light, who freely gives mystic enlightenment (XVII). Ephrem is said to have experienced trance states,

as did his contemporary, Julian Saba of Edessa, who reputedly lived in his visions day and night.

151 In closing, we may consider the thirty-second of Ephrem's *Hymns on Faith*, as a moving example of his mysticism, in which meditation is depicted as commerce, producing a treasure to contemplate.

> Turn me towards your teaching,
> for I sought to turn myself away,
> but I saw that I was impoverishing myself,
> because the soul can only be rich
> through commerce with you. . . .
>
> Whenever I have meditated on you
> I have received from you a treasure;
> and wherever I have contemplated you
> a spring has flowed from you,
> and I have drawn as much as I was able. . . .
>
> Your spring, O Lord, is hidden
> from anyone who does not thirst for you;
> and your treasure room is empty
> for anyone who hates you;
> love is the treasurer of your celestial treasure.
>
> When I withdraw from your company,
> your beauty arouses my desire;
> and when I am in the presence of your majesty,
> your glory fills me with fear;
> whether I withdraw or approach,
> I am conquered, in every way. . . .
>
> I meditated, and I spoke of you,
> without comprehending you;
> then I was overcome, and I fell silent,
> without losing you;
> I became lost in you, and speechless.
> Glory to you, hidden Being.

The spirituality of Ephrem achieves through purification and prayer a climax of loving wonderment and silent adoration in the presence of the beauty, and majesty, and mystery of the Beloved.

152   From the time of Aphrahat and Ephrem in the fourth century, or shortly afterwards, comes the *Book of Degrees* (or *Book of Steps*, *Ketaba demasqata*), a collection of thirty discourses on moral and spiritual matters. This work is an important witness for the early history of Syriac asceticism and mysticism. The anonymous writer has produced an original composition, which has affinities with the *Spiritual Homilies* of Pseudo-Makarios, but not literary dependence. The originality of its theology consists in a tripartite view of the Christian *ekklesia*: the visible church; an invisible church (of the heart); and the celestial church. Each of these three levels has a different degree of glory. Christians are divided into two main categories (of the weaker and stronger brethren kind): the *righteous* (ordinary good and faithful church-members); and the *perfect* (the ascetics).

153   The 'righteous', or the 'upright', are the 'disciples of faith', and they obey the 'lesser commandments' summed up in the golden rule, which the author formulates both negatively and positively: 'one should not do to anyone else what is hateful to oneself; and what one wishes others to do to oneself, one should do to those whom one meets' (Discourse 1.4; cp Mt 7:12, Lk 6:31). The upright thus practise active charity: they give food to the hungry; they give drink to the thirsty; they welcome strangers; they clothe the unclad; they visit the sick and the imprisoned. And for this they are called 'blessed of the Father', and they 'inherit the kingdom' (Mt 25:34-40).

154   The 'perfect' are the 'disciples of love'; they perform the 'great commandments' which prescribe complete renunciation of family and property. The pattern for being 'perfect' is to give away everything one owns and expect 'treasure in heaven', meanwhile following Christ (Mt 19:21). Like their Lord, they 'empty themselves' (cp Phil 2:7); they 'fast from the world', having become 'strangers to the world'. Having no possessions they are in no position to feed the hungry or to take in strangers; what they have to offer to others is their prayer and their instruction. The 'perfect' do not judge

others, but consider themselves inferior to everyone. Ultimately 'the upright will have an inheritance this side of the city of the perfect, while the perfect will be with our Lord in Eden and the Jerusalem above, because they have imitated him' (Discourse 14).

155   Whereas the upright have a 'pledge' of the Spirit, and experience the Holy Spirit only partially, the perfect achieve the fulness of the Spirit, namely, 'baptism in fire and the Spirit'. The lower order Christians are given 'milk' to nourish them (Heb 5:13), but those at the higher level receive the solid food that is appropriate to the 'mature' or 'perfect' (Heb 5:14). This metaphor of milk versus solid food is developed in Discourse 12, 'On the ministry of the hidden and the manifest church', from which a mystical extract is offered in the anthology (XVIII). In this discourse the author articulates his doctrine of the Church. Over and above 'the visible church' on earth there is 'the church on high', the celestial church, in which Christ officiates as great high priest. The perfect take part in the liturgy of heaven, but the writer insists that to enter the heavenly church one must first pass through the earthly church and receive baptism by water at the hands of its priests, in order to prepare for eventual baptism by fire and the Spirit (12.4).

156   The visible church is 'the blessed mother who nurtures everyone as children' (12.2). By its altar and its baptismal rite, the church here below 'gives birth to men and women as children, and they suck her milk until they are weaned'. When they are taken off mother's milk, they begin to consume solid food; they come to true knowledge; their bodies become temples and their hearts altars; they become perfect and feed on Christ in their hearts (cp Jn 6:58); they attain to the church on high; they enter the city of Jesus the King (12.3).

157   Like Aphrahat (paragraph 134 above) the author of the *Book of Degrees* bases his hope of the beatific vision on the dominical beatitude which promises that 'the pure in heart' shall see God (Mt 5:8). Purity of heart is achieved by defeating Satan and his demonic hordes, and banishing evil thoughts. Those who have overcome Satan 'become worthy of this church which is above all, upon which our Lord shines openly, and they experience the glorious light of his countenance' (12.7; XVIII below).

158   Clarification on the question of the beatific vision is given in
         Discourse 18, 'On the tears of prayer'. When Christians are deliv-
         ered from sin, tears of sorrow, caused by compunction and repen-
         tance, are replaced by tears of joy inspired by love: 'they weep with
         joy as they encounter our Lord, just like a person seeing a dear
         friend unexpectedly, and falling on his neck, and weeping over him
         with sobs and tears of joy' (18.2). Those who are 'in Christ' will
         engage in prayer, shedding tears 'in their love and yearning for our
         Lord, waiting for when they shall come and see him face to face;
         as it is written (Mt 5:8), "Blessed are the pure in heart, for they shall
         see God", *in this world*, as Paul said (1 Cor 13:12), "as in a mirror",
         with the eyes of our hearts we behold our Lord, but *in that world*
         "face to face"' (18.3). Here we have the familiar mirror motif: the
         heart or soul, when purified of the dross of evil, becomes clear,
         like a polished metal mirror, and reflects the glory of God shining
         upon it; and the ecstatic mystic gazes on this with the interior eyes,
         the eyes of the heart.

159   The mystical scheme of the *Book of Degrees* can be viewed as
         having three stages equivalent to the *purgation, illumination, unification*
         framework. The *visible church* provides the *cleansing* through bap-
         tism. In the *church of the heart*, after the demons and evil thoughts
         have been vanquished, the *illumination* of 'the glorious light of his
         countenance' is experienced (12.7; XVIII). Entry to the *church on
         high*, after death, results in *unification* with God.

160   The author sets up a hierarchy of relative glory for the quality
         of life (and afterlife) offered by 'these three churches and their
         ministries' (12.4). Someone who dies while still at the level of the
         visible church, is assured of salvation; such a person 'departs from
         this world without sins'. Anyone who has attained the level of the
         church of the heart fares 'even better' on departing. Finally, someone
         who 'attains in his heart to the *church on high* and then passes away,
         blessed is his spirit; he will become *perfect* and will go to see our
         Lord face to face'. And here it is affirmed that 'by striving in this
         visible church', a person can move up to the church of the heart,
         and then to the church on high, in this life.

161   Other elements in this author's mystical theology should also
         be mentioned. The 'perfect' person is a complete renouncer (like

the *sannyasin* of Hinduism). The 'perfect' renounce property and reject marriage. In Discourse 15, in which the subject of carnal concupiscence is discussed, the author explains sexual desire as a consequence of the fall of Adam. Sexuality, he avers, did not exist in Adam before his fall from grace; and because 'perfection' is defined as a return to the adamic state, the 'perfect' abstain from sex and marriage. In this they are like the angels (15.3; cp Mt 22:30).

162   To be perfect one must practice humility to the point of considering oneself inferior to everyone else (6.2). Accordingly, one does not distinguish between righteous and sinful persons, but honours all humans equally, 'kissing their feet' out of love for them. In this perfect state one would gladly die in the place of others in order to save them, a sentiment also expressed by John the Solitary (XXII). This kind of humility, combined with compassion, is also set forth in the *Makarian Homilies*, and in later Syriac mystics (paragraphs 93–98).

163   This form of universal love is inspired by the Holy Spirit, and the *Book of Degrees* teaches that the Spirit, as the Paraklete, also imparts perfect knowledge of the divine mysteries, leading disciples 'into all truth' (John 16:13). This combination of love and knowledge was noticed in connection with the robe of glory in the Song of the Pearl (XII; paragraph 46). The robe gained entry for the pearl-prince at the gate of the king's city (XIII). In the *Book of Degrees*, when the Paraklete reveals the truth to the perfect, they see the celestial portals opening to them, and thenceforth, while remaining on the earth, they live in the heavenly realm in spirit, and they continue to grow until the Lord takes them, after their decease, into the heavenly Jerusalem (6.2).

164   Clearly this *Ketaba demasqata* belongs to the category of 'Syriac Christian mysticism', and it sets a number of patterns that recur in the subsequent history of this subject. One basic question to be asked before we proceed further is whether the author is laying new foundations or merely affirming ancient fundamentals. It has been said that in the *Book of Degrees* a time-honoured principle is restated: the real church consists entirely of the company of the ascetics (Vööbus, **101**). This is in line with the view that, in early Syriac Christianity, 'the sons and daughters of the covenant' were

the only ones who received baptism, celibacy being a requirement for entry into the covenant-community, the Church (Vööbus, **25**). This case is improbable and not proven, but it can be compared with Buddhism: the celibate monks constitute the 'church' (*sangha*), the community of those who have formally vowed to follow the Buddhist path, which entails renunciation of all family ties and personal property, and devotion to austerity and meditation. This was certainly the ideal of Tatian and the hero of the *Acts of Thomas* (who did his missionary work in India, it should be noted): baptism meant acceptance of asceticism and celibacy. But was this the absolute rule and norm?

165   The possibility that Buddhism may have influenced the Judeo-Christian tradition has not been seriously explored. But if Zoroastrianism could influence Judaism with eschatological ideas like resurrection and last judgement, then Buddhism could have provided the Essenes of Judaism and the apostles of Christianity with their monastic ideas of asceticism and renunciation of the world. The trade routes by land and sea were available to missionaries of the Buddha as well as emissaries of the Christ. Thus in the third century before the Christian era, the Emperor Ashoka of India sent messengers of Buddhism to the Iranian and Mediterranean worlds. And in the third century of the current era, the Iranian prophet Mani and his followers produced *Manicheism*, an amalgam of Judeo-Christian and Indo-Iranian religion. Like Buddhism, Manicheism was a two-tiered system: the Elect were ascetic and celibate (like Buddhist monks and nuns); the Hearers were permitted to marry (like Buddhist lay people). Incidentally, Manicheism could have mediated Buddhist concepts to Iranian and Syrian Christianity.

166   Established religions tend to have a lower path and a higher way: a basic course for beginners and ordinary believers, and a more advanced course for the spiritual elite. As in the *Book of Degrees*, the higher way leads to some kind of unification experience: in Hinduism it is the union of *atman* and *brahman* (the soul is united, or 'yoked', by *yoga* to the ground of all being); in Buddhism it is enlightenment and attaining Nirvana (transcendent bliss); in Islam it is the Sufi union with God. Adepts of mysticism, who have been to the centre or heart of their own particular religion, are inclined to

say that they have all been to the same ineffable place. This is the characteristic 'irenicism' of the mystics, exemplified in the present anthology by Bar Hebraeus (XCVIII; paragraph 280)

167   This irenical attitude is also found in the *Book of Degrees*, with some interesting ramifications. In Discourse 30, the last chapter of the book, the author notes that the 'perfect', as 'disciples of love', have a peaceable and loving attitude towards all humans, including heretics and pagans; in return, they are relatively safe from persecution by non-Christians. By contrast, the ordinary church members, the 'disciples of faith', are violently persecuted by outsiders. Ironically, the 'upright' are prone to attack the 'perfect' Christians, because they cannot understand their behaviour and their doctrine; and church leaders are suspicious of the mystics' 'superior' aspirations to 'perfection' ('a more excellent way', we may call it with I Cor 12:31). The perfect accept this harassment in the spirit of 'love bears all things' and 'endures all things' (I Cor 13:7).

168   The author also speaks of the incompatibility of holding ecclesiastical office and treading the path of pefection. A bishop must be harsh towards sinners and heretics, but the perfect must exercise universal love and compassion. To be perfect one must regard oneself as inferior to everyone else, but the bishop (*episkopos*, 'overseer') is by definition in a position of superiority. Here we should note that in the eastern churches priests may marry, but bishops must be unmarried. This means that if at any time no suitable candidates are available among the clergy for ordination to the episcopacy, then bishops have to be recruited from monasteries. The famous seventh-century mystic Isaac the Syrian (Isaac of Nineveh) had this dignity thrust upon him, but he made a hasty retreat back to the monastic life (paragraph 240).

169   Inevitably, suspicion and conflict arose between ecclesiastics and mystics. In the eighth century, the great Nestorian Patriarch Timothy banned the mystical writings of Joseph the Visionary (Yausep Ḥazzaya) and John the Venerable (Yoḥannan of Dalyatha); and their works have been preserved through the subterfuge of attributing them to other writers, such as Philoxenos in the case of Joseph, or putting them under the vague designation 'a holy old man' in the case of John. Accounts of their visions were considered heretical

by their church; they were deemed to be tainted with Origenism (Evagrianism) and Messallianism.

170   *The Book of Degrees* is anonymous, though its foreword (not by the author) suggests that it was one of the last disciples of the Apostles who composed it; and the name of Evagrios (or else John the Monk) is sometimes attached to the discourses by Syriac scribes. What is the reason for this anonymity? Possibly its author was writing from personal experience when he pointed out the antipathy between the 'upright' and the 'perfect' (among whom he numbered himself) and either he or someone else thought it expedient to suppress his name. (Note, however, that anonymous books are common enough in Syriac literature, sometimes because the first and last pages of manuscripts have been lost.) There are a number of names of mystics contemporary with this manual which could be considered for its authorship, notably Julian Saba of Edessa, who has been mentioned already as a fervent ascetic (paragraphs 8 and 145). Another candidate is Adelphios of Edessa.

ADELPHIOS OF EDESSA

171   Adelphios of Edessa was a disciple of Julian Saba, whom he accompanied on a journey to Egypt sometime before 363. Philoxenos of Mabbug (in his letter to Patrikios, **127**, 108–110) says that in Egypt young Adelphios met some of the illustrious fathers, including Antony the Great. From them he learned, according to Philoxenos, 'that the intellect has contemplations after being purified, and that the soul can through the grace of God be made worthy of impassibility, when it sheds its old passions and stands in the original wholeness of its nature, and is as if in the kingdom of God, while still having its habitation in this life'. Adelphios returned to Edessa, and though still a young man he set himself up in a hermitage. There he engaged in austerity and prayer, but without humility, Philoxenos adds. This left him a prey to Satan, who appeared to him in the form of light and claimed to be the Paraklete-Spirit sent by Christ to

reward his labours with the desired impassibility and contemplations. After being accorded adoration by the deceived solitary, the disguised Devil filled Adelphios with demonic hallucinations. The monk then ceased mortifying his body and struggling against his passions. Adelphios thus became the founder of the Messallian heresy, Philoxenos tells us.

172   Whenever the *Book of Degrees* is discussed, the question always arises whether it is a Messallian work, to be placed alongside the *Spiritual Homilies* of Pseudo-Makarios as another handbook of Messallian spirtuality (an *asketikon*; see paragraphs 80–83). The portrait of Adelphios that Philoxenos paints for us certainly bears a resemblance to the anonymous author of the *Book of Degrees*. Accordingly, as a matter of interest and as a means of confronting the Messallian issues, let us call in a kind of devil's advocate to argue that the book was written by Adelphios. The first thing he would bring to our notice is the scenario of Philoxenos, as a bishop, attacking Adelphios as a Messallian (too charismatic by far). This is precisely what the *Book of Degrees* describes: the mystic being persecuted by the ecclesiastic (paragraphs 167, 169 above). From another point of view, Philoxenos is like the modern church-based charismatic who sees other people's mystical experiences as Satan working in them, but is convinced that his own spiritual experiences occur through the inspiration and operation of the Holy Spirit. Philoxenos was a mystic himself; but, as the *Book of Degrees* says, as a bishop he must be severe where heresy is apparently in evidence; he cannot be irenical like the spiritually perfect (paragraph 168). Philoxenos has to keep pneumatism within orthodox bounds, under ecclesiastical control. His own theology, eventually and ironically, would bring the Church's wrath upon his head (paragraph 209).

173   Although Philoxenos accuses Adelphios of lacking humility, in desiring spiritual blessings that were above his station, and of being under the power of the passion of vainglory and having a high idea of himself, Adelphios would doubtless have denied this. Humility is a cardinal characteristic of the perfect, according to the *Book of Degrees*. In Discourse 20, 'On the difficult degrees that there are on the way to the City of our Lord', the three principal degrees are humility, poverty, and chastity.

174   To test the hypothesis that the *Book of Degrees* is Messallian, the core doctrines of established Messallianism, as summarized by its opponents, have been brought to bear on its contents. Here are four basic propositions of Messallianism:

(1) the indwelling of the soul by a demon, from the time of one's birth;

(2) the inefficacy of the sacraments to purify the soul of this demonic power;

(3) the exclusive efficacy of prayer to achieve this purification;

(4) the resultant impassibility, and the coming of the Holy Spirit.

Differing 'results' have been obtained from this 'experiment'. One scholar finds no trace of these doctrines in the *Book of Degrees*. Other scholars see them there in their germination stage. In my opinion, this is essentially a Messallian book. This is not a value judgement, condemning it as being full of vile heresy. My suggestion is that these four statements are distorted versions of ideas that actually appear in the book.

175   Heresy-hunting bishops have been known to misrepresent the beliefs of the people they condemn: they find offending doctrines in passing remarks, and they take words out of context. The Katholikos Timothy could be accused of doing this to Joseph the Visionary and John the Venerable in the eighth century (cp. paragraph 169). An examination of their writings shows that this kind of misrepresentation has occurred.

176   We also have to take account of the phenomenon of expurgated editions of banned books. Works can be purged of offensive matter if they are otherwise considered to be of spiritual value, as happened when Syrian Orthodox scribes edited and preserved the writings of the aforementioned Joseph and John. In the case of John, one of his discourses has been excluded from the major recensions of his works. In Joseph's case we have copies of East Syrian and West Syrian editions of some of his treatises, which, when compared, show that alterations have been made by scribal editors. Even more pertinent is the analogy of the two different Syriac versions of the *Kephalaia Gnostika* of Evagrios. Remarkably, one of

these texts contains none of the proscribed evagrianisms. This purged edition may well have been the work of Philoxenos, who valued the mystical teaching of Evagrios—up to a point, as shown by the allusions and quotations in his own spiritual writings (always made, however, without naming Evagrios). Accordingly, there is a real possibility that the extant copies of the *Book of Degrees* contain alterations, omissions, and interpolations.

177   Consider now the *first* of the four Messallian 'errors': the doctrine of the demon inhabiting the soul from the time of one's birth. The New Testament accepts that people can be possessed by demons, but this pronouncement seems to imply that everyone is indwelt by a devil that needs to be exorcized. Before seeking this idea in the *Book of Degrees*, the way should be prepared with a few clarifications. Syriac monks unanimously agree that demons attack and invade them; furthermore, 'demons' and 'passions' and 'sins' are very closely related; the demon of pride stirs up the emotion of pride and causes the sin of pride, for example. In his portrait of Adelphios, Philoxenos says that this young monk had the passion of vainglory burning inside him; Satan appeared to him in the form of light; and the demon (*shi'da*) took control of him. Notice that 'passion', 'demon', and 'Satan' are almost interchangeable here. These variations are also observable in the formulations of Messallian tenets set down by Theodoret, Timothy of Constantinople, and John of Damascus (**75a**, 244–279). Timothy of Constantinople states that Messallians say that, as a result of the condemnation of Adam, each person is united with a 'demon' from the time of birth; Theodoret mentions an 'indwelling demon'; while John of Damascus speaks of 'Satan' dwelling with a person, or 'Satan and the demons' possessing the mind, or 'Satan and the Holy Spirit' dwelling together in a person, or the nature of humans being in communion with 'spirits of evil'. It therefore seems that the picture of a personal made-to-measure demon need not be interpreted literally. And what does the *Book of Degrees* say of evil inhabiting the soul? In Discourse 3, the author extends Paul's idea of the pledge (*arrabon*, 'guarantee') of the Spirit (2 Cor 1:22: 'God has put his seal on us, and given us a pledge, his Spirit, within our hearts'). He sets alongside 'the pledge of the Spirit' the concept of 'the pledge of Satan'

or 'the pledge of sin' (3.11). This seems clear enough, but the Syriac word used in the *Book of Degrees* (*'urbana*) is not found elsewhere; its root can mean either 'to pledge' or 'to mix', and so it might be translated as 'admixture' or 'commixture', and this has been the usual interpretation (**75a**, 198–203), hence 'an admixture of sin', rather than 'a pledge of sin'. In any case, those who are not at the 'righteous' stage, and who do not keep even 'the lesser commandments', have no part in the Spirit, because anyone who is captive to Satan cannot receive the Spirit of the Lord (3.10). The 'righteous' have a proportion of the pledge of the Spirit within them, together with a proportion of the pledge of Satan (or sin). The 'perfect' have by degrees attained the state of being filled with the Spirit, and so sin and Satan have no place in them any more. The state of being 'captive to Satan' (and having the pledge of Satan within) may be considered as reasonably equivalent to the first Messallian doctrine, of 'Satan cohabiting substantially with the person and controlling him' (John of Damascus).

178   The *second* Messallian error is the inefficacy of baptism or the sacraments to remedy this situation. They say that 'baptism does not perfect the person, nor does reception of the sacred mysteries (the Eucharist) purify the soul'; 'and it is not through baptism that the faithful receive the divine and incorruptible garment' (John of Damascus). This simply says that baptism and the Eucharist cannot deal with this particular problem, but it has also been taken to mean that Messallians are anti-ecclesiastical and anti-sacramental; by contrast, the Book of Degrees respects the church, its priesthood, and its sacraments.

179   As to the anti-ecclesiastical accusation, practising Messallians certainly had a 'hippy' reputation in their day: they were unemployed vagabonds, men and women mixing together freely and sleeping in the streets. But perhaps the Messallians were only heretics and sectarians because the bishops of the Church branded them as such. Or if they were in fact a sect, they would probably (like most Christian sects) claim to be the true church (as the first Christians claimed to be the true Israel, but were cast out of the synagogues). Yet the history of Messallianism seems to show that it was a movement within the Church, and its members did not deliberately seek

to break with the established Church. Initially the movement was led by Adelphios, in the fourth century; it spread to Antioch, and there the bishop condemned him. In the following century another leader, Lampetios, succeeded in gaining ordination to the priesthood, though his writings were refuted by Severos of Antioch and he was placed under condemnation. The ordination of the leader to the priesthood seems to show that the Messallians were not seeking to supplant the Church but simply wanted their teaching to be accepted by the Church. This irenic approach was also characteristic of Syriac Christian mystics, but they were frequently under attack from the Church hierarchy. In their time Saint Francis of Assisi and his followers were never above suspicion either.

180   If we invoke the *Book of Degrees* as a hypothetical source of Messallian doctrine, we can see perhaps what the root of the trouble was. Ecclesiastics could accept that that there is a church on earth and a church in heaven, but they might well balk at the idea of yet another church, namely the church of the heart, as proposed in the *Book of Degrees*. This is obviously a mystical church: it stands closer to the celestial church than does the established 'visible church', and its members are 'the perfect', who do not need the ministry of the lower order church any more. That would surely cause bishops considerable concern.

181   The Messallian attitude to the Church's sacraments, according to the testimony of the *Book of Degrees* (paragraphs 155–156 above), is that baptism, administered by the clergy, produces the 'children' of the Church, 'the blessed mother', and that the Eucharist feeds these children, preparing them for maturity, when they will have a new baptism by fire and by the Spirit. (There is perhaps an analogy to this in the present-day church, with 'charismatics' insisting on the baptism of the Holy Spirit as a higher experience, but not dispensing with water baptism as the means of entry to the church.) As for the Eucharist, in the higher church the person's body becomes the temple and the heart becomes the altar (12.2), and there the perfect 'consume our Lord himself in truth' (12.3). Remember that the homilies of Ephrem express similar ideas about monks not needing the Church, because their own bodies are temples of the Spirit and they act as their own priests (paragraph 149 above).

182   If the sacraments cannot deal with the evil in the soul, what can
eradicate it? The answer is found in the *third* alleged error of the
Messallians. In the words of Timothy of Constantinople: 'They say
that only assiduous prayer can remove this demon' (75a, 245). And
it is here that the so-called Messallianism of the *Book of Degrees* is
plainly manifested: 'When we no longer have any external sins and
outward faults, we should offer up supplication and *prayer*; for until
we find ourselves in anguish in prayer, just as our Lord did (Lk 22:43)
. . . we will not be delivered from *the sin that dwells in the heart*, or
from the evil thoughts that it devises within us' (18.3). As reported
by Timothy, Messallians believe that baptism does nothing towards
the expulsion of the 'demon', because it is incapable of removing
the roots of the sins' (**75a**, 247, 249). Here 'demon' and 'sins' are
virtually synonymous, as are 'Satan' and 'sin' in similar contexts in
the *Book of Degrees*, as we noted earlier (paragraph 177). Here we
are apparently told that the only way to uproot the sin that is
entrenched in the heart is to pray assiduously, like Jesus in the
Garden, shedding abundant tears and groaning forcefully. This is
surely the very essence of Messallianism, which by definition means
'prayerfulness'.

183   It is not sufficient to retort that the *Book of Degrees* also advo-
cates asceticism, notably fasting and vigils. It is in the visible church
that fasts and vigils are performed, in order to deal with the 'external sins and outward faults' mentioned above (paragraph 182).
At the higher level the practice is known as 'fasting from the world',
that is, denying oneself all material things and worldly pursuits (cp
paragraph 154); and there is also 'mystical [concealed] fasting of
the heart', which is 'fasting from evil thoughts' (12.1). As a consequence of this kind of dynamic prayer, 'people who have struggled
and battled alone with evil spirits and have purified their hearts of
evil thoughts', thereby becoming 'pure in heart' and therefore
worthy to 'see God' (Mt 5:8), have the experience of seeing the
Lord in his celestial church, in this life (12.7; XVIII).

184   In Discourse 18 ('On the tears of prayer') the 'Messallian' author
affirms that it is prayer that cleanses the heart and soul. Over and
over he declares that prayer is the only recourse we have. In order
to be 'without any sins' we must '*ask* our Lord to deliver us from
sin' (18.2). He then restates this formula (18.3):

> Once we have cut off those of our sins that are visible, we can
> take up the struggle against the sin that dwells right inside us,
> those evil thoughts which *sin* forges in our heart; and we can run
> towards the contest that awaits us, engaging in it through *prayer*,
> just as our Lord did before us . . . 'with a mighty groan and many
> tears' . . . and he was made *perfect* (Heb 5:7, 9).

The same remedy is then reiterated:

> The heart does not become pure unless hidden sin has dis-
> appeared from it and evil thoughts that had been hidden away in
> it through the strength of *the sin that dwells there* have come to
> a complete end. This sin will not be eradicated from our heart,
> nor will the evil thoughts and the sin's other fruits disappear
> unless we *pray* as our Lord and all who preached him prayed
> (18:4).

Notice the recurring phrase 'the sin that indwells'. If we applied
the principle outlined above (paragraph 176), that heretical works
are frequently purged and altered, then we might read 'the demon'
for 'the sin', in line with the formulation of the first Messalian error.
But this would be unwise, since the author is surely borrowing this
phrase from Paul (Rom 7:17): 'it is no longer I that do it, but *the sin
that dwells in me*'.

185   The *fourth* alleged error is twofold: the achievement of impassibility (Greek *apatheia*) and the coming of the Spirit. The latter
phenomenon would be the 'baptism in fire and in the Spirit' of the
Book of Degrees, an experience which is available only to those who
have already been baptized with water in the visible Church (12.4).
This can be compared with 'the enkindling of the Spirit' and 'the
fire of the love of Christ' in the *Makarian Homilies* (paragraph 88
above), and similar images found in later Syriac mysticism (paragraphs 85–87, 89–91). This is followed by the state of being 'filled
with the Spirit' (cp paragraph 177). This is the state of the perfect,
who 'have received the greatest of all gifts, the one known as the
Spirit, the Paraklete' (3.12). Elsewhere it is said (20.7):

> When we have ascended by these degrees [or steps], and have
> removed the sin and its fruits from our heart, we will be *filled
> with the Spirit, the Paraklete*; the Lord will dwell in us perfectly,

and we will eat freely of the tree of life, from which we were
excluded because of the transgressing of the commandment.

This divine spiritual gift restores the person to the adamic state,
the original innocence of Adam, before he sinned. The breath of
God that brought the created body of Adam to life (Gen 2:7) is
the Spirit that dwells in the perfect (28.1). Moreover, since the role
of the Paraklete is to lead the disciples into all truth (Jn 16:13), 'as
soon as one receives the great gift, the Paraklete, one knows all
truth' (28.2). As regards the gift of impassibility, freedom from
passions, the *Book of Degrees* has the perfected person returning
to the state of Adam before he sinned, and becoming like a little
child, with no concupiscence (15.3).

186   For additional clarification, we now look at what Theodoret of
Kyrrhos (Cyrrhus) said about Adelphios and his Messallian doctrines. Theodoret was a native of Antioch; he was educated in its
monasteries early in the fifth century, and in 423 he became a
bishop of a town in its vicinity. His language was Syriac, but he wrote
in Greek. He was an expert on Syriac monasticism, as is shown by
his *History of the Monks* (biographies of three women and twenty-
eight men, including Simeon Stylites). His *Ecclesiastical History* has
a section (IV.10) 'on the heresy of the *Messalianoi*.' He begins by
stating that they were known as Eukhites (*Eukhitai*, Greek *eukhe*
'prayer'); they were also called 'enthusiasts', because they came
under the influence of a certain demon, which they supposed to
be the Holy Spirit. This is precisely what Philoxenos says about
Adelphios, whom he names as the founder of Messallianism (paragraph 171 above). Theodoret names Adelphios as one of the ring-
leaders, alongside Dadoes, Sabbas, Hermas, Symeon, and others,
'who did not separate themselves from ecclesiastical communion'.
It is not clear whether Theodoret included Adelphios in this statement about not seceding from the Church, but he goes on to single
him out as the eldest of the group that was called to account by
Bishop Flavianus of Antioch. This Messallian stance of attempting
to stay within the church is consistent with the position taken by
the author of the *Book of Degrees* (paragraph 155 above).

187   The bishop, Flavianus, won the confidence of the monk Adelphios by saying that his accusers were slanderers and false wit-

nesses, and were too young to have discernment in spiritual matters; but they themselves, being men of more advanced age, both understood the machinations of demons and the workings of divine grace. On being asked to explain in what sense the opposing spirit retreats and the grace of the Holy Spirit comes in, Adelphios (in the words of Theodoret) 'vomited out all his concealed poison'.

> He [Adelphios] said divine baptism is of no use to those worthy to receive it, but only earnest prayer drives out the indwelling demon. Everyone who is born derives from his forefather [Adam] not only his nature but also servitude to the demons, he said, and when these are driven away through earnest prayer, the All-Holy Spirit then comes in visitation with perceptible ['sensible and visible'] signs of personal presence, freeing the body from the impulse of the passions, and ridding the soul entirely of its inclination towards evil, so that there is no longer any need for fasting to subdue the body, or for instruction to bridle it and to train it to go the right way; and not only is the recipient liberated from the wanton impulses of the body, but also clearly foresees things to come, and with the eyes beholds the divine Trinity (**75a, 244ff**).

188   In defence of Adelphios, the *Book of Degrees* can be invoked on all these points. *Firstly*, the inefficacy of baptism relates only to the expulsion of the demon; Adelphios would not mean that baptism is unnecessary and useless; the *Book of Degrees* has baptism as the essential requirement for proceeding along the path to the celestial city (12.4; see paragraph 155 above). *Secondly*, concerning slavery to 'the demons', we have seen (paragraph 177) that 'demon', 'demons', 'evil', and 'Satan' seem to be fairly interchangeable in these reports on Messallianism; and in the Book of Degrees we read of 'those who are bound in spirit to Satan, and do not receive the Spirit of the Lord, as it is written' (3.10; 1 Cor 2:14). *Thirdly*, the idea that only assiduous prayer can remove the evil entrenched in the soul is frequently affirmed in the *Book of Degrees* (see paragraphs 182 and 184). *Fourthly*, the perceptible coming of the Holy Spirit corresponds to the 'baptism by fire and the Spirit' of the *Book of Degrees* (2.4; cp. Mt 3:11), and the fiery impulse of Joseph the Visionary and of the *Makarian Homilies* (paragraphs 85–89 above); furthermore,

the full awareness of the spiritual experience doubtless goes with the statement that 'as soon as one receives the great gift, the Paraklete, one knows all truth' (28.2). Note that John of Damascus, in his seventh proposition against Messallians, speaks of their 'reception of impassibility (*apatheia*) and perception of the Holy Spirit's presence with total awareness and complete certainty' (**75a**, 251). *Fifthly*, the lack of passions would follow logically from the idea that 'the sin and its fruits' have been removed from the heart when a person is 'filled with the Spirit, the Paraklete' (20.7). The perfect are without desire (15.1), in the state of original purity (15.3; paragraph 185 above). *Sixthly*, with body and soul freed from passions and evil inclinations, 'there is no longer any need for fasting to subdue the body'; the emphasis needs to be placed on the 'no longer' (*mêketi*); the *Book of Degrees* has a whole chapter (29) on the subjugation of the body (based on Paul's dictum, 'I buffet my body and subdue it': 1 Cor 9:27), but a distinction is made between the fasting of the 'upright', from food and drink at set times, and the mystical fasting of the 'perfect', which is 'fasting from [*or* to] the world' (7.20; cp 2.4, 4.4, 15.16, 29.6) and 'a mystical (hidden) fasting of the heart, fasting from evil thoughts' (12.1; cp paragraph 183). The *seventh* accusation is that there is no more need for education and training in correct behaviour, and this is to be explained by the distinction between the 'lesser commandments' followed by the upright and the 'great commandments' practised by the perfect, the disciples of love (paragraphs 153–154). The apostolic distinction between 'milk' for the immature Christian and 'solid food' for the 'mature' or 'perfect' ('who have their faculties trained through experience to distinguish good from evil', Heb 5.14) is taken up in the *Book of Degrees* (12.3): if a suckling child went to a house of evil men he would perish, but a mature person (one of the impassible perfect) could go there without being affected, and might even convert them, because the perfect are no longer learners but instructors (12.6). *Lastly*, the visionary experiences are to be connected with the ability of the perfect to see into the church above and to behold the Lord in this life, not with the physical eyes (as implied by Theodoret) but with the eyes of the heart, as in a mirror (paragraphs 157–159 and 163; cp what Philoxenos says about the mystical experience of Adelphios, paragraph 171).

189   Theodoret says of Messallians in general that 'they shun all manual labour as a vice' (75a, 262); this has been fairly typical of Syrian contemplative monks, knowing nothing of Saint Benedict's principle that work is a form of prayer (*laborare est orare*). In the *Book of Degrees*, the perfect take up their 'mystical cross' and separate themselves from 'the earth and its work and all its labour and worry'. On their cross they will be lifted up above all the things of this world (3.10). The labours of the perfect are contemplation and instruction (14.2-3), and if they are to 'admonish, pacify, exhort, and teach', and be shepherds (though not bishops) of Christ's flock, 'then they cannot follow the plough or labour on the visible land' (12.6).

190   In the light of all these comparisons, it is reasonable to suggest that the *Book of Degrees* might have been read or written by Adelphios. Theodoret's list of prominent Messallians runs: Dadoes, Sabbas, Adelphios, Hermas, Symeones. The last-named, Symeon (of Mesopotamia), was possibly the author of the *Spiritual Homilies* transmitted under the name of Makarios (paragraph 81), and one of the others may have produced the *Book of Degrees*; Adelphios is the most likely candidate, but our extant sources do not attribute any books to him.

191   *The Book of Degrees*, whether it had a Messallian author or not, was considered worthy to be handed on in Syrian monasteries, as the manuscript tradition shows. Its doctrine that a vision of God is achievable in this life by those who have become pure in heart through victory over demons, may have influenced the great Syriac mystics of subsequent centuries, although they apparently never quote from it or refer to it by name. However, there is possibly an echo of its idea of the hidden church' (Discourse 12) in Sahdona's *Book of Perfection* (2.8.57): 'the soul becomes a hidden church where the Godhead is ministered to in an excellent way'. Similarly, the theme of prayer as an interior offering of the heart is developed by Sahdona (2.8.19-20): when the heart's sacrifice of prayer and tears is accepted, 'the fire of the Spirit' descends and raises these sacrifices and the mind of the offerer to heaven for divine revelations. And Isaac of Nineveh, who distinguishes himself from the Messallians, could say in excusing himself from regular attendance at congregational worship: 'our work is not only that which is

accomplished before the eyes of men, but we also have a service
that is concealed from the eyes of men, one that is not known to
novices and lay folk' (extract XXXVII).

JOHN THE SOLITARY

192   Nothing is known about John the Solitary (John of Apamea), apart
from the few things he reveals about himself in his writings. It seems
that he lived in the second half of the fifth century in Apamea, in
Syria. The oldest manuscript containing examples of his work is
dated 581. His influence was great among Nestorians and Jacobites
alike. His own theology seems orthodox but original, he shows no
real connection with Neo-Platonism or Evagrianism, even though
he obviously has a good knowledge of Greek philosophy and
medicine.

193   The mystical theology of John is one of *hope*, of longing for 'the
new world', the world to come. The present world is set in stark
contrast to the future world, but humans can comprehend the
dimensions of the upper realm by means of this very contrast. The
greatness of those above is an aid to human understanding, for it
gives us knowledge of a more excellent hope. The inferiority of
those below demonstrates the excellence of those above and the
omnipotence of God. The pearl appears in the course of the
author's examples (Strothmann, 110, IV, 38–39):

> The sun and the moon are great because the stars are smaller.
> Do we learn the richness of God because all the luminaries are
> like the sun, or because there are in fact great differences in the
> luminaries? Similarly, do we wonder at the richness of God's
> work because of the great variety of birds, or because there are
> only eagles? . . . If all stones were pearls then amazement over
> the divine workmanship would not be as great as when there
> are great differences among stones. Also, pearls would not be
> considered to be valuable if all things were pearls.

194   Christ is the supreme revelation of the mystic's hope: 'He is for us the symbol of the new world, such that through him we can see and grasp how great our hope is' (Rignell, 108, 29*). As our light he comes to awaken us who are under the dominion of wickedness and passions (see extract XXI below). This is similar to the awakening of the prince in the *Song of the Pearl* (V); he was under the rule of 'wickedness' in the person of the king of Egypt, and he ate the Egyptian foodstuffs which caused his 'sleep' and which correspond to the 'passions' of John the Solitary.

195   Then comes a passage that is very enlightening for our understanding of the Song of the Pearl. We have already seen that the presence of the child (the Christian pilgrim) with the royal father (God) in the kingdom (heaven) before his descent into Egypt (the world) can be explained by the doctrine of predestination (paragraph 14), and John substantiates this hypothesis (Strothmann, 110, IX, 104):

> 'Before the foundation of the world he chose us in him' (Ephesians 1:4). Thus, before the heavens were separated and the firmament was stretched out, before the earth appeared and everything visible was set in order, he in his foreknowledge had prepared and equipped us who are weak and small, had chosen, renewed, sanctified, and formed us in the image and likeness of his son, so that we who had lost and forgotten our greatness, our honour, our excellence, and the glory we received at our creation, should through Christ be renewed and perfected, and be replete with life and truth, and a wealth of wisdom and of mysteries of God in his holy realm.

'We' are 'weak and small' (or 'inferior'), and the pearl child was so 'young' to set out on the road to Egypt (III), but his divine parents had 'equipped' him (I), as God 'prepared and equipped' us; we had 'forgotten' our 'greatness' and 'glory', as the pearl prince, 'forgot' that he was of royal birth (V); the 'wealth of wisdom' relating to divine mysteries can be compared to the 'wealth' of the prince, namely his 'bright ornamented robe' (XI).

196   John concludes this part of his case for Christ as the manifestation of the mystic's eternal hope, in the following words (Strothmann, 110, IX.105):

> When he is crucified and dies for our sake, we learn how we
> are seized and bound by destructive passions, and how we
> descend and sink into the darkness of error. When he rises up
> from the dead in the majesty of his Father, he reveals and shows
> to us our hope, our resurrection, and our true life.

197   This leads to the baptismal area of John's mystical theology.
Through the gift of baptism Christ communicates the substance of
his revelation. Again we find comparisons with the Song of the Pearl,
where the prince is delivered from bondage to a foreign king
(Pharaoh, that is, Satan) and receives the mark of the true king who
saved him, and this guarantees him entry to the kingdom of light,
as son and heir with his elder brother (Christ).

> Baptism is also an occasion for being separated and estranged
> from the knowledge of demonic mysteries and for receiving
> knowledge of the kingdom of heaven. And because through bap-
> tism we are made worthy to be sons and heirs of the kingdom
> of God . . . and be freed from all this subjection, we receive from
> the divine hand the gift of forgiveness for previous sins. For even
> as people who have been subjected to a foreign kingdom, after
> they are saved by their true king, receive the likeness of his image
> . . . even so the human race, because through baptism it is freed
> from this entire evil dominion, receives the likeness of Christ
> and forgiveness of sins is given to it (109, 2, 19*).

198   The prince in the Song of the Pearl (XIII) wraps himself in his
scarlet toga (receives forgiveness of sins), and puts on his shining
robe (equivalent to putting on the new person or putting on
Christ), and he returns home to be reunited with his royal family
and the nobles of the realm. John declares that this experience
comes through baptism into Christ (**109, 2, 22***):

> You who have been baptized into Christ, have put on Christ;
> there is no Jew or Aramean, no slave or freeman, for all are one
> in Christ' (Gal 3:27-28). These freedoms, riches, felicities, joys,
> blessings, and this truth, life, delight, kinship with God, divine
> communion, fellowship with the angels, knowledge of the king-
> dom of heaven, undivided unity, everlasting life, these the human
> race receives through the mystery of baptism.

199   Notice, however, that baptism only sets us on the path to attaining the new world. It is only 'a prefiguration (*tupos*) of the
resurrection from the dead' (**109**, 2, 16*). Moreover, John speaks
of a twofold aspect in baptism: 'By baptism I mean not only this
visible baptism, but that by which we are baptized in order to become totally removed from all participation in this world'. (**110**, X,
117*). Baptism, John of Apamea says, involves a new birth, without
which one cannot experience 'contemplation of the sight of the
true world'.

> If a person is not first born through baptism, one can not see the
> kingdom of heaven, as indeed Christ said to Nicodemus (Jn 3:3);
> but by seeing the kingdom he means that in one's soul one ex-
> periences and knows the glorious riches of the wisdom of God.
> (109, 2, 22*)

200   John insists, however, that a path of spiritual progress must be
followed after baptism, and he sets forth Christ as the model for
imitation:

> After his baptism by John he applied himself to the labour of
> fasting . . .; thus our Lord became a helpful model (*tupos*) for
> the baptized, so that after their baptism they would not be
> uncommitted to the labour of repentance. (**109**, 3, 38*).

201   The spiritual path is divided by John into three stages or orders
(*taxis*):

     1. *somatical* (or corporeal), relating to the *body*

     2. *psychical*, relating to the *soul*

     3. *pneumatical* (or spiritual), relating to the *spirit*.

This bears a close resemblance to Paul's three classes of Christians
in 1 Corinthians:

'fleshly' (3:3, *sarkikos*)

'soulish' (2:14, *psukhikos*)

'spiritual' (2:15, *pneumatikos*).

Paul also implies a tripartite division of a person when he says: 'May your spirit, soul, and body be kept blameless' (1 Thess 5:23). Here the word 'body' goes with the 'somatic' or 'corporeal' category of John's three stages of spiritual development.

202   The writings of John the Solitary thus constitute another 'Book of Degrees', with a similar tripartite set of churches (cp paragraph 152): the *visible* church is the assembly of people in their gathering together; the *true* church is found in agreement of thought and of understanding, one in faith; and the *heavenly* church has knowledge of the truth and its members partake of the divine mysteries (**106, 88***). But John insists that perfection is only attained on the other side, after the resurrection of the dead, in 'the new world'. He is appalled at the audacity of those who claim to be 'perfect' in this life, when all they have done is abandon their possessions (in accordance with the Lord's command in Mt 19:21) (**108**, Letter 2.59-64). He may have in mind here the 'perfect' of the *Book of Degrees*, but they were expected to be humble (paragraph 162 above).

203   In John's ascetical and mystical scheme of stages and states, the 'somatical' person achieves 'purity' (*dakhyutha*) and enters the ranks of the 'psychical', who go on to a higher state of purity known as *shaphyutha* (from a root meaning to 'plane' or 'clear'; see paragraph 133), variously translated as 'serenity', 'integrity', 'transparency'; and the final goal is the attainment of 'perfection' at the end of this 'spiritual' ('pneumatical') stage. His analogy for this pilgrimage of faith and hope is a traveller making his way over an uneven terrain which is difficult and tiring; he eventually comes to a plain where he finds journeying easier, towards the magnificent city which is his destination. The perilous part of the journey represents the battle with the passions; the plain is 'serenity'; and the city is 'perfection' (**108**, Letter 2.58).

204   John is fond of categorizing the aspects of each of the three levels. Thus the corporeal fasting is abstinence from food; the psychical fast involves hunger and thirst for righteousness and abstinence from evil deeds; the spiritual fast is complete absence of remembering evil actions and odious things, but this happens perfectly only after the resurrection. He declares that a few individuals reach the 'pneumatical' order, some people enter the

'psychical' stage, but everyone experiences the 'somatical' stage (**106**, 3.66).

205   The possibility that ascetical and mystical ideas were flowing back and forth between India and the Syriac Orient receives apparent support from a comparison of John's *Letter to Hesykhios* (Brock, **114**: 1, 81–98) with Buddhist meditation literature from the early centuries of the current era (Edward Conze, *Buddhist Scriptures*, 1959, 103–116). Thus in the *Saundaranandakavya* of Ashvaghosha (a Buddhist monk of first century CE), the basic step towards the attainment of Nirvana is 'mindfulness', which means withholding sense-objects from the senses. The Buddhist monk is told to apply 'mindfulness' to all activities; when walking, he thinks 'I am walking', and so on; and if sight-objects appear before his eyes he must not classify them as 'man' or 'woman', or 'lovely'. John urges his reader to be 'fully aware' in all his activities; when walking he should not let his eyes wander, but look straight ahead, not 'sating his eyes on the faces of other people' (**114**, paragraph 31–32).

206   John and Ashvaghosha both advocate seclusion and solitude (in the monastery), and the ascetic practices of fasting and keeping vigil. Ashvaghosha lays down the Buddha's 'middle way' between starving the body and stuffing it with excessive food. After spending the day in keeping his mind collected, the monk should also practice yoga meditation at night, and repeat long passages from the Buddhist Scriptures before taking any rest. John sees usefulness in fasting, in that it dispells cravings ('craving' is the root cause of all suffering according to the Buddha, and Ashvaghosha reiterates this fundamental doctrine here); but John rates 'vigilance' more highly than fasting, because it makes the mind luminous, and alert, and makes the body still; he also enjoins reading of the Scriptures, not just standing in prayer, for the solitary will be illumined in prayer as a result of his reading (**114**, paragraphs 23–24, 44, 65).

207   Both monks acknowledge the problem of distracting thoughts which ruin concentration, and evil thoughts which, for the Christian, invite God's judgement if the mind takes pleasure in them (John, 114, 42–43), and which, when nursed in the heart, will grow and breed misfortune for the monk, and others too, and may well lead to punishment in hell (Ashvaghosha). Detachment and non-attachment

are required; the Buddhist monk is told how to deal with thoughts of family and homeland by those means; the Christian monk must not be tied down by anything, but should release himself from the yoke of the world by means of the freedom of the new life (29); he should be friendly to everyone, by all means, but he should not seek attachment to his loved ones, that is, his family (33).

208   The Buddhist is advised to be mindful of death and its inevitability (and rebirth into another life of suffering is the usual result of death). Hesykhios is counselled constantly to hold the image of his death before his eyes, so that his life will be preserved through good works (114, 69). The Buddhist goal is the state of absolute peace, the supreme place of rest where all worldly activity ceases, and where the passions are stilled. For John the aim here and now is peace (51–52), to be tranquil and serene (10), to come near to perfection before we depart from the body (24, 59), and to attain to an exalted state of glory when the Saviour is revealed at the judgement (70).

PHILOXENOS OF MABBUG

209 Philoxenos (in Syriac: Aksenaya) was born of Persian parents at Tahad in Beth Garmai, east of the Tigris and outside the Roman Empire. He was educated at the famous theological college of Edessa known as the Persian School, and he became a monk. He rejected the school's espousal of Theodore of Mopsuestia and turned towards Cyril of Alexandria. He held the episcopate of Mabbug (between Antioch and Edessa) from 485 to 519. Together with Severos of Antioch, he was deeply involved in the Christological controversies of his age; as a result he was banished to Philippopolis in Thrace, and subsequently to Gangra in Paphlagonia, where he met his death in 522 or 523.

210   Besides Bible commentaries and doctrinal writings, Philoxenos produced discourses and epistles on asceticism and spirituality

(124). He is revered by the West Syrian Church as one of their best writers of Syriac language; his name is attached to a Syriac translation of the New Testament, known as the Philoxenian version. He is also regarded as a great teacher of mysticism. The problem is that West Syriac scribes sometimes put notable works of East Syriac mystics under the name of Philoxenos to make them acceptable and available to their own monks. One example of such false attribution is an epistle on the three stages of the spiritual path, by Joseph the Visonary, of which specimens are given in the anthology (XLIII–XLVIII).

211   The letter to Patriq (Patrikios), a monk of Edessa, is thought to be genuine. In its early Greek translation it was attributed to 'Isaac the Syrian', an East Syrian mystic (see paragraph 240) whose writings are accepted by the Orthodox churches, and the name of its recipient was changed to Simeon the Stylite, though Isaac lived in the seventh century and Simeon in the fifth. The subject of the epistle is the relationship of asceticism to mysticism. Patriq asks whether there is a short route to the goal of spiritual contemplation, one that would bypass all the ascetic hardships, which he sees as obstacles. For Philoxenos the spiritual life is inseparable from ascetic 'practice' (exercises of austerity and mortification), 'keeping of the commandments', and 'virtue'. Mysticism is the attainment of 'purity of soul': when the soul is purified of passions the result is 'contemplation' (*theoria*). Typically, this idea stems from the beatitude of 'the pure in heart' (Mt 5:8).

> He has commanded us to seek his revelation within ourselves, as he said to the Jews: 'The kingdom of God is within you' (Lk 17:21). This contemplation of spiritual things is not something for our own will to decide whether we are worthy of it or not; rather it is a gift of his grace. However, whether to keep his commandments or not is the responsibility of our will; and that we should keep the commandments which he has established for us, he teaches us in all his sacred scriptures; but asking him for spiritual contemplation is not there at all. In one of the beatitudes he has given us, which are also commandments, he has told us this: 'Blessed are those who are pure in their heart, for they shall see God'. By this word he has taught us what the

commandments give us when they are kept, namely purity of
heart; and purity of heart brings a person to vision of God. So
he has told us what comes of this, but he has not allowed us to
ask for it. (**127**, 122)

212   The spiritual theology of Philoxenos is baptismal in its emphasis,
another typical Syriac feature:

> Even in our own day the Holy Spirit is given through baptism to
> those who are baptized, and like the first believers, they truly
> receive it (*or* her); but in none of them does it (*or* she) manifest
> its operation visibly; for although it is in them it remains hidden;
> and unless a person abandons the world, sets out on the path
> of spiritual morality, keeps all the commandments given by Jesus,
> and walks straitly and steadfastly in the narrow way of the gospel,
> then the operation of the Spirit received at baptism is not mani-
> fested upon the person. (**127**, 120)

213   Philoxenos warns his reader to distinguish true visions from the
hallucinations of pagans (90–94) and the false revelations of heretics
(107). He relates a cautionary tale concerning 'a certain Adelphios,
who was at one time in the city of Urhai (Edessa) and was the
inventor of the heresy called Messallianism' (108; see above, paragraphs 171–173). Other heresiarchs named by Philoxenos (105)
are Valentinus, Marcion, Bardaisan of Edessa (Bardesanes), Mani the
founder of Manicheism, and 'John the Egyptian'. The last of these
had appeared on the scene 'recently', and may have been John the
Solitary of Apamea.

214   Evagrios, who was condemned in 553, was apparently not considered to be a heretic by Philoxenos. In the Epistle to Patrikios
there are quotations from his *Praktikos* (65 and 133) and *Gnostikos*
(112, twice); Evagrios is not named, but is cited as 'one of the
blessed' (65), or 'one of the fathers' (133), or 'one of the saints'
(112). That Philoxenos accepted some of the teachings of Evagrios
is shown in the following extract, in which the eight passions (or
passionate thoughts), as formulated by Evagrios, are set out in
pairs:

> It is not only the desert which calms the passions, but the pas-
> sions themselves very often calm one another. Thus the passion
> of vainglory calms that of lechery, and vice versa; the passion of
> avarice ('love of gold') that of gluttony ('love of the belly'), and
> vice versa; the passion of sadness that of anger; and the passion
> of acedia ('torpor') that of pride. (**127**, 18)

This procedure of applying opposites is already found in the *Praktikos*
and the *Antirrhetikos* of Evagrios.

215   Philoxenos also knows the five contemplations of Evagrios (*Kephalaia Gnostika*, **54**, I:27), contemplation of the Trinity, of bodiless
beings, of embodied beings, of Divine judgement, of Divine providence:

> The contemplations of the natures are three in number: two of
> them are for the created natures, the rational and non-rational,
> the spiritual and corporeal; and one is for the Holy Trinity. Be-
> sides these there is another order of contemplation: everything
> that is incomprehensible has an intelligible contemplation, namely
> the creation and providence of God, and the judgement on all
> and the holy commandments that we are instructed to keep.
> Moreover, the intellect has a contemplation of itself ('its soul'),
> and all the words contained in the Scripture which are not com-
> mands but mysteries, as also the holy and divine mysteries cele-
> brated by us, all have a spiritual and intellectual contemplation.
> (**127**, 74)

216   The paragon of mystics, for Philoxenos, is Saint Paul (127, 100–
107), who was made worthy of hearing the voice of Christ on the
road to Damascus (102); and after his baptism he received the Holy
Spirit, who 'told him all the mysteries and the revelations of all the
hidden things' (103). Thereupon, according to Philoxenos, Paul lay
on the ground for three days, while his intellect ascended to the
regions above the sky and experienced various contemplations
(103). For Philoxenos, this was the mystical experience that Paul
related 'fourteen years later' in his letter to the Corinthians (2 Cor
12:1-4): 'I know a man in Christ who, fourteen years ago, whether
in his body or out of his body I do not know, God knows, was

raptured to the third heaven . . . into Paradise . . . and he heard things that cannot be told'. Philoxenos uses this as a supreme example of Christian mysticism and its 'spiritual contemplations' (104–106).

217   In his thirteen *Discourses* (**124**, on faith, serenity, fear of God, renunciation of the world, gluttony, abstinence, and mental fornication) Philoxenos distinguishes two Christian ways of life: the way of righteousness and the way of perfection. This is comparable to the 'righteous' and the 'perfect' in the *Book of Degrees*, as two classes of baptized Christians (paragraphs 153–154 above). For Philoxenos, the righteous Christian who lives in the world can obtain justification, but only the spiritual Christian, the monk, can obtain perfection (Discourse 8). Philoxenos thus has three types (Discourse 9):

1. the righteous, who have the wealth of the world and give it to the needy;

2. the spiritual, who renounce the riches of the world for the love of God;

3. the perfect, who have attained the stature of the knowledge of the fulness of Christ, as Paul says.

The stages of the path to perfection are (Discourse 9):

1. avoidance of doing evil;

2. doing good, under the fear of the Law;

3. doing good willingly, beyond fear of the Law;

4. complete abandonment of the world;

5. labours of asceticism for eliminating the old self;

6. carrying the cross and attaining the fulness of the perfection of Christ.

All these steps are based on commands of the Lord.

218   Philoxenos does not seem to allude to the parable of the merchant and the pearl in the *Discourses* or the *Letter to Patriq*; but in

the Greek version of the letter, the pearl appears when these words are put into the mouth of Paul: 'I who am baptized in the Holy Spirit and filled with grace wish to receive the precious pearl within me, through Christ who dwells in me'. In Discourse 9 Philoxenos uses the pearl to represent Christian discipleship, more particularly monasticism; it is not to be sullied with unclean hands, by which he means impure motives for becoming a monk (extract XXIII below).

STEPHEN BAR SUDAILI

219 A younger contemporary of Philoxenos of Mabbug in the first half of the sixth century, Stephen Bar Sudaili was originally a monk of Edessa. A letter of Philoxenos warns two priests of Edessa about the heterodox ideas that Stephen was propagating: he had allegedly imbibed the gnostic doctrines of John the Egyptian, who had studied philosophy and medicine in Alexandria. Stephen moved to Palestine, to the region of Jerusalem, and was there involved in the outbreak of Origenism in the monasteries of Saint Sabas. He returned to Edessa and died there sometime after 543.

220 No writings have survived under the name of Stephen Bar Sudaili, but works of his were circulating in his own lifetime. A thirteenth-century West Syrian scholar and mystic, Gregory Bar Hebraeus, knew that Bar Sudaili was the author of *The Book of the Holy Hierotheos*. The only copy of this work that was available to its modern editor was the one in the British Library, and it was the very same manuscript that Bar Hebraeus had obtained for his own use after a long search. The book purports to be by Hierotheos, the teacher of Dionysios the Areopagite, and to have been translated from Greek into Syriac. Both claims are improbable in the extreme, as critical examination of the text has shown. Whether this fictional framework was devised by the author or an editor is not known. This case is reminiscent of the editor of *The Book of Degrees* attributing it to a disciple of the Apostles (when it was, perhaps, really composed by some suspect monk such as Adelphios of Edessa). It also

follows the pattern of the earlier mystical collection attributed to Dionysios the Areopagite, but there is little or no connection between the Hierothean and Dionysian books.

221   *Hierotheos* is an example of the Origenism of Evagrios taken to extremes, and it may have helped fuel the fire to which Evagrianism was consigned in 553 by the Council of Constantinople. The teachings of Bar Sudaili have been described as eschatological pantheism, which went further than the idea of eschatological unity that was running through the Eastern Christian tradition. In *The Gospel of Thomas* an eschatological unity of male and female is urged. In the last saying in this *Gospel* (112), Jesus declares to his disciples that Mariham (Mary Magdalene) will be made like a man, so that she will become 'a living spirit' like them, because 'every woman who makes herself a man will enter into the kingdom of heaven'. In an earlier saying (23), in explanation of 'little ones receiving milk' being like 'those who enter into the kingdom', Jesus states that dualism must be transcended in unity to ensure entry to the kingdom: 'make the two one . . . the man and the woman a single one, so that the man is not the man, and the woman is not the woman.' It is 'the single ones' who 'enter into the bridechamber' (75) who 'will find the kingdom', because they come from it and will enter into it again (50; cp *Song of the Pearl* I–II); and it is like a wise man who 'sold his cargo and bought for himself the pearl alone' (76). Similarly, in *The Acts of Thomas* (129), there is an allusion to the Pauline assertion, 'all one in Christ Jesus' (Gal 3:20), when Mygdonia (one of the Apostle's converts who has given up 'filthy intercourse' with her husband) looks forward to being in the presence of God, where there is 'neither male nor female', but also 'neither good nor bad'.

222   The next step is taken by Stephen Bar Sudaili, alias Hierotheos: he moves from eschatological unification to eschatological monism (in which the influence of Hinduism may be conjectured). His pantheism is based on another of Paul's pronouncements (taken out of context): 'God will be all in all' (1 Cor 15:8). For Stephen, everything is of a single nature with God, and at some point in the future everything will become identified with God and identical to God. All distinctions will vanish, the good and the evil alike will be united in God, and hell will be no more. The word to describe this consummation is not 'union' (ḥedayutha) but 'commingling' (ḥebikutha),

because those that are united can be separated again, but not those that are commingled (so that their identity is lost).

223   'Hierotheos' states that he is revealing the things that Paul did not dare to tell (2 Cor 12:4). And so he warns his reader that these secret and mystical teachings are only to be communicated to the purified minds of the initiated. This secretiveness can be seen in the extract in the anthology (XXIV), which speaks of not casting pearls before swine, and compares this secrecy with the necessity for the oyster to be concealed within the ocean, or it will not produce pearls.

224   The mystical system of Bar Sudaili begins with an ascent of the mind through successive celestial levels, under attack from demonic beings at each stage. The intellect undergoes a mystical crucifixion at the hands of angels, for its purification. After three days in the tomb, the mind experiences its mystical resurrection and becomes reunited with its body and soul. A descent of the mind then takes place, as it confronts evil in the form of a great tree, and in suffering and in tears it journeys down to the roots of the tree of evil to deal with the demons in the underworld, with the assistance of Christ, 'the great Intellect'. The next step is the second baptism, administered to the mind on high, a baptism of spirit and of fire, for union with the Good. The Spirit descends on the mind and it is no longer called 'intellect' but 'Christ'. Paul's statement, 'we have the mind of Christ' (1 Cor 2:16) might be the doctrinal source here. The intellect now reigns as Christ, entering the Holy of holies to perform the mystical sacrifice and to distribute the mystical bread of perfect knowledge to the angels. Descending again from the spiritual Paradise with its Tree of Life, wielding the mystical sword, he finds the demons pleading for mercy from him. Ultimately, after reascending and redescending, the mind encounters the same luminous Essence that he had seen on high, and thus there is now neither height nor depth for the mind. The perfected intellect passes beyond love, which supposes a distinction between the lover and the beloved, and becomes absorbed, commingled, in the Unity. All names disappear; there is no God, Christ, or Spirit; God has become 'all in all'.

225   The influence of this book cannot have been great; two West Syrian prelates were impressed by it, but endeavoured to cover up

its heterodoxy. Theodosios wrote a commentary on it in the ninth century, apparently accepting its first-century attribution; and in the thirteenth century Bar Hebraeus removed some of the offensive material and rearranged the work.

ABRAHAM OF NATHPAR

226   Abraham, surnamed Nathperaya ('of Nathpar', near Mosul), flourished around 600. After three years of living in a cave as a hermit in the mountains of Adiabene, he travelled to Egypt to visit the Pakhomian monastic heartland. He returned to his own cave for another thirty years of the solitary life. His disciple Job (Ayyob or Ahob) established a monastery at this cave. This disciple had an interesting background. As the son of a pearl trader he had fallen sick while on a business trip; while being nursed in a monastery at Nisibis, he vowed to take up the ascetic life.

227   Job translated Abraham's writings from Syriac into Persian. The surviving Syriac works attributed to Abraham of Nathpar are ten in number: one of these is simply the *Admonition on Prayer* of Evagrios, and another is the discourse *On Prayer* by John of Apamea, prefaced by a few sentences from Aphrahat's *Demonstration on Prayer*. One therefore hesitates to include anything under his name in an anthology. But here is Abraham's response to the purity beatitude (Mt 5:8), in his own or borrowed words (141, 347):

> Make your conscience resplendent with purity, and the Almighty will impart pure thoughts to your soul, with rectitude. He will illumine your conscience; he will be like the purifying cloud before you; all the obstacles of life will be levelled ahead of you. He will bring your little boat to the harbour. The life to come will commence for you here and now: you will do the will of God completely, on earth as in heaven. According to your way of life, and also according to your wisdom, your joy will grow and increase, and you will finally achieve the same vision as the saints receive.

GREGORIOS THE HERMIT

228 Gregorios the Hermit (the Syriac term translated 'hermit' denotes
a 'desert-dweller') seems to have belonged to the sixth or seventh
century. He was a Persian merchant who had visionary experiences.
He went to Edessa and studied in the theological school, subse-
quently moving to Mount Izla near Nisibis to practise the solitary
life. For some reason he travelled to Cyprus, where he entered a
monastery, hence his other appellation, Gregory of Cyprus. Being
unable to speak Greek, he first worked as the monastery's gardener,
but he eventually became the superior of the community. He returned to Mount Izla, died at an advanced age, and was buried in
the sepulchre of Mar Awgin, the reputed founder of Syriac monasticism (paragraph 3 above).

229 Gregorios produced a book of discourses 'On Holy Contemplation' (*theoria*), and a collection of letters. His book owes something
to Evagrios Pontikos, and he employs John the Solitary's framework
of corporeal, psychical, and spiritual stages. His starting point in
discussing 'holy contemplation' is the purity of heart that leads to
seeing God (Mt 5:8). He gives advice on defeating passions and
demons, such as gluttony, vainglory, and depression (*akedia*). The
goal, as with Evagrios, is 'impassibility' (*apatheia*). Then the Father
and Son, and even the whole Trinity, can come and dwell in him (cp
Jn 14:23). He says that when Paul reached the third stage, that of
'spirituality', he was transported to the third heaven, where he saw
and heard ineffable things (2 Cor 12); prayer then becomes speaking with God with 'familiarity' (*parrhesia*, 'boldness'), a technical
term in Syriac mysticism.

SAHDONA-MARTYRIOS

230 The variant names Sahdona (Syriac) and Martyrios (Greek), given to
this seventh-century monk, carry the idea of 'witnessing' (or even

'martyrdom'). It seems that he spent his last years in exile in a cave near Edessa, after being hounded by his own East Syrian Church for alleged heresy. He was born at Halmon in Persia, son of a pious Christian woman whose prayers (like those of Monica for Augustinus) brought him into the monastic life, while he was still a young man. He was apparently educated at the School of Nisibis, and was accepted into the Mount Izla monastery of Beth Abey by its founder Jacob. Around 635 he became a bishop, but at some time before 650 he was deposed by the Patriarch of the Church of the East, and he left Persia.

231   *The Book of Perfection* is his most important work, an ascetical and spiritual book which, he claims, was written when he was twenty-eight years old, though it reads like the wisdom of a person with long experience. There are traces of the intellectual mysticism of Evagrios in Sahdona, but his mentors are rather Saint Basil of Caesarea and Saint Gregory of Nazianzus. He distinguishes cenobitic monks, 'who renounce marriage', and solitary monks, who are 'strangers to the world and united to God' (1.3.82); but he rejects absolute eremitism in favour of semi-anchoritism, in which contemplation and action are balanced.

232   Sahdona's paragon of the solitary life is given an enthusiastic pen portrait in his book. His mother had frequently taken him to visit this holy hermit, who became an inspiring example to him, namely Shirin, 'blessed among women' (Jdg 5:24-27); who was in her eighties when he knew her:

> Like Jael (cp Jdg 4:22) she plucked desire out of herself as a peg from the tent of her body, wielded it, and laid out at her feet the hidden enemy who fights against the saints; by outward labours and by mystical prayer, she humiliated all his manly strength and nailed his head to the earth. He, the evil one, is thus put to shame: having originally been victorious and sown his error through a woman, he is now defeated by women, through him who was born of the virgin and who has made their nature strong. She appeased the continual hungering of the belly with a meagre ration, to sustain her body and not for the demands of its desires. A small cake of lentil bread was her meal each evening, with boiled vegetables; and although she sustained

herself with this food only, and drinking only water, her face was
radiant with the grace of the Spirit who nourished her, so that
anyone would have imagined that she was regaling herself with
luxury foods; and yet mostly she was dining only once in every
four days, or even once a week. She was so diligent in prayer
and so vigilant in the lengthy office that it would not be a lie to
say that she was continually engaged in it. She spent most nights
without sleep, constantly singing psalms and praying; moreover,
by day she was also occupied with reading the Scriptures, stories
of righteous people, and instructional literature for reforming
morals and teaching reverence for God. She was so peaceful
and so gentle, so pure and so simple, generous with love and
charity to everyone, ever ready to receive strangers. (1.3.69-79,
abridged)

233   Martyrios bases his mysticism on Paul's antithesis between the
outer and the inner person (2 Cor 4:16: 'our outer person is wast-
ing away, our inner person is being renewed day by day'), rather
than in the typical Syriac tripartite scheme of body, soul, spirit
(1.3.11-32). The outer practices include renunciation, repentance,
prayer, austerity, and struggling with passions and demons; these
produce in the interior person 'the fruits of the Spirit' (Gal 5:22),
of 'faith, hope, and love' (1 Cor 13:13).

234   The extract in the anthology (XXV) twice uses the metaphor
of pearls. Some of the imagery in the *Song of the Pearl* can also be
found in Sahdona's *Book of Perfection*. There is the prospect of 'the
delights of the kingdom of heaven, endless repose, praise and
honour from God, and the sheen and beauty of the robe of glory,
sparkling with light' (1.3.27; cp XI–XIII). Like John of Apamea (paragraph 203) Sahdona uses the analogy of a plain and a city as the
last stage of the path of perfection: the monk traverses a narrow
track, surrounded by sea and brigands; eventually he comes to a
broad plain, where peace and repose are enjoyed; finally he enters
the city of the kingdom and beholds the King on his glorious throne
and in his ineffable beauty (1.3.156-163).

235   In Part 2, Chapter 8, Sahdona treats prayers as an interior offering
of the heart, which must be pleasing to God. Perfect prayer without
blemish, purified of passions and accompanied by attentiveness and

tears, will be accepted by God, who will in return send the fire of his Spirit to consume our sacrifice, and will raise our mind to heaven in the flames of the sacrifice. 'Then we shall behold the Lord, to our delight and not to our destruction' (cp Ex 33:20, and Ex 24:9-11), 'as the stillness of his revelation falls upon us, and the hidden things of the knowledge of him are portrayed in us; our hearts will be given spiritual joy, together with hidden mysteries which I am unable to disclose in words to the simple' (2.8.20; cp 2.8.55).

SIMON TAIBUTHEH

236   Shem'on de-Taibutheh or Simon the Gracious (literally 'of his grace') was an East Syrian monk of the seventh century. He was also a physician, and he produced a medico-mystical book, in which he attempted to relate his medical 'knowledge' of the bodily organs to his ascetical and mystical experience. He is, for example, very technical about the workings of the heart: the right ventricle, he says, receives the blood from the liver and purifies it, and sends it on to the brain and the rest of the body; the left ventricle is understood as the seat of the animal spirit, which it subtilizes and sends to the lobes of the brain, where rationality is created, together with memory and understanding. If the 'tablets of the heart' are inscribed with good (as a result of fulfilling commandments, victory over passions, knowledge of divine things), then the heart radiates light, peace, and life, and the memory and the understanding are thereby purified and illuminated (**152**, 198a–199a). He divides the mystical path into seven stages (167b–168a):

1. novitiate, the struggle to show obedience to authority;

2. change, to a life of discipline;

3. warfare, against the passions, through fulfilling the commandments, to achieve purity of heart;

4. mental labour, to discern the providence of God;

5. mental contemplation of the incorporeal beings;

6. contemplation and ecstasy over the mystery of the Godhead;

7. divine grace works mystically and ineffably in the mind, sometimes overwhelming it with love.

This scheme, with its contemplation of providence, incorporeal beings, and the Trinity, owes something to Evagrios, who is in fact named in another connection (169b).

237   Simon has another set of spiritual stations, in which he speaks of 'three ascents' (174b–176a):

1. The novice makes his exodus from Egypt and proceeds across the broad and restful plain of Egypt, unaware of the trials and pitfalls that lie ahead of him; and when he encounters them, he may turn back, or he may stop and mock those who go further, or he will join them in their exertions.

2. The middle ascent involves mountains, seas, winds, darkness, dejectedness, grief, and 'the fourteen impediments of Abba Isaiah', as 'they mount up to the heavens and go down again to the depths' (Ps 107:26). When they see the monks on the plains of the first and third stages, they mistakenly rebuke them for their seeming idleness. Eventually they become 'illuminated', and worthy to enter the third realm.

3. In the stage of perfection, the 'spiritual' person rests on the plain of serenity and reaches the harbour of peace, the haven of impassibility, and while still in this world his soul dwells in the next world.

238   This last idea is developed in extract XXVI: a person from India and China who lives in Syria has a different culture and does not really belong to the Syrian world. Similarly the spiritual monk who has experienced the mysteries of the New World (the next world) is an alien in this world; he is in the world but not of the world. At the same time (extract XXVIII) Simon reprimands himself: In my garb (as a monk) I am a stranger to the world, but I keep a deposit on it; I am stronger than it, yet I am caught in the snares of its desires. Come and marvel, he says, at a merchant who trades with a purse that has holes in it.

239　　　Simon does not use the pearl symbol in his book, but he has musk as a metaphor for the essence of monasticism. Musk becomes adulterated as it is passed on from person to person, and it loses its precious qualities. The earliest monks obtained the gift of grace, received spiritual knowledge, worked miracles, and experienced the mystery of revelations. When the mystery was handed on, all these things were lost in monasticism (XXVII). And Simon has the treasure metaphor for the beauty and glory hidden in a person, waiting to be brought to light through ascetic exercise (XXIX). He also has a word of comfort for the non-achiever: he invokes a blessing on the person who has not experienced the blissful operation of grace, but who can (by knowledge, theory, and understanding obtained through reading) investigate and learn about this operation, which is performed on those who have been purified (176a).

ISAAC OF NINEVEH

240　Isaac bishop of Nineveh, known in the Eastern Orthodox churches as Isaac the Syrian, was born in Qatar, a peninsula on the Arabian side of the Persian Gulf. After his monastic training in Mesopotamia, he was ordained bishop of Nineveh (Mosul) by the Katholikos Mar Giwargis (660–680). He lasted only five months in this office, abruptly retreating to the solitary life in the mountains of Huzistan in south-western Iran. He lived to a great age but eventually suffered blindness, for which his ardent reading was blamed, and thereafter he dictated his books to his disciples.

241　The writings attributed to him are: firstly, a collection of some eighty-two discourses on spirituality which were translated from Syriac into Greek in the ninth century by the monks Abramios and Patrikios of the Laura of Saint Sabas in Palestine, and in this form Isaac the Syrian was welcomed into the fold of Eastern Orthodoxy; secondly, four 'centuries', sayings in groups of one hundred each; thirdly miscellaneous epistles and discourses; fourthly, a work en-

titled *The Book of Grace*, in seven sets of 'centuries'. Only the first
of these collections has had wide dissemination.

242   In Isaac's mystical teaching four main streams meet: Evagrian,
Makarian, Dionysian, and Johannine (Apamean). Evagrios is frequently quoted by name in the eighty-two discourses. In Discourse
22 (Bedjan's edition, **153**, 163–175), for example, he is invoked more
than once as an authority on the highest forms of prayer, in opposition to the Messallians who claim they can perform 'spiritual prayer'
at will (171). And Isaac has the Evagrian image of 'the light of the
Holy Trinity' being like 'sapphire or the colour of heaven, as the
place of God was called by the elders of Israel, to whom it appeared
on the mountain' (174–175; cp paragraphs 69–71 above). And the
combined weight of Evagrios and Pseudo-Makarios is brought to
bear on the Messallians (495 and 500; cp paragraph 83). Isaac speaks
of 'fiery impulses' clothing the mystic, and this is a Makarian motif
(367, extract XL below; paragraphs 85–89 above). The Dionysian
contribution (cp paragraph 124) is seen in Isaac's use of *Divine
Names* 4.11 (**76**) to show that names and words pass away when
mystical unification is achieved (169), and *Celestial Hierarchy* 6–7
(**76**) to distinguish the nine classes of heavenly beings (187). He also
follows Pseudo-Dionysios in designating the three stages of the
spiritual life as: novitiate, intermediate, and perfection, that is, firstly
the beginners or novices, secondly the intermediates, thirdly the
perfect (Discourse 12, **153**, 121–123). But his main schema for
separating the three types is borrowed from John the Solitary of
Apamea, whom he apparently mentions once, as the blessed John
(334).

243   In speaking of the relationship between faith and knowledge in
Discourse 51, 'On the three degrees of knowledge' (360–377; cp
XL below), he uses John the Solitary's 'body, soul, spirit' framework
(369–375). The *first* stage of knowledge is concerned with love for
the *body* (369–372). The *second* or *intermediate* degree involves
psychical love (372–373). The *third* is the degree of *perfection* and
spirituality. Isaac has thus combined the two systems of classification.
He also has the two goals, *purity* and *serenity*, for the somatical and
psychical stages respectively. In the first stage the monk defeats the
passions, which have their seat in the body, and it is purified of them.

The psychical stage involves the purification of mind and soul, ridding them of thoughts that are foreign to the person's true nature. The result is serenity and impassibility. The distinguishing feature of this second stage is the continual outpouring of tears; such tears are absent from the corporeal stage because the mind is immersed in passions. When the gift of tears comes, the monk will find that they will be so constant and profuse that he will be drinking them in with his meals (245). This is a sign that the soul is moving into the spiritual stage where the flow of tears ceases, where the integrity of the soul is restored, and where ecstasy occurs, so that the person is rapt in wonderment, in a state of deep spiritual inebration, and no longer in this world (174).

244   This spiritual state corresponds to the life in the new world after the resurrection (304). There are temporary foretastes of it through the intervention of the Holy Spirit, but the mystic must wait patiently, with joy and hope, for the final consummation and the unending bliss. The extracts in the anthology (XXX–XL) are concerned with the voyage towards the harbour of rest and the last mooring (XXX–XXXIII); the solitary life (XXXIV–XXXIX); and faith (XL). The pearl acts as a metaphor for Christ (XXXIV), treasures of grace (XXXVIII), and faith (XL). Isaac's uniting of faith and knowledge (XL) could be compared with the pearl and the robe in the Song of the Pearl (paragraph 46–47). Isaac also uses the pearl as a symbol for chastity, a pearl of great price which the monk is ever in danger of losing (543).

245   Some of Isaac's descriptions of mystical experiences are revealing. Here is an example of the illuminations of the second stage, experienced at the time of prayer, when the monk is on his knees.

> When God opens your mind from within, and you give yourself over to frequent genuflexion, do not give your heart up to anxiety about anything, even though the demons secretly seek to persuade you. Then gaze in wonder at what is generated in you by this. . . . Sometimes a person will be on his knees at the time of prayer, with his hands outspread or stretched heavenwards, and his face gazing at the cross, and, so to speak, his whole attention and his whole mind directed towards God in supplication, and while he is thus engaged in beseeching and groaning,

suddenly a fountain of delight will spring up from his heart, his limbs will slacken, his eyes will be shut, his face will be bowed down, and his thoughts will be interrupted, so that his knees are just not able to rest on the ground, because of the exhilaration from that act of grace, spreading through his whole body. Consider, man, what you are reading. Can such things be communicated through ink? Can the taste of honey be conveyed to a reader's palate through writing? (57–58)

The ascetic exercise of keeping vigil and foregoing sleep can bring the reward of divine revelations, while the monk is standing.

It is said of one particular saint that because the demon of lechery was waging war against him on all fronts, he committed himself to the labour of vigil, and imposed on himself the rule that he would not bend his knees at all, but would stand all night, with his eyes open, not going down on his knees until morning. . . . Through the labour of vigil, ascetics cast off the old person, depraved with improper desires, and they put on Christ, and are saved. Through this kind of labour performed with wisdom, the saints become worthy of wondrous divine revelations, higher than fleshly thought. When ascetics are enjoying such things in their vigils, they pass the whole duration of the long hours of the night without tiring, as their soul exults and rejoices and forgets that it is wearing a coat woven of passions. And because of the delight and the elation of their heart, they do not think about sleep. They imagine that they have cast off their body and are already in the state that comes after the resurrection. Because of their great joy they sometimes leave off their psalmody, and fall on their faces, from the excitement of the joy aroused in their soul. And the whole length of the night is like the day to them, and the darkness like the sunrise, because of the hope that lifts up their heart and intoxicates them with its ideas, and through the blazing of their mind, enkindled by reflecting on things to come (549–550).

246   But illumination and ecstasy can also surprise the monk while he is sleeping, as Isaac shows in describing what is apparently an experience of his own (492):

I know a person who even during his sleep was caught up in
ecstasy with God through the contemplation of something he
had read in the evening. While his soul was stupefied in this
contemplative meditation, he perceived that he had been meditating for a long time, while going through the motions of sleeping, and observing the ecstatic vision. It was in the deep of the
night, when he suddenly woke from his sleep; tears flowed like
water, down onto his breast; his mouth was full of praises and
his heart meditated in contemplation protractedly, with in-
exhaustible delight.

247   There is no doubt that Isaac is the most famous of the Syriac
mystics. His writings (translated into Greek with a few necessary
alterations) were and are admired in all the Eastern churches (cp
paragraph 259). In the West, in the Middle Ages, they were translated from Greek into Latin under the title *De contemptu mundi*,
and there were also Spanish, French, and Italian versions. The
Slavonic translation found its way into the Russian edition of the
Philokalia.

DADISHO QATRAYA

248 Dadisho Qatraya was a contemporary and a compatriot of Isaac
of Nineveh: both lived in the second half of the seventh century,
and both came from Qatar (hence the surname Qatraya, 'Qatarian').
Two surviving works of Dadisho have been published: his commentary on the *Asketikon* of Abba Isaiah (Esaias of Sketis, paragraph
77 above); and a set of pieces making up a *Discourse on Solitude*
(*shelyutha*; solitude, stillness, silence; Greek *hesukhia*). The second
of these gives an insight into the life of the solitary monk. Dadisho
is speaking primarily to young monks who need guidance on their
obligatory seven-week retreat in a secluded cell.
249   The three great struggles that confront the solitary in the desert
are terror in the night, weariness in the daytime, and mental delu-
sions caused by demons (**169**, Syriac text, folio 7ab). For the monk
who undertakes solitary seclusion, there are three requirements:

right intention, faithful performance of his spiritual service in the cell, and a guide (8a). This is where extract XLI comes in to emphasize right intention. The performance of the services and prayers in the cell will ward off the demons, and the monk will be rewarded with spiritual understandings, divine consolations, and victory over passions and demons (9a). For the young solitary, two major problems will be dejectedness and passions aroused by demons, and he will need an experienced leader to visit him on occasion, to console him and admonish him through the aperture of the cell.

250   In extract XLII the benefits of solitude, the spiritual treasures, are enumerated, notably the familiar 'purity of heart' which brings divine vision, so that the solitary 'sees in himself the holy light of his mind', and 'the divine light of the glory of Christ shines in his soul through the inspiration of the Holy Spirit' (11ab). In the section on 'pure prayer' (34a–36b), Dadisho says that this is the means by which passions are healed, sins are forgiven, and purity of heart is acquired, leading to contemplation of God.

251   Dadisho shows himself to have been a well-read scholar. Besides the Holy Scriptures, the desert ascetics, and the Doctors of the Church, he also quotes non-christian philosophers on the advantages of solitude (26b–29b). He is fond of quoting Evagrios, Esaias of Sketis, and Mark the Hermit; he knows the *Apophthegmata* of the Desert Fathers, the Makarian writings, and works of such earlier Syriac writers as Ephrem.

JOSEPH THE VISIONARY

252 Yausep Ḥazzaya (Joseph the Seer) was born early in the eighth century, of Zoroastrian parents, his father being a Magian priest. At the age of seven he was captured and enslaved by Arabs. After serving an Arab master for three years, he passed into the service of a Christian. When Joseph received baptism he was released by his master, and this left the young man free to enter a monastery in the Qardu region of northern Iraq. Eventually Joseph took up the solitary life, but returned to be the abbot of a monastery. A further

sojourn in the desert was followed by another period of abbacy in a different community of monks. He died at an advanced age.

253   He was reputedly the author of many writings on mysticism, but not all of them have survived; and those that are still extant are not always under the name Joseph Ḥazzaya. We are told that he was condemned at a synod in 786/787, along with John of Dalyatha and John of Apamea, by the Patriarch Timothy I, head of The Church of the East. This may be why some of his works have been transmitted under the name Abdisho (said to be the name of his brother, who was also a monk). West Syrian scribes preserved his important letter on the three degrees of the spiritual life, but they put it under the name of their own illustrious teacher, Philoxenos. Joseph wrote commentaries on the books of Evagrios, Pseudo-Dionysios, and Abba Esaias, so we would expect to see their influence in his own doctrine. His commentary on the *Asketikon* of Esaias has not survived, though it is quite possible that the anonymous fragments of such a commentary (published by R. Draguet, 182) belong to this book, but Draguet does not accept Joseph as their author. The writer refers to Mar Isaac (of Nineveh) as his teacher, and while it is possible to fit such an encounter between Joseph and Isaac into the time span of 650–750 (both lived long lives), in their biographies there is no mention of them ever meeting. Joseph (Abdisho) does, however, quote 'Mar Isaac' once in his published works.

254   Joseph's basic framework of three stages of mysticism is borrowed from John of Apamea (John the Solitary): he relates them to the body (corporeal), the soul (psychical), and the spirit (pneumatical) (paragraph 201), and sets forth the goals of purity, serenity, and perfection (paragraph 203). In his letter on the three degrees, Joseph draws an analogy with the Exodus of the Israelites. The coming out of Egypt and the entering into Sinai is symbolic of abandoning the world for the monastery. The Hebrews were placed under the Ten Commandments as servants of God; likewise the novice monk. In this *first* stage the goal is purity, so the body has to be tamed and purified by the practices of fasting, vigil, prayer, psalmody, and reading. This corresponds to the 'practice' of Evagrios and the 'purification' of Dionysios. The *second* phase is the crossing of the Jordan river and the entering of the promised land to con-

quer the foreign nations, equivalent to entering the cell of solitude and battling with the demons, to cleanse the *soul* of their evil influence, and to achieve serenity. The status here is that of a *worker* expecting his daily pay; and the solitary monk receives gifts of grace as reward for his labor, the Dionysian 'illumination' and the Evagrian 'natural contemplation'. The *third* level is the state of *perfection*, entry into glorious Sion as son of God (cp *Song of the Pearl*, paragraphs 53–56), the stage of the *spirit*, with revelations of divine mysteries (LV). This is the Dionysian 'unification' of 'the perfect', and the Evagrian divine vision or contemplation of the Holy Trinity.

255 The remarkable thing about Joseph's writing is his unexpected willingness to talk about the experiences of the spiritual stage, albeit in language that is both guarded and ecstatic. In the 'sphere of spirituality', above the level of 'serenity', the experiences are ineffable, and also ethereal; God is perceived as being formless, without image ('On the prayer that comes to the mind in the sphere of serenity; and against those who claim that there is a material image and likeness to the vision of the mind that has reached the sphere that is above that of serenity . . . in which God has no image or likeness'; see LIV–LV).

256 When Joseph describes the mystical operations of the Holy Spirit originally received at baptism, he relies on Evagrios and Pseudo-Makarios, as we have seen (paragraphs 70–71, 84–85, 93–97). The *first* operation is the love of God burning like fire in the heart and producing contempt for the world and desire for asceticism (XLIX); this is already described in the Makarian *Spiritual Homilies* (paragraphs 85–88 above). The *second* sign is true humility, whereby all people are seen as 'great and holy, and there is no difference in his mind between good and bad, righteous and sinner' (L; cp XLVIII); Makarios expresses the same idea (paragraphs 93–95), and it is also affirmed in the *Book of Degrees* (paragraph 162 above). The *third* sign is universal charity and compassion, for all human beings (LI); this is also known to Makarios (paragraphs 96–98). The *fourth* operation is divine love engendering mystical revelations (LII); here Evagrios is a likelier source (see paragraphs 70, 84). The *fifth* is the reception of the light of the Godhead (LIII), and the other four of the five contemplations of Evagrios (70–71).

257   Joseph is fond of the *pearl* metaphor; he does not shrink from using it to describe one of his own books (XLIII). Like Sahdona (XXV) he has a variation on the theme of 'casting pearls before swine', whereby foolish people cannot discern the value of the pearl (XLVII). The merchant-monk labours for the pearl, the experience of divine mysteries (XLVIII, cp XLVI).

JOHN THE VENERABLE

258   A glance at the anthology will show that more pages are allotted to this mystic than to any other person in this collection. The bibliography for John the Venerable reveals that I have a particular affection for this author; hence the special place he holds in this book. Fortunately this bias can be justified on the valid grounds that hardly anything of his work has been published in English translation before this. And yet he is the most approachable of all these mystical writers. He is less technical than Joseph the Visionary and more lyrical too. He uses metaphors and symbols in joyous profusion, and he carries his reader on high with him in his ecstatic descriptions of mystical experience (LXIII, LXXI–LXXII, LXXIII–LXXIV, LXXV–LXXIX, LXXXI–XCIII).

259   A Syriac corpus of two dozen discourses (or homilies), approximately fifty epistles, and some 'chapters of knowledge', have been bequeathed to us, almost anonymously, ascribed simply to 'the holy saba' (old man) or (in their Arabic translation) 'the spiritual sheikh'. But the manuscript tradition lets slip that the author's name was Yoḥannan, and so he has come to be known as Yoḥannan Saba, that is 'John the Old Man', John the Elder (Sebastian Brock's designation for him), or John the Venerable, as we shall call him here. One biography of this author, attributed to one 'David the Phoenician', has John Saba identified with John bar Penkayé (or John of Penek), who was also known as John of Dalyatha. However, the best solution to the John Saba mystery is to distinguish the scholastic historian John of Penek from the mystical writer John of

Dalyatha, the author of the works attributed to John Saba. One reason for concealing his identity was that John of Dalyatha was condemned for alleged Messallianism by the East Syrian Patriarch, Timothy I. No East Syriac manuscripts of his mystical writings are known today, but his works were rescued from oblivion by West Syriac scribes and were preserved in monasteries as far away as Mount Sinai and the Egyptian Desert. They also passed into Arabic and Ethiopic translations, and four of the pieces in the Greek version of Isaac's discourses (paragraph 247), which was made in the Saint Sabas monastery in Palestine, are actually by 'the holy Saba', John of Dalyatha of the eighth century (not to be confused with Saint Sabas, in Syriac Mar Saba, who died in 532).

260   Briefly, John Saba came from Beth Nuhadra. As a child he read all the books in the local libraries, and as soon as possible he became a monk. He had two brothers who also entered the monastery, and when he moved on into the solitary life he sent his thoughts, written on scrap materials, to his brothers; these writings were eventually combined into books. He lived in the mountains of Beth Dalyatha, and later in the hills of Qardu, where he set up a monastery. He died at a great age and was buried in the monastery.

261   Like Saint Francis he had a reputation for being at ease with animals. Wild beasts would not harm him because they sniffed the scent of their Creator on him, he being so close to God. And he was an expert on how to overcome demons: he wrote discourses on the demons of lechery, anger, distraction, distress, pride, and blasphemy. Here is an example of his strategy against the demon of blasphemy (Vatican Syriac MS 124, 289b–290a):

> As the Lord showed me in a spiritual vision, we write the stratagems of this blaspheming demon, for the consolation of those who are tormented by him. I have seen this wicked demon; he is fouler in odour and more hideous in appearance than all the unclean demons. He will cling to a brother at any time, and blaspheme while the brother is praying, chanting, reading, praising, celebrating the life-giving mysteries, or partaking of them; . . . the demon clings to him and blasphemes against their Maker, producing his blasphemous voices in the soul, which becomes troubled and distressed, thinking that these outrageous blasphemies

are impulses of its own. Far from it. . . . Give unceasing praise,
beloved soul, because your Lord has distinguished your pure and
lovely praises from the blasphemies of the deceitful one, for even
if they are mingled and coupled with them they are not confused
by him, but are pure and holy and without blemish.

262   The spiritual life starts with repentance, the mother that gives
new birth to the repentant soul (LVII–LVIII). Motherhood imagery,
including the comforting and nurturing maternal breast, is characteristic of John Saba (LVIII). The Holy Spirit is also the *Genetrix* who
gives suck (XCI). This is a natural motif in Syriac theology, as we
have seen (paragraph 19). And the vision of God depends on the
usual Syriac precondition, namely purity of heart (Mt 5:8): 'He
whose heart is purified of passions sees God perpetually' (LIX);
'You who desire for yourself purity through which the Lord of all
may be seen, do not commit slander or listen to words of calumny
concerning your brethren. . . . Heaven is already within you if you
are pure, and there you see angels rejoicing, with their Lord among
them and within them' (LX; cp LXIV).

263   The fiery impulse which Makarios saw as the motivating force
for renouncing the secular world (85–88) is known to John Saba.
The monk who returns to the world is like a fish leaving the water
to live on the land, only to be stifled; similarly 'the fiery impulses
emanating from God vanish from the heart of the solitary who likes
worldly society and business' (LXII). It is the demon of lechery who
cools the monk's spiritual ardour and fills his soul with 'fantasies
and vanities' when he is asleep, 'so that the beloved angels withdraw
because of its putrid odour' (LXV). On the other hand, the pure
soul has resplendent beauty 'a hundred times more glorious than
the orb of the sun' (LXIII).

264   In isolation from the world, the ascetic sheds tears of compunction (LXV), and in a moving prayer, a veritable meditation on the
Passion, he says:

You who wept and shed tears of sorrow over Lazarus, accept
my bitter tears. May my passions be allayed by your Passion;
may my wounds be healed by your wounds, my blood be blended
with your blood . . . (LXVI).

Because this supplication passed to the West among the Isaac discourses, in Greek and Latin translation, it is possible that it had an influence in the Orthodox and Catholic churches, notably in the *Anima Christi* prayer (**201**).

265 Besides Makarian motifs (paragraphs 86 and 98), John Saba refers to such Dionysian concepts (126–127) as 'the cloud of essential light' and 'union and perfect commingling with God' (LXVIII). He has a system of three stages of spiritual development, which in its features and terminology (first stage; intermediate stage; psychical state; stage of perfection) is an amalgamation of ideas from John the Solitary of Apamea (who was condemned along with John Saba and Joseph Hazzaya), and from Dionysios, Makarios, and Evagrios (LXIX–LXXII).

266 The pearl-merchant and the pearl-diver are at the forefront of his imagery (paragraph 1, LXXVII, LVI). The prayerful mystic has access to all the divine treasures:

> Through prayer the mind opens the door to the treasuries of God and becomes his treasurer and the divider of his riches. Through prayer it is made worthy to behold the glory of God, and to abide in the Cloud of his majestic light, within the place of the spirits, in stupefaction and silence, void of impulses, in ecstasy, and wonderstruck at the beauty of the many-splendoured rays of light dawning upon it (LXXV).

ABRAHAM BAR DASHANDAD

267 Known as 'the Lame', Abraham bar Dashandad lived in the eighth century. He taught at the Christian school of Bashosh in Persia, and two of his pupils became patriarchs of The Church of the East, namely the Katholikos Timotheos I (780–823), and his successor Isho' bar Nun (d. 828). As we have seen, the first of these was very suspicious of some of the mystics under his jurisdiction: Joseph the Visonary and John the Venerable were condemned by him (paragraphs 253, 259).

268   Only one mystical text by this writer has been published in recent times: 'The letter of Mar Abraham bar Dashandad which he wrote to his brother, who had gone forth to the itinerant ascetic life'. The 'brother' (not necessarily a sibling) would have been following the age-old Syriac pattern of 'going forth' to lead the life of homeless wandering advocated in the Gospels; he was going to be a 'solitary' (**202**, 61a).

269   The ascetic and devotional exercises recommended by Abraham are: 'silence, solitude, prudence, watchfulness' (61a), reading in silence, recitation of Psalms, prayers, labours of repentance (61a, 63b, 64a, 65b). He cautions his reader against excessive sleeping, eating, and talking (60b); but vigil and fasting should be practised with moderation (61a). 'Victory over his passions' should be the monk's goal, and this can be achieved by depicting before one's mind the sight of the rich man in Hell (Gehenna), suffering torments because of the pleasures he enjoyed in this world (64b).

> Do not possess anything but the love of God, in complete renunciation of this world and of all its possessions, because it is in him that we live, move, and have our being (Acts 17:28). He is the life of everything, and everything is from him; everything is in him, and everything is for him (64b).

270   The basic remedy prescribed by Abraham, with repeated dosage, is remembrance of death (202, 62a, 62b, 63b, 64a, 65a; cp paragraph 208 above). 'Blessed is he who continually has the image of his death before his eyes, and who prepares himself provisions that will help him in the new world' (63b).

271   The mystical objectives are neatly summarized in this statement: 'Silence finds God; purity sees the living God'. In outlining the spiritual path depicted by Abraham, who offers 'the reward of *pearls*' to those who persist in meditation, virtues, good works, and pure thoughts (XCVII), we shall note some remarkable comparisons with The Song of the Pearl (I–XIII). This will serve to reinforce the argument that this poem is simply based on the spiritual teachings of the Bible; and the same is true of Syriac Christian mysticism.

272   The mystic monk has to be a solitary (61a), as the pearl prince was 'solitary and alone, a stranger' in the evil land of Egypt (IV). The dedicated monk must not commune with men of loose conduct or 'anyone who does not care about the salvation of his life', who will dissuade him from communion with Christ (62b); similarly the prince apparently spoiled his communion with his 'anointed' intimate friend, when he began to conform to the Egyptian way of life (IV).

273   The solitary must realize that filling the stomach, sleeping excessively, and distracting the mind with thoughts of the outside world separate one from eternal happiness (61b). Conforming to the customs of the Egyptians (meaning worldlings) and eating their food made the prince fall into heavy sleep, and he forgot his glorious destiny (V–VI).

274   'You have been called to heavenly things; do not be bound to earthly things', says Abraham (66a). The prince is similarly reminded of his bondage to the world of Egypt, and his forgotten task, and the rewards awaiting him in the celestial realm of 'the East' (VI). This reminder comes in the form of a letter (VII), representing the Holy Scriptures (cp paragraph 35). The Bible, Bar Dashandad declares, 'will teach you all that is helpful to your life', on such matters as faith, hope, and love (65a). This 'holy reading' is associated with 'the hope of the promises' and 'the reward of your works', in the admonitions appended to the letter (67a); such ideas appear in the pearl poem (promise, II, XIII; works or labours, XII).

275   'Remember that you are a son of kings . . . and that with your brother our viceroy you shall be heir in our kingdom' was the call to the prince in Egypt (VI). Similarly Abraham affirms: 'Remember that you are the son of God and the brother of the Beloved of the Father' (67a), and he expounds 'the inheritance of the saints', including participation in 'the glorification of the angels', comparable to the prince's experience on his arrival home to join the 'servants' of the king in their praise and glorification (XIII).

276   'The pure children are the children of the Kingdom, and the children of the new world despise everything in this world' (64b). The prince, after he remembered his ancestry, stripped off the 'filthy abominable clothing' of Egypt, and headed homewards to the

realm of light (VIII). Abraham says that social intercourse is 'the domicile of all the demons, and of straying, and complete separation from God' (61a), and 'Blessed is he who has not slumbered throughout his voyage, right to the haven of decease' (65a), apparently quoting Isaac of Nineveh (XXXIX). Unfortunately the prince did fall asleep, but he awoke, performed his task of dealing with the serpent, and proceeded past Sarbug, where the demons were entrenched (VII), and arrived at the haven of Maishan (IX), with his pearl intact (representing faith, and perhaps also purity; cp Isaac XXXIX, and paragraph 244).

277   There the prince received his ornamented robes (X–XII) as the reward of his labours (XII), and he arrived home to be reunited with his brother ('the splendour of my father', paragraphs 18 and 52), who 'rejoiced and welcomed' him (XIII). 'Adorn yourself with good works and enter into the joy of your Lord', and 'inherit everlasting life', Bar Dashandad exclaims (63b).

278   Finally, the donning of the shining robe (XI–XIII), with its allusions to grace and love, faith and knowledge, and putting on the Lord Jesus Christ (par. 46–50), finds a parallel in Abraham's closing admonition (67b): 'Let us pray sorrowfully at all times that *grace* will *shine* in our heart. *Truth* is the measure of *love*, and *works* are the *knowledge* of *faith*; but as for the soul that is far removed from these, what profit has it gained in *putting on Christ?*

279   In the extract included in the anthology (XCVII; 66b), Bar Dashandad refers to spiritual 'pearls and precious stones'. He also says: 'Your soul is truly more precious to you than all the world and everything in it. Blessed is he who has acquired the love of God in his soul, and blessed is he who is continually kindled with the love of Christ' (65b).

GREGORY BAR HEBRAEUS

280   The last mystical writer to be mentioned in this book was a scholar and a gentleman. He was the shining light of the silver age of Syriac literature (thirteenth century), and a veritable polymath. He held

the highest office in the West Syrian church, and was so irenical and ecumenical in spirit that he enjoyed excellent relations with leaders of other religions. Grighor Abu'l-Faraj was his Arabic name; he was born the son of a physician of Jewish descent, hence his surname Bar 'Ebraya ('son of a Hebrew'); he was baptized under the name John and became a bishop at the age of twenty. He died in 1286, after a fruitful life of sixty years, and was laid to rest in the monastery of Mar Mattai (Saint Matthew) at Mosul.

281   Bar Ebraya produced many books: on theology, ecclesiastical history, philosophy, science, linguistics, and ethics. One of his works in the field of mysticism has already been mentioned: he obtained, with difficulty, a copy of *The Book of the Holy Hierotheos* (paragraph 220) and edited it along orthodox lines (225). We are fortunate in having his own spiritual testament, in the fourth and final section of his mystical manual, *The Book of the Dove*. His experience was similar to that of Islam's Al-Ghazali and Western Christianity's Thomas Aquinas: they all found that the production of weighty theological tomes can leave a scholar spiritually unsatisfied. Ghazali found refreshment and repose for his soul in Sufism. Bar Ebraya looked into the mystical writings of Evagrios and the whole Syriac Christian tradition of mysticism, West Syrian and East Syrian alike, and he was thereby lifted 'out of the whirlpool of disintegration and destruction' (XCIX). He says that some of the scales covering his eyes were taken away, and revelations came to him. These he recorded in the hundred sentences with which the book ends, and many of them are represented in the anthology (CII–CXXX).

282   He frequently invokes the Sinai cloud motif, borrowed from Pseudo-Dionysios (paragraph 125). He uses the maternal metaphor: he speaks of suckling at the breasts of Providence (paragraph 19; CXXV). He also has the mirror of the mind image (CIII, CXIX, CXXI). The *pearl* is not prominent in the *Book of the Dove*, but it is combined with the mirror thus: 'What profit is there . . . in a mirror decorated with pearls and gems if it is not cleansed of dross? (CIII).

283   When he says in his introduction (Bedjan's text, **204**, 522) that his book is divided into four chapters, small in extent but great in power, we perhaps hear an echo of Joseph the Visionary's Letter on the Three Degrees, which is said to be of limited extent but

large in profit, like the Pearl of Majesty (XLIII). His book has the same three levels as Joseph's letter, namely the body, soul, spirit framework of John the Solitary of Apamea:

(1) the *bodily* labour in the monastery;

(2) the *psychical* labour in the cell;

(3) the *spiritual* rest of the perfect.

In the third part, section nine, on varying states (**204**, 573–575), Gregory has taken over the twelve operations of divine grace set out by Joseph the Visonary in his Letter to a friend on the workings of grace (**2**, 169–175, Ms 158a–162b). This epistle is found in some manuscript collections of the letters of John the Venerable, and perhaps that is where Gregory saw it. Section two of part three (**204**, 565–566) has been reworked from a similar passage in the *Ethikon* (497) which is clearly based on John the Venerable's discourse on the three stages. The divine agent Grace, in John's original setting and also in the *Ethikon*, is changed to the Dove, in conformity with Gregory's unifying theme.

284   The Dove of *The Book of the Dove* is the Holy Spirit (cp paragraph 42 above), and also the dove of Noah's ark. The four periods in Noah's life (Gen 6–9) are correlated with the stages of the mystical path:

(1) performing works of righteousness, which made him pleasing to God, corresponding to the monk's *corporeal* labour in the monastery;

(2) entering the ark, which saved him from destruction in the flood; the ark represents the cell in which the monk performs his *psychical* exercises;

(3) leaving the ark, when the dove had announced that the waters had receded; this signifies the *spiritual* rest that the consoling Dove imparts;

(4) the revelations he received, the covenant established with him, the planting of the vineyard, drinking the wine and becoming intoxicated; the Dove elevates the perfect to royal rank, and introduces them into the cloud where the Lord is said to abide.

In section four of part three, Bar Ebraya speaks on 'the unification of the mind' using Dionysian terminology, with echoes of John the Venerable (paragraphs 125–126 above); 'It sees itself in the likeness of God, and because of the full cups it drinks in that room, it loses its senses, and in this inebriation it says: I and my Father are one, and my Father is in me and I am in him, together with other things which should be kept secret, the Dove warns' (Bedjan, 567).

On this sublime and mysterious note our introduction ends. We are now invited to dive into the deeps of the anthology, in quest of mystical pearls.

THE ANTHOLOGY

THE SONG OF THE PEARL

I

When as a little child I dwelt
in my father's palace in my kingdom,
content I was with the luxury and riches
of those who saw to my upbringing.
Then from our homeland the East,
my parents sent me forth equipped;
from the riches in our treasure store
they made me an abundant load;
large it was and yet so light
I could carry it by myself:
there was gold from Beth-'Ellâyê,
silver from noble Gazak;
there were rubies from the Indies,
agates from Beth-Kushân;
and they girded me with adamant,
which pulverizes iron.

II

They took my shining robe away,
which they in their love had made for me,
and likewise the scarlet toga,
measured and woven to my stature.
A covenant they made with me,
writing it on my heart lest it be forgotten:
If you will go down into Egypt
and bring out a certain pearl,
the one in the midst of the ocean,

109

hard by the hissing serpent,
then you shall wear your shining robe again,
and the toga that goes over it,
and with your brother, our next in rank,
you shall be heir in our kingdom.

⌖ III ⌖

I left the East and wended my way down,
having two guardians with me,
for the journey was perilous and difficult,
and I so young to set out on it.
I passed through the borders of Maishan,
resort of the Orient's merchants;
I arrived in the land of Babylon,
and entered the walls of Sarbug.
I went right down into Egypt,
and my guides then parted from me.
I made my way straight to the serpent
and lodged close by his lair,
waiting till he slumbered in sleep,
when I would take my pearl from him.

⌖ IV ⌖

I was solitary and alone,
a stranger to those I lived with.
Then one of my own kind, a freeman,
someone from the East, I saw there,
a comely and gracious lad,
a consecrated person, who joined me;
I made him my intimate friend,
and took him as partner in my pursuits.
I warned him against the Egyptians,
against joining with the unclean.
Yet I myself wore their manner of dress,
lest they abhorred me for coming from outside

to take the pearl away,
and lest they stirred up the serpent against me.
But by some means or other they perceived
I was not a fellow-countryman of theirs.
They dealt with me deceitfully;
they gave me their food to taste.

꙳ V ꙳

I forgot I was a son of kings,
and I served a king of theirs;
I forgot as well the pearl
for which my parents had sent me.
With the heaviness of their foodstuffs,
I sank deep into sleep.
But all the things that befell me
my parents perceived, and grieved over me.
Proclamation was made in our kingdom,
that all should hasten to our gate,
the kings and princes of Parthia,
and all the nobles of the East.
They drew up a plan for my sake,
that I might not be left in Egypt;
and then they wrote a letter to me,
and each noble signed his name to it.

꙳ VI ꙳

From your father, the king of kings,
and your mother, mistress of the East,
and from your brother our second in rank,
to you, our son in Egypt, greeting!
Awake and rise up from your sleep,
and listen to the words of our letter.
Remember that you are a son of kings;
look at your bondage to the one you now serve.
Call to mind the pearl,

for which you were sent into Egypt.
Be mindful of your shining robe,
and think of your splendid toga,
which you shall put on to adorn yourself,
when your name is called in the honour roll,
when you and your brother our viceroy
are together again in our kingdom.

⌁ VII ⌁

My letter was an epistle
that the king sealed with his right hand,
to protect it from the wicked Babylonians
and the cruel demons of Sarbug.
It flew in the form of an eagle,
the king of all winged creatures;
it flew and alighted beside me,
and became entirely speech.
At its voice and the sound of its rustling
I started and rose from my sleep.
I took it up and kissed it,
I broke its seal and read it;
in line with what was inscribed on my heart
the words of my letter were written.

⌁ VIII ⌁

I remembered I was a son of kings;
my free-born nature asserted itself.
I remembered too the pearl,
for which I had been sent into Egypt.
So I commenced to work enchantments
on the fearsome hissing serpent.
I hushed him and lulled him into slumber,
pronouncing my father's name over him,
and the name of our second in rank,
and of my mother, queen of the East.

I snatched up the pearl,
and turned to go home to my father.
Their filthy abominable clothing
I stripped off and left in their country;
I directed my course to bring me
to the light of our homeland, the East.

◦: IX :◦

My letter, which was my awakener,
I found ahead of me on the way;
and as with its voice it had woken me,
so now with its light it was leading me.
Enwrapped in silk as it was,
it shone before me with its form,
while with its voice and with its guidance,
it encouraged me to make haste,
and with its love it drew me on.
I went on my way beyond Sarbug,
and passed by Babylon on my left.
Then I came to Maishan the noble,
that haven of the traffickers
which sits on the shore of the sea.

◦: X :◦

My shining robe which I had taken off,
and my toga with which it was covered,
from the heights of Hyrcania
my parents had sent to me there,
by the agency of their treasurers,
whose honesty they could trust.
I had not remembered its fashion,
having left it with my father in childhood;
suddenly, as I encountered the garment,
it seemed like a mirror of myself.
I beheld its all in my own all,

and I encountered my own all in it;
for though we were two in distinction
we were still one, in one likeness.

✻ XI ✻

The treasurers too, who brought it to me,
I saw in the very same way,
that they were two yet one in likeness,
for one sign of the king was marked on both,
by his own hands, who returned through them
my deposit and my wealth,
my bright ornamented robe,
adorned with glorious colours,
with gold and beryls,
with rubies and agates,
and the sardonyx of varied hues,
it had also been fashioned on high;
and with stones of adamant
its every seam was fastened;
and the image of the king of kings
was all embroidered over it;
and like the sapphire jewel
were its manifold colours.

✻ XII ✻

And now I saw that all over it
impulses of knowledge were stirring,
and I saw it preparing itself
to give forth utterance.
I heard the sound of its tones,
as it murmured on its way down:
I am his who is diligent in doing,
for whom I was brought up before my father;
truly I have been aware in myself
that my size has been growing with his labours.

Moving in its regal manner
it was giving itself completely to me,
and on the hands of its presenters,
it was impatient for me to receive it.
For my part I was impelled by love
to run to meet it and take it.

◌ XIII ◌

I stretched out my hand and accepted it;
I decked myself out in its beauteous colours;
my toga with its lustrous colours
I wrapped right around myself.
Thus clothed I made my way up
to the gate of greeting and homage;
I bowed my head and made adoration
to its sender, the splendour of my father;
for I had carried out his orders,
and he had done what he had promised.
Standing at the gate of his princes,
I mingled with his noblemen,
for he rejoiced and welcomed me back,
and I was now with him in his kingdom.
With the voice of glorification
all his servants were praising him,
and he promised I would once again be brought
with him to the gate of the king of kings,
and with my present and my pearl,
I would appear with him before our king.

APHRAHAT THE PERSIAN

⌐: XIV :⌐

Profitable is the word I speak and worthy of acceptance.

Rom 13:11   Let us now awake from our sleep, and lift up our hearts and our hands towards God in heaven, so that if the Lord of the house comes suddenly, when he comes

Mk 13:35f   he shall find us in watchfulness.

Let us observe the appointed time of the glorious bridegroom, so that we may enter with him into his bridal chamber.

Mt 25:1-13   Let us prepare oil for our lamps, so that we may go forth to meet him with joy. . . .

Let us put away and cast from us all uncleanness, and put on wedding garments.

Mt 25:14-30   Let us trade with the silver we have received, so that we may be called diligent servants.

Let us be constant in prayer, so that we may pass beyond the place where fear dwells.

Mt 5:8   Let us purify our heart from iniquity, so that we may see the Lofty One in his glory.

Mt 5:7   Let us be merciful, as it is written, so that God may have mercy upon us.

Mt 5:9   Let there be peace amongst us, so that we may be called brethren of Christ.

Mt 5:6   Let us hunger for righteousness, so that we may be satisfied from the table of his kingdom.

Let us be the salt of truth, so that we do not become food for the serpent. . . .

Mt 13:45-46   Let us sell all our possessions, and buy for ourselves the pearl, so that we may be rich.

Let us lay up our treasures in heaven, so that when we　*Mt 6:19-20*
arrive we may open them and have pleasure in them. . . .
Let us honour the Spirit of Christ, so that we may receive
grace from him.
Let us be strangers to the world, as Christ was not of it.　*Jn 17:14*
Let us be humble and meek, so that we may inherit the　*Mt 5:5*
land of life.
Let us be constant in his service,
so that he may let us serve in the abode of the saints.
Let us pray his prayer in purity,
so that it may have access to the Lord of majesty.
Let us be sharers in his suffering,　*1 Pt 4:13*
so that we may also rise up in his resurrection.
Let us bear his sign upon our bodies, so that we may
be delivered from the wrath to come.　*1 Th 1:10*

EPHREM THE SYRIAN

∻ XV ∻

Mt 13:45-46   Blessed be he who compared
the Kingdom of the Most High to a *pearl*.

On a certain day, my brethren,
heirs of the Kingdom, I picked up a *pearl*;
I saw in it symbols, images, and types
of that Majesty, and it became a well
wherein I drank symbols of the Son.

I placed it, brethren, in the palm of my hand
to consider it; I set to looking at it
from one side, but it had faces
on all sides; so it is with examining the Son;
both are unsearchable, being all light.

In its clearness I saw the Clear One
who is unsullied; and in its purity
the great mystery, the body of our Lord,
which is spotless; in its undividedness
I saw the truth that is undivided. . . .

When I asked the *pearl* if there were in it
yet other symbols . . .
it answered me saying: A daughter am I
of the immense sea; and vaster than that sea
from which I have risen is the treasure
of mysteries in my bosom; you may search the sea
but you can not search the Lord of the sea.

I have seen the divers who come down for me;
after a short time in the midst of the sea
they return to dry land in distress;
they can endure no longer; who then can expect
to search the depths of the Godhead?

৵ XVI ৲

In symbol and truth is the sea-monster* crushed   *lwytn*
by mortals; the divers strip themselves,   *Leviathan*
then put on oil, a symbol of the Anointed Christ;
they grasp you and ascend, as Apostles would seize
a soul from the ferocious jaws.

By nature, *Pearl*, you are like the silent lamb
in its gentleness; for if one pierces a pearl,
then lifts it up and hangs it on one's ear,
as on Golgotha, it sheds more brightly
all its rays on those who gaze upon it.

৵ XVII ৲

O free gift that came up
with the diver, akin to that light,
the manifested one, which shines freely
upon human beings, you represent the mystic* one   *'hidden'*
freely giving mystic enlightenment.

The painter has painted you in a picture,
with colours; but in you is depicted
faith, in types and symbols, as with colours;
and in place of a picture, in you
and in your appearance your Creator is portrayed. . . .

You are uniquely great in your smallness;
O *Pearl*, diminutive is your size,
and small is your measurement and your weight,

but great is your splendour; solely on that diadem which
is beyond price are you set.

Anyone who does not perceive in your smallness
how great you are, who despises you
and loses you, will be censured
for their stupidity; but having seen you
on a king's crown, they will be drawn to you. . . .

Unclothed men dived to bring you up,
O *Pearl*; kings were not the ones
who first presented you to human beings,
but the unclothed, symbolic of the poor,
and of fishermen and Galileans.

For they could not, with bodies clad,
come to you; but they came unclothed,
like new-born babes, entombing their bodies
and descending to you; you welcomed them
and took refuge with them, who so cherished you.

Their tongues gave tidings of you
before they opened their pockets; poor as they were
they brought forth and showed their new riches
in the house of the merchants; in the hollows
of the hands of people they placed you,
as the medicine of life.

THE BOOK OF DEGREES

⌁ XVIII ⌁

Blessed is the person who enters the celestial church, upon which our Lord shines openly, as the visible sun shines upon the visible church and upon these temples that are our bodies. No matter how often the sun may set on these, the church above never loses the light of the countenance* of our Lord and Saviour Jesus Christ.

Num 6:26, Ps 4:6

Even though our Lord is in every place, he is only seen openly in that church in heaven, and only by those who have humbled themselves, and become peaceful, and gentle towards everyone, who have struggled and engaged in single combat with evil spirits, and have purified their hearts of evil thoughts. As the Apostle said*: Your struggle is not with humans of flesh and blood, but with rulers and powers, with evil spirits, and with Satan the destroyer.

Eph 6:12

Those who have fought with Satan and have overcome him, become worthy of this church which is above all, upon which our Lord shines openly, and they experience the glorious light of his countenance. For our Lord said*: Blessed are those who are pure in heart, for they shall see God.

Mt 5:8

JOHN THE SOLITARY

~ XIX ~

At all times you should be offering to Christ constant
thanksgiving out of the fullness of the love in your soul;
for he has deigned to accomplish in you his glorious
parable: The Kingdom of Heaven is like a merchant who
sought fine *pearls*, and when he discovered a very precious
pearl he went and sold all he had, and bought it.* So it is
with you, our dear friend. After you had set out to seek
much wisdom and had found the knowledge of the mystery of Christ, which is more glorious, more exalted, and
more abundant in great virtues than any other wisdom,
you then forsook all other knowledge and kept only the
knowledge of Christ within your soul. Through him you
have become rich, and you reign in his magnificent Kingdom of God . . .

Mt 13:45f

> God almighty, perfect and complete in himself,
>   is himself the Kingdom,
>   the sheen of his splendour,
>   the majesty of his sway,
>   the honour of his glory,
>   the tranquillity of his person,
>   the immensity of his power,
>   the loftiness of his truth,
>   the fullness of his substance,
>   the vision of his loveliness,
>   the tabernacle of his joy,
>   the blessedness of his rest;
>   his riches are not present without him,

his secrets not without his wisdom,
his appearing not without his knowledge,
his likeness not without his fullness.
He himself is the appearing,
the secrets of his knowledge,
the wealth of his treasures,
the restfulness of his will,
the sphere of his being,
the realm of his glory.
He is in his perfection single and unique;
there is no duality in him . . .
His might is incomparable,
his beauty indescribable,
his love immeasurable,
his serenity inexpressible,
his worth incomprehensible.

◡ XX ◠

Anyone occupied in virtuous conduct and not ruled by
wickedness and passions is freed from the corruption
and darkness of this world and the tyranny of sin,
whereby a person serves the forces of deception, from
whose dominion he cannot escape. . . . As a person
asleep is held captive by fear and terror in idle dreams
until waking comes and delivers him, so people are held
at the mercy of deception and evil passions until Christ,
our true dayspring and holy light, comes to rouse us and
bring us to ourselves, and from their power he saves and
delivers us. . . .

◡ XXI ◠

Although he worshipped with the Father,
he was sent as a messenger;
he put on our garment, to be seen by us;
walked as a servant,

appeared as a healer,
became as a brother,
served as a slave;
spoke as a teacher,
listened as a student;
fought as a mighty man,
succumbed as a vanquished one;
he was sold as a vassal,
he freed as a lord;
he reproved as a judge,
he was condemned as a malefactor.
With the needy he was needy,
with the almsgivers he gave to the poor;
with the fasters fasting,
with the diners dining;
with the persecuted he was persecuted,
with the fighters he fought;
with those subject to the law keeping the law,
with God a rewarder of those who labour;
with the sons an heir,
with the Father a giver of inheritance;
with the supplicaters entreating,
with the Father granting petitions;
with the envoys an emissary;
with the sinners a sacrificed lamb,
with the priests an atoning high priest;
with the departed slain,
with God raising the dead;
with the persecuted persecuted,
with God vindicating the persecuted;
with the reviled reviled,
with the wounded smitten,
with God healing,
with the sick as an invalid,
with the strong strong,
with the perfect perfect,
with the deprived as one deprived,

that he might perfect them;
with the redeemers a redeemer,
with the imprisoned a prisoner,
so that when he was subjected to death
he might redeem the captives.

◌ XXII ◌

As at the rising of the sun over the horizon the shroud
of darkness is removed from the face of the earth, so
that it shows itself in all its beauty, so likewise when the
love of Christ shines forth in the soul and the veil of the
old nature is taken away, the light of Christ shines forth
in it, and the hidden things that were not visible before
are now seen by it. And as iron when placed in a fire has
the fire pass into it to become one substance with it, the
iron united with the fire assuming its likeness and colour,
no longer appearing in its former aspect, but becoming
like the fire, because they have become absorbed in each
other and have become one, so it is when the love of
Christ has come into the soul as a living fire which burns
away the thorns of sin from the soul; it becomes one
substance with him and he with it; then the soul which
was old, becomes new; dead it comes alive; and the
likeness of its own nature is changed into the likeness of
God. And now everything it sees appears to it as the
likeness of God (for it is granted to created beings to
behold the works of God spiritually), and it becomes
absorbed in love for all humankind, so that if it could it
would let itself perish, so that all humans might live.

PHILOXENOS OF MABBUG

∻ XXIII ∾

If you intend to become a disciple, do as the will of your Master requires; otherwise remain in the world. Do not aspire to be honoured with a title you do not deserve; do not take a pure *pearl* with unclean hands; do not put on the purple of discipleship if you do not possess the knowledge to keep it. Calculate for yourself what discipleship demands of you, and then take its yoke upon yourself*. . . .

Mt 11:29-30

Be a perfect disciple; otherwise remain in the world and work within the righteousness of the Law, which is below the spiritual life. . . .

So long as sin lives in you, whether in deed or in thought, and corporeal care arises in you from the world, you are an old bottle and cannot receive the new wine of the wisdom of Christ. Abandon everything, as the Apostles did, and then freely ask to become master of the spiritual treasures.

STEPHEN BAR SUDAILI

↙ XXIV ↘

I am in fear of those strict injunctions which have been
laid upon me . . ., that I should not expose the secret
and hidden mysteries before minds that are not pure,
thereby transgressing the word that says, Do not give
a holy thing to dogs, and do not throw *pearls* to
swine*. . . .   *Mt 7:6*

My son, I have seen many men to whom there came a
rapid fall from heaven because they disclosed this divine
mystery; as with our Lord, I too have seen Satan and the
man who is like him fall from heaven.*   *Lk 10:18*

Therefore, my son, honour with perfect and mystic
silence those things which give you life; and consider also
the ant* and learn from its ways, how it stores up its   *cp. Pr 6:6-8*
bread and conceals its food; and the oyster, which if it
were not concealed within the deep, would not produce
pearls. . . . When the mind has been accounted worthy
to ascend above the firmament, it then becomes as a
babe that has just been born, that has just arrived out
of darkness into light.

SAHDONA-MARTYRIOS

⊰ XXV ⊱

I think that it has already been revealed to you, my brethren, how glorious and excellent is this holy path of the fear of God; it has been seen as resplendent, limpid, pure, and filled with light. But bear with me a while yet, and you will behold anew its magnificent beauty. For it becomes much more attractive to us when we examine one by one its spiritual beauties and its infinite virtues. We acquire greater prudence by learning about the struggles and athletic labours in it, and we do not stray from it as easily as those who are not aware of its great glory and have not even reached the outer portals of its knowledge.

How often, in their stupidity, they disdain and despise it and account it as nothing, because they do not comprehend the power of its knowledge. They are to be compared with a child who has not yet acquired understanding, who regards pebbles as equal in value with *pearls*, not knowing their superiority and preciousness, and will lose both with indifference while amusing himself with them; or the stupid man who makes bronze equal with gold, or emeralds and rubies equal with clay beads, or considers tin to be silver; or like someone whose palate is ruined and who cannot distinguish the sweetness of honeycomb from the bitterness of wormwood.

So it is with these ignorant people: their sense of discernment being corrupted, they cannot appreciate the delicious sweetness of that spiritual food which is the accomplishing of the will of God, which through its sweetness brings back to life those who eat it with discernment.

And so the service of perishable food (which delights their palate for a mere moment and is then gulped down to become dung in those sewers of the belly, the intestines) is valued more highly by them than the spiritual service of divine food, which remains alive for ever, such as the Son of God has bestowed on us through the gift of his Spirit.

They are in no way different from senseless youths who prefer a tasty fig on their palate to a *pearl* set in a diadem.

SIMON TAIBUTHEH

∴ XXVI ∾

The things that happen to those whose mind perceives
the mysteries of the New World, are like what befalls a
man who comes to our country from China or from
India: he goes in and out of the houses of many people,
he gives and takes, eats and converses with many people,
but although he performs his actions in his body, and is
seen here by all, yet in his mind and in his thoughts he
is in his own country and among his own people; his manner of life is just as it is in his own country, even though
he superficially displays the manners and customs of
those among whom he is now living; the manners and
customs of those with whom he is living are not acceptable to him, nor are his acceptable to them; he does not
know how to live with them, nor they with him; if he
meets a man of his own country and of his own language, he rejoices and sees his fellow-countrymen in his
imagination.

cp. IV

So it is with the man who becomes aware of the mysteries
of the New World: his mind is captive, and in his char-
acter and thoughts he is an alien to the ways and customs
of the world in which he is sojourning.

∴ XXVII ∾

An old monk was asked what the monasticism of the
ancients, in relation to ours, might be likened to, and he
replied: There was a wise rich man who wished to ac-

quire valuable musk, and, not finding the genuine article of his desire, he traversed mountains, sea, and land, and reached China. He presented gifts to the king of that region to gain permission to cut the musk with his own hands. He then returned and gave it to his sons, who little by little introduced sham substances into it. They adulterated it as they handed it down from one to another, until only the sham was left in place of the true musk, with no odour or perfume remaining.

In the same way the early fathers, desiring what is true, trod life and death underfoot, experienced all tribulations, endured all trials, delivered their very beings up to spiritual sacrifice, and implored Christ with sorrow and tears until they obtained the gift of grace, were found worthy of spiritual knowledge, became an abode for God, worked miracles, and perceived the mystery of revelations. And the mystery was handed down little by little until we alone were left, having only the name and garb.* *of monk*

⁓ XXVIII ⁓

What am I to do? I hate evil deeds, but I zealously perform them; and although I love good things, I do evil things. I am zealous for the things that I hate, but lethargic about what is of advantage to my being. I hate the passions, yet I love their objects; I am distant from them, yet I embrace them. In my garb I am a stranger to the world, but I keep a deposit on it. I am stronger than it, yet I am caught in the snares of its desires. I am upright, yet it teaches me wiliness. I have not learned its craft, yet it requires it of me. When I think I am moving forwards, I am really running backwards.

Come and laugh at an able man who is entangled in cobwebs and who labours in voluntary servitude.

Come and laugh at a rational man who forgets his own resolutions and works in a retrograde manner.

Come and weep over a free man who has deliberately turned his freedom into slavery under his enemies.

Come and marvel at a merchant who trades with a purse that has holes in it.

Great is my shame, for when victory is set within my grasp I run to my defeat. The world shows me a beautiful flower, but puts thorns into my hands. It places enticing bait in my mouth, but casts a snare round my neck. Why do I not flee from it when I know about all these snares, and not one of them could then overcome me?

Worst of all, I fail to notice my own foul sores, but I observe other people's tiny scratches. The foul festering of my own wounds is not loathsome to me, but I abhor the perspiration of others. The beam in my own eyes is not too heavy for me, but I am assiduous in setting right the

Mt 7:3   specks in other people's eyes.*

⌁ XXIX ⌁

A great and glorious treasure, without equal in the creation, is hidden within you, O man. If you had become aware of it, even by accident, you would have cried out like the prophet: I will not give sleep to my eyes or slumber to my being, until I find a place for this divine treasure that is hidden in me.

Glory, glory, glory to you, merciful God, for you have hidden in this clay from the ground and in this dust from the earth (a substance which is always melting and dissolving) an ineffably beauteous treasure that has no equal in Heaven or Earth. Had you but known, O monk, what

beauty is hidden within you, you would not have bestowed blessing on the illustrious men of this world, but
you would have changed night for day in your pursuit of
the treasure hidden in you.

ISAAC OF NINEVEH

᪥ XXX ᪥

The mind that has found spiritual wisdom is like a man
who has found ready at hand in the midst of the ocean
a ship on which to embark, to take him from the ocean
of this world and bring him safely to the islands of the
world to come. Thus the apperception of things to come
in this world is like a small island in the midst of the
ocean, and whoever has attained to it will no longer be
agitated by the storms of transitory illusions.

᪥ XXXI ᪥

When the merchant has completed his season of business he makes haste to return home. While the monk
still remains in his time of service he is distressed about
departing from the body; but when he realises in his soul
that he has redeemed his time and has received his
pledge, he yearns for the world to come.

᪥ XXXII ᪥

While the merchant is on the sea, apprehension takes
possession of him: a storm may rise and the gain he
hopes to make from his toil will be swallowed up. And
while the monk is in this world, anxiety reigns over his
service lest a tempest be stirred up against him to destroy what he has toiled for from his youth till his old
age. The merchant looks towards the dry land, the monk
towards the time of his death.

❧ XXXIII ❧

The mariner looks to the stars while he is sailing over the sea, and he steers his ship by them as they point him to the harbour. The monk looks to prayer, for it steers him towards the haven to which his course is to be directed. Through prayer the monk is on the watch at all times, to be shown the island where he may anchor his ship free of anxiety and take on provisions to enable him to voyage to yet another island.

Such is the course of the solitary while he is in this life; he departs from island to island, or from knowledge to knowledge; and like different islands he encounters different stages of knowledge, until he leaves the sea behind and makes his way to the city of truth, whose inhabitants no longer engage in commerce, but everyone is content with his riches.

Blessed is he whose voyage is not disrupted on this wide ocean. Blessed is he whose ship is not wrecked and who reaches that haven rejoicing.

❧ XXXIV ❧

The diver plunges naked into the sea to find a *pearl*, and the wise monk will go naked through the desert places to find the *Pearl*, Jesus Christ himself. When he has found it he will not wish to acquire anything else. A *pearl* is kept in an inner room; the solitary takes delight in silent seclusion.

❧ XXXV ❧

A dog licking a file is drinking his own blood, but he does not notice his injury because of the sweet taste. A solitary who stoops to lapping up glory is sapping his own life without giving thought to his injury, because of the momentary sweetness.

⁖ XXXVI ⁖

Glory from worldly people is like a rock hidden in the sea; it is not perceived by the mariner until his ship strikes against it, so that its bottom is holed and it fills with water. Accordingly it is said by the Fathers that through glory all the passions that have been overcome and dispatched from the soul are now able to return to it.

⁖ XXXVII ⁖

It frequently happens at various hours of the day that a brother, even if he were offered an earthly kingdom, would not be persuaded to leave his cell at that hour or to answer the door when someone knocks. A time for (spiritual) business has come upon him suddenly. So often this can happen on days considered to be for relaxation and for going out: suddenly grace visits him, with tears beyond measure, or a lively affection moving the heart, or gladness without cause, or delight in genuflexion. I know a brother who put the key in the door of his cell

Qo 1:14   to lock it, as he was going out to feed on wind,* in the words of Scripture, and then and there grace visited him, so that he went straight back in again. Well then, no one should blame a brother if, on days when he does not have to observe canonical solitude, he sometimes happens to stay away from congregational worship.

You know, my brothers, that our work is not only that which is accomplished before the eyes of men, but we also have a service that is concealed from the eyes of men, one that is not known to novices and lay folk. As you are aware, the solitary is under indenture and is not his own master. Accordingly, if any of one's brethren happens to call and receives no answer, he should turn back immediately without blaming his brother. For he does not know what the brother is doing at that moment. The cell of a solitary is, in the words of the Fathers, the cavern in the rock, where God spoke with Moses.* *Ex 33:22*

⏑ XXXVIII ⏑

Sometimes a brother is suddenly confronted with some unavoidable struggle, and with his hands laid on his heart he is in danger of expiring. Falling down on his face he beseeches God, and he is unable to hear the voice of any person. Those who have done the crossing of this ocean are aware of the winds that blow there. . . .

Many are the variations of this sea. Who knows its toils and its multitude of merchandise, the wondrous *pearls* in its deeps, and the creatures that rise up from within it? Blessed is he who does not slumber during his voyage, right to the haven of his decease.

⏑ XXXIX ⏑

No one can occupy himself with divine things unless he renounces and scorns temporal things, becoming a stranger to the pomp and pleasures of the world, cleaving to the shame of the cross, every day drinking vinegar and gall because of passions, devils, people, and poverty.

Be diligent, my brother, like a prudent merchant, carrying your *pearl* as you roam through the world, lest its resplendent beauty be marred. Take care that it is not stolen from you through your laxity, and as a result you go to Hell in anguish.

⏑ XL ⏑

Everything is possible to one who has faith*. . . . What *Mk 9:23*
unspeakable riches, a swelling ocean rich in wondrous

treasures, the overflowing power of faith! How full of consolation it is, and how pleasant and reassuring its course is; and its burdens, how easy they are; and how pleasant its service is. Anyone who has been deemed worthy to taste faith and who then turns back to psychical knowledge is no better than someone who has found a *pearl* of great price and exchanged it for a copper penny, because he has given up absolute freedom and turned to the meagre resources of fearful bondage. Knowledge is not to be rejected, but faith is superior to it. . . . When knowledge is united to faith and becomes one with it, through faith it is clothed in fiery impulses, and it glows spiritually; it acquires the wings of impassibility and is lifted up from the service of earthly things to the place of its creator. . . . Knowledge is made perfect by faith, so that it acquires the power to ascend and to experience what is above all experience, and to behold the splendour of the one who is not attained by the mind or by the knowledge of created beings. So knowledge is a stair by which a person ascends to the height of faith, and for which, when he has attained faith, he has no further use.

DADISHO QATRAYA

∺ XLI ∾

Right intention is a necessary requirement for a monk, because without it his virtuous work will all be accounted worthless and unprofitable. As a high tower erected on a base that is not right will fall down easily, so too a tower of virtuous conduct which has a crookèd intention will rapidly lean over and fall down. Right intention consists in this, that a man lives in solitude solely for the sake of God and for love of our Lord Jesus Christ, with absolutely no thought or expectation of reward for his labours in anything of this world, whether bodily repose, or personal gain, or primacy in leadership, or honour, or commendation, or passing glory. Neither does he desire or yearn or ask that it be granted to him by our Lord, as a reward for his labours, to perform miracles and signs or any of the gifts of the Spirit, for which he will be recognized and honoured by men. Rather, his whole aim and intention is to be deemed worthy of the perfect love of our Lord Jesus Christ and the spiritual vision of him, like a virgin princess, who is betrothed to a king and does not look for or yearn for anything from the wealth of her betrothed, but only the sight of him, and his love and companionship. This is the praiseworthy kind of right intention that a monk ought to possess in his cell in the glorious exercise of solitude.

∺ XLII ∾

When we make progress in this work of solitude, rejection of evil thoughts, and praying without ceasing, we find not only hope in God, but also true faith, sincere charity, unmindfulness of evils, love for the brethren, abstinence, patience, inner knowledge, deliverance from temptations, spiritual gifts, gratefulness of heart, tears of compunction, endurance of the vexations that befall us, guileless forgiving of our neighbour, knowledge of the spiritual commandments, recognition of the righteousness of God, indwelling of the Holy Spirit, and gifts of spiritual treasures. All these things are bestowed, through solitude and prayer, on monks living in seclusion. For the acquisition of these benefits one should therefore desire solitude.

Anyone who does not rid himself of all memories and concerns, and does not withdraw from all business, to be steadfast in solitude with right intention and love for labours, will not remember his former sins, nor will he see his daily failings; he will not be aware of his passions, nor will he understand the provocations of the demons; he will not be prepared for the struggle against the passions and the demons, nor will he attain purity of heart; he will not practise pure prayer, nor will he be worthy of spiritual prayer; he will not see in himself the holy light of his mind, nor will the divine light of the glory of Christ shine within his soul through revelation by the Holy Spirit.

JOSEPH THE VISIONARY

⋈ XLIII ⋈

Among astute merchants who are expert in the art of
trading, whenever their commerce brings in multiple gain,
in order to avoid being overwhelmed by the great weight
of the cares of commerce and being agitated in mind by
the reckoning of their accounts (something that would
occasion losses to their purse-strings) it is customary
for them to give up the heavy load of secondary trading
ventures and concentrate in each affair on the essential,
of limited extent but of considerable profit; like the *pearl*
called Pearl of Majesty (*shomarworid*), small in dimension
but for commerical value extremely profitable.

Now just as Christ has said: The Kingdom of Heaven is
like a merchant who sought after many *pearls*, and having
found one of great price he went and sold everything he
had and purchased it,* so, my very dear friend, having   *Mt 13:45f*
looked around everywhere, I have perceived that the aim
of your thinking was that your commerce should bring
in a return several times above the investment. Like an
astute merchant you have asked me for something
limited as regards extent but large as regards profit. You
have said: Write to me by letter briefly on these subjects,
namely on silence and the solitary life in the cell, on the
temptations which come upon those who perform spiritual exercises in silence, and on the visitation of grace
that is bestowed on them through the mercy of Our
Lord, as well as other matters. . . .

⋈ XLIV ⋈

The first impulses prompting us to withdraw from the
world are the natural seeds of goodness sown by God in

us, in the nature of our first creation. Constantly springing up within us, when they find a will that is slightly inclined towards goodness they immediately provide an opportunity for a guardian angel to approach the soul. When he does, the first impulse he arouses in it is fear and terror about the judgement to come, by depicting before its eyes the bliss of the righteous and the torment of the sinners. Standing between these two different states the soul is sometimes tormented by fear and sometimes exhilarated by joy, and then the guardian angel stirs up in it a further impulse, which plunges it even deeper into suffering and moves it nearer to repentance, by depicting before the soul all the failings and weaknesses it has. And the more it recognizes its weaknesses the more the world, with all the passions and desires that belong to it, becomes to the soul an object of contempt.

⁓ XLV ⁓

Just as darkness is dissipated by light, so love of the world is dissipated by the impulse of which I speak. This impulse infuses and instils into a person the desire to renounce wealth and possessions, so that he gives all he owns to the poor. . . . Then the guardian angel, wishing to strip him completely of possessions, inspires in him the thought of going out into the desert and living with animals, reminding him of the great many people who, out of tender love for Our Lord, have given away their possessions and gone out into the desert, where their food was the roots and herbs of the ground.

⁓ XLVI ⁓

When day is dawning the solitary should wash his hands and make genuflections before the cross, until his thoughts are gathered in from distractions and his heart is on fire with love of Our Lord, when he will pray to Our Lord amid tears of contrition, saying: O God, make my mind worthy to find delight in understanding the dispensation of your beloved Son. O Lord, take away the veil of passions that lies over my mind, and let your holy light shine into my heart, so that my mind may enter into the interior of the outward ink-written text, and that with the enlightened eye of my soul I may behold the sacred mysteries that are hidden in your Gospel. And by your grace, Lord, grant that the thought of you shall not depart from my heart by night or by day.

Having collected your thoughts with such words of supplication, salute the cross and take the Gospel in your hands; place it on your eyes and on your heart. Then go and stand on your feet before the cross, not sitting on the ground. After reading each chapter you should place it on its cushion and fall down before it up to ten times while giving thanks. . . .

Truly I know a brother who, when one day he prostrated himself before the divine Gospel with hands and eyes directed to heaven, had his heart opened and filled with an ineffable light. . . . That brother declared to me: For two days I took neither food nor sleep; my thoughts were carried away from this world and everything in it. All I know is that my mind was lifted up and that I saw and heard, but what I saw and heard I cannot express to you, as these are mysteries that cannot be spoken by a tongue of flesh, or cannot be written by pen and ink; for they are the pledge of those ineffable rewards which God the Lord of all will grant after the resurrection from the dead; those things which Saint Paul contemplated, as it were in ecstasy, saying: That which eye has not seen, and ear has not heard, and has not entered into the heart of man, is what God has prepared for those who love him.* *1 Cor 2:9*

When you have read from the Gospel and have received a blessing from it, one which sanctifies your soul through the Holy Spirit hidden in the living words of Our Saviour, the Lord Jesus Christ, then read from the Epistles and *9 AM* the Acts until the third hour,* when you finish the office of obeisance before the Gospel; for frequently in reading these also you may find that life-filled pearl.

ᴥ XLVII ᴥ

When thoughts begin to move in your heart, differentiate, on the one side, those that come from serenity of thinking, or from the guardian angel, or from the grace of the Holy Spirit, or from perserverance in reading, or those springing up from natural seeds in your heart, and, on the other side, the thoughts that are sown in you by an accursed demon.

Recognize that it is from the right-hand side that come all the thoughts which, when they begin to stir in your heart, draw your mind to composure of thought and fill your soul with joy, affection, and tears, and plunge your intellect into humility and abasement. All the while the fountain of your heart wells up with them, give them the opportunity to operate. Lock all the doors of your cell, go into the inmost part, and sit in darkness and stillness, where you cannot even hear the sound of a bird. If the time for divine service comes, see that you do not rise up at all, lest you be like a little child who in his ignorance exchanges a talent of gold for a fig which sweetens his palate for a mere moment. Rather, you should be like a wise merchant: when a *pearl* of great price is presented to you, do not change it for cheap things that are always available to you.

ᴥ XLVIII ᴥ

While the solitary is experiencing this operation of thoughts, this movement of humility, and these tears, in his view there is no sinner in creation, but all men are deemed righteous by him. Blessed is he who is judged worthy of this operation, and whose mental palate tastes the delights of these divine mysteries.

Many a time from the vehement force of these operations a person falls to the ground and remains there for a day or two without being able to rise, since the body cannot stand before this joy. He neither takes food nor has his usual sleep, because body and soul alike are fed on spiritual nourishment through the sweetness of these thoughts.

While a person remains in this situation a light shines over him by night and by day, because night and day are identical to one who has merited this gift.

While the solitary continues under this operation there is no need for him to perform the offices or the labour of readings, for that is the whole labour of the merchant up to the time when the *pearl* of great price falls into his hands. At these times God asks of you no more than the observance of solitude.

⁓ XLIX ⁓

The first sign of the operation of the Spirit's visitations is this: the thought of the love of God burns in a person's heart like a fire. This engenders in his heart hatred for the world, renunciation, and love for the eremitic and ascetic life, which is the mother and nurse of all virtues.

⁓ L ⁓

The second sign, through which you perceive that the Spirit you received at baptism is working in you, comes when true humility is born in your soul. I do not mean humility of the body but rather the true humility of the soul, whereby a person, notwithstanding the great and

Gen 18:27

Ps 22:6

wonderful things done to him considers himself dust and
ashes,* a worm and no man.* All men are considered in
his eyes as great and holy, and there is no difference in
his mind between good and bad, righteous and sinner.
And it is from humility that peace, meekness, and endurance of tribulations are born in the soul.

⁓ LI ⁓

The third sign of the operation of the Spirit in you is the
mercifulness that fashions within you the image of God,
so that when your thought is extended to all people,
tears are shed from your eyes like fountains of water. It
is as if they are all dwelling in your heart, and you lovingly
embrace them and kiss them, pouring your kindness over
them all in your thought. Whenever you remember them
your heart is kindled by the power of the Spirit working
in you like a fire. This engenders in your heart goodness
and kindliness, so that you cannot bring yourself to speak
any [unkind] thing to any person, nor does your imagination think evil of anyone, but you do good to all, in
thought and deed.

⁓ LII ⁓

The fourth sign by which you know that the visitation
of the Spirit is operating in you is true love, which does
not leave any other thing in your thinking save the remembrance of God alone. This is the spiritual key by which
the inner door of the heart is opened, wherein is hidden
Christ our Lord, whose dwelling-place is spiritual and
spacious, and the sight of whom is light that is ineffable.
From this love there is engendered faith to see the hidden
things that the mind is not allowed to commit to parch-
ment, and which the Apostle called the substance of

Heb 11:1

things hoped for,* unknown to the eyes of the flesh but
clearly known to the eyes of the mind, in the inner room
of the heart.

LIII

The fifth sign that the Spirit you received at baptism is
working in you is the illuminated vision of your mind,
which is seen in the firmament of your heart like sapphire,
namely the reception of the light of the Holy Trinity. It
is this sign that leads you to the vision of the material
natures, from which you rise further to the knowledge
of the intelligible natures, from which you then ascend
to the revelations and mysteries of Divine Judgement
and Providence.

This ascent by steps next brings you to commingling with
the holy light of the vision of Christ our Lord.

From this glorious and holy vision you will pass into
wonderment over that spacious world, the boons of
which are inexpressible.

From this wonderment you will derive a flow of spiritual
speech and knowledge of both worlds, of the one that
has been and the one that shall be, and also consciousness of the mysteries of future things, together with a
sanctified sense of smell and taste; the ethereal sounds
of the spritual intelligences: joy, jubilation, exultation,
glorification, psalms, hymns, and magnifying praise; communion with the spiritual hierarchies; seeing the souls
of the saints; beholding Paradise, eating from its tree of
life, and meeting the saints who dwell in it, together with
other things that are unutterable.

LIV

We say that we see light in the sphere of spirituality; but
this is not like material light. We also say that we have
spiritual food there; but that food is not like what we
have here. We further say that our mind perceives there
the sound of the spiritual hosts and that it there has
speech and conversation; but that speech is not like the

speech that we have with one another. The sound heard there by our mind is so ethereal that our senses are not able to receive it, and a fleshly tongue is unable to speak or tell that which is revealed there to the understanding.

∻ LV ∻

After a person has risen to the sphere of serenity and has been recorded as an adopted son, he will constantly take part in the revelation of God's mysteries, and will consequently see and hear everything there in a spiritual way, and his service and his sanctifying singing* will constantly be joined with that of the spiritual beings. Blessed is the man who has been found worthy of this gift and of this liberty, and has seen this glorious vision with the eyes of his mind, and has heard with the ears of his heart the ethereal sound which, above the level of serenity, is revealed to a spiritual man. . . .

Is 6:3

Even if the body is asleep, these faculties of the mind have no rest, on account of their service with the spiritual beings. This is why night and day are alike to the mind found worthy of this gift by the grace of our Lord.

JOHN THE VENERABLE

⌁ LVI ⌁

Blessed is he who constantly dives into the endless sea to gather up *pearls* from its treasures. His is happiness beyond compare. Blessed is he who gazes within himself and sees the glorious ineffable light of the Holy Trinity and rejoices in it with infinite joy.

⌁ LVII ⌁

O Mercy, how munificent you are. To us who were dead in sins you have granted the holy womb of repentance, giving birth to new sons for old, pure instead of unclean, enlightened instead of benighted, pleasant and fragrant instead of foul, desirable and comely like their Heavenly Father instead of hateful and loathsome like their task-master Satan.

⌁ LVIII ⌁

Glory be to you, O Father of all, for giving us repentance as a new mother for a new birth; for though our infancy pollutes us entirely with filthiness, she cleanses, purifies, beautifies, and cherishingly shelters under her wing those who are born of her, until they come through to you enlightened and dearly loved, to be gods and kings, and sons of your possession, to take their delight freely at your breast, in the breath of the nostrils of your Holy Spirit, to be made resplendent in your glory, to see your likeness as their own likeness, and to be changed through your Spirit into your glory.

◦⁝ LIX ⁝◦

He who holds his mouth back from talking preserves his heart from passions.

Mt 5:8   He whose heart is purified of passions sees God perpetually.

He who perpetually meditates on God drives devils away and destroys the seed of their evil.

He who fixes his gaze within himself continually, his heart will exult in revelations.

He whose contemplation is collected within his mind sees there the splendour of the Father.

He to whom all pleasures are contemptible will see his Lord within his heart.

◦⁝ LX ⁝◦

cp. Mt 5:8   You who desire for yourself purity through which the Lord of all may be seen, do not commit slander or listen to words of calumny concerning your brethren. If a quarrel is going on near you or if you hear angry words, stop up your ears and flee away, lest your soul cease from living. The heart of an irascible man is devoid of the mysteries of God, but anyone who is innocent and peaceable is a fountain of the mysteries of the New World. Indeed, Heaven is already within you if you are pure, and there you see angels rejoicing, with their Lord among them and within them. Anyone who deserves to receive glory lacks nothing; but if glory is sweet to a person, then he labours without reward. The treasure of a humble man is within him: it is the Lord.

∴ LXI ∻

Just as dolphins float about on the calm stillness of the sea, so in the stillness of the sea within the heart that is free from anger and wrath there are hidden mysteries and divine revelations ever stirring for its delight.

∴ LXII ∻

What happens to a fish when it has an experience of dry land is the same as what happens to the intellect when it turns from the knowledge of God to be absorbed in remembrance of the world, for as far as a man is removed from human society and business, to that extent he is deemed worthy of speaking freely with God in his mind. In proportion as he resolves to cast off worldly comforts, he is deemed worthy of rejoicing in God through the Holy Spirit. And just as fish perish and die from deprivation of water, so the fiery impulses emanating from God vanish from the heart of the solitary who likes worldly society and business.

∴ LXIII ∻

The habitat of the person whose soul is pure is within him, and the sun that shines there is the light of the Holy Trinity; the air breathed by its inhabitants is the Holy Spirit the Paraklete; his fellow-dwellers are the holy spiritual natures; and their life, their pleasure, and their exultation is Christ, the splendour of the Father. Moreover, this person is always exulting over the sight of his soul and marvelling at its beauty, a hundred times more glorious than the orb of the sun. This is Jerusalem and the Kingdom of God concealed within us,* in the words of our Lord, this place which is the Cloud of God's Glory, which only the pure in heart may enter to behold the face of their Lord, and to have their mind made resplendent in his dazzling light. *Lk 17:21*

ᵔ LXIV ᵕ

The passionate man, the irascible man, the lover of glory, the miser, the glutton, the man engrossed in worldly things, the self-seeking person, the gabbler, the vehement man, the emotional person, all these grope about in the darkness outside the place of light and life, because this is the inheritance of the meek and the gentle and those that are pure in heart.*

Mt 5:8

ᵔ LXV ᵕ

When we are moved to flee from the world and to become strangers to the world, there is nothing that keeps us so far removed from the world, so dead to passions, so alive in God, and so stirred in spirit, so much as weeping and heart-felt compunction, with discretion, and a reverent attitude that imitates the humility of the Beloved. Nor is there anything that makes us associates of the world, vain foolish worldlings, strangers to God, and bereft of God's wisdom or God's treasure of mysteries, so much as amusement and diversion in licentious pleasure.

This is the craft of the evil demon of lechery. That is why, my dear friend, knowing your wisdom as I do, I urge you lovingly to beware of the evil one's guile, lest with words of trumpery he cool your soul from the warmth of its love for Christ, who for your sake drank bitterness on the tree; and lest in place of a single-minded contemplation and a gaze fixed on God he fill it with great fantasies and vanities when it is awake, and lest he subject it when it is asleep to dreams that reek of dissoluteness, so that the beloved angels withdraw because of its putrid odour, and it becomes a stumbling-block to others and a thorn in your own flesh.

⌁ LXVI ⌁

You who wept and shed tears of sorrow over Lazarus, accept my bitter tears.

May my passions be allayed by your Passion; may my wounds be healed by your wounds, my blood be blended with your blood, and the lifegiving fragrance of your holy body be mingled with my body.

May the bitter drink that was given to you by your enemies soothe my soul, which has been made to drink wormwood by the evil one.

May your body, which was stretched out on the tree, stretch my mind out to you, for it has been shrunken by demons.

May your head which was bowed down upon the cross lift up my head, which has been buffeted by impure men.

May your pure hands, which were transfixed with nails by unbelievers, draw me up to you from the abyss of evil, as your mouth has promised.

May your face, which has received spit of derision from accursed men, cleanse my face, which has become odious through its sins.

May your soul, which on the cross you committed to your Father, bring me up to you by your grace.

⌁ LXVII ⌁

I will now show you, my brother, how the grace of the Spirit commences the purification of your soul through the holy angels, if you will pay heed to it and persevere in solitude, wrestling in labours and combats; how it is purified and polished, how it is sanctified and illuminated, for the reception of gifts and revelations, and the perception of divine mysteries; and through what signs the mind acquires perception and knowledge in its passage through them; how it is absorbed in profound ecstasy in the vision of light, and its perception and free will are cut off and it forgets itself.

⋲ LXVIII ⋺

When Grace descends upon the solitary at the start it produces unfamiliar sensations, pleasures, and consolations in him and gradually enlarges his mind with pleasures, visitations, wondrous sights, and revelations, until he reclines in the cloud of essential light without passing thence. There the mind will look upon and shine in the rays of light that dawn upon it from the Essence. Thereby it ascends and penetrates day by day, in proportion to its diligence and watchfulness, from glory to glory through the Lord the Spirit, being transformed into the likeness without likeness, in union and perfect commingling with God.

⋲ LXIX ⋺

The visitations of the first stage.

cp. L   Sometimes Grace sows humility in his heart and makes his thoughts lower than dust and ashes.

Sometimes it causes him to shed tears through the remembrance of his sins.

Sometimes it makes recitation of the Psalms sweet to his heart, giving him facility and enjoyment in his lengthy service.

Sometimes it makes him love frequent genuflection, stirring up in him impulses of sorrow and humility, or of joy and confidence.

Sometimes it consoles him with dreams; the solitary should be wary about these, however wonderful they may be, because of the Adversary.

Sometimes it stimulates him with the remembrance of the saints and their labours and accomplishments, giving him the fervent desire to emulate their labours.

Sometimes it reproaches him with the remembrance of his faults and how Grace has borne him patiently like a loving nurse, and in this recollection he will shed tears of sorrow and of joy. Here, if Grace were not sustaining the solitary's heart, he would expire because of the multitude of burning tears.

Sometimes it grants him constant praises and delight in them.

Sometimes it causes him to love constant reading and it mingles tears or delight with it.

Sometimes it brings the life of our Lord to his mind, and he becomes humbled but joyful; or it portrays the Passion to him and causes passionate tears to flow without measure from his eyes.

Sometimes it inspires in him love of doing things for the pleasure of his brethren.

Sometimes it will bestow stillness on him to quell the impulses of the passions.

Sometimes it will arouse in his heart pity for the oppressed and ministering to the sick.

By these things the Grace of the Spirit purifies and polishes the soul of the novice solitary and of any one who turns back from his heedlessness and vile actions, and drawing near to it places himself under its yoke of obedience.

~ LXX ~

The middle stage, which is the psychical state.

Henceforward the Spirit alters his operations in the soul notably, so that it is thereby illuminated and sanctified for the reception of gifts, for the vision of revelations, and for the perception of hidden mysteries.

Sometimes Grace comes to rest upon him during his service and stills his mind from wandering thoughts, and even interrupts the service, sending his mind into ecstasy over the understanding of some mystery.

Sometimes it interrupts his service with tears over the love of his Lord.

Sometimes it imparts a stillness to his mind, and it makes his chanting cease, without thought, memory of anything, or meditation, though it sometimes holds back his service for more excellent meditation.

Sometimes it stirs up hot fiery impulses in his heart in the love of Christ, and his soul is set on fire, his limbs are paralysed and he falls on his face.

Sometimes it works up a fervent heat in his heart, and his body and soul are enkindled so that he supposes every part of him is being consumed in the blaze, except what is in his heart. Whenever you perceive such in only one of your members or in only one of the places on your body, then that comes from the Adversary. If he scrapes your head as if with a hand, or if he clings to your heart, breast, or belly, you have the feeling in your body that you are being stung. Whereas the action of Grace is associated with tranquillity and pleasure, that of the Adversary is either with mental derangement and coldness of impulses, or else turmoil.

⁓ LXXI ⁓

The stage of perfection.

Here begins the entering into the treasury, the place of glorious visions, the place of joy and exultation, the place without shadow, the place of light where no mention of darkness is made, the place of life and delight, the place of peace, whose inhabitants are illuminated by the sight of the beauty of the King.

Now their heart will rejoice, those who sought the Lord in adversities, who thirsted for the sight of him, and to whom he has shown his face. Enter now and take your rest, you who were wearied and exhausted. Recline with your Lord in the bridal chamber,* you who were weep-   *or: feast* ing at the door. The tears of sorrow have been stopped, and the struggles and battles have been taken away; the travail and conflict have ceased. Now is the time of rest. Fear has been removed out of the way of ardent love. The mind's impulses are stayed in amazement at the wondrous sights.

⁓ LXXII ⁓

This is the place in which the inhabitants inhale the Spirit; their mind stilled of impulses, the Spirit speaks his secrets into it.

This is the place of serenity and beauty; it is called light without likeness.

An invitation to enter it comes from the Spirit to the energetic mind, the impulses of whose visionary powers are wearied, to gaze, to behold the One who is in all and in whom is everything. And when it comes to prayer it sees its own glory, and upon the soul there dawns the beauty of its nature and it sees itself as it really is, and sees the divine light dawning in it and changing it into his likeness, while the likeness of its own nature is taken away out of its sight, and it sees itself as the likeness of God, being united with the light without likeness, which
cp. X–XI   is the light of the Trinity, shining forth in the soul itself.* It becomes immersed in the waves of its beauty and remains in ecstasy for a long period.

⸰ LXXIII ⸰

O solitary, acquire for yourself charity by keeping the commandments, that you may be deemed worthy to receive love. The solitary taken up with charity hates the world, together with everything in it, and desires to perform the things to which he is called.

Love is a fire that inflames: it does not allow anyone in whom it burns to carry out the rule laid down for him, but it rises up and does not permit him to finish, staying the service with gladness as it rises.

Love bursts forth within the heart, and the heart becomes hot, so that it kindles and burns the whole body with the force of love. So the person is not able to stand upon his feet but falls on his face as if dead, and his cither is broken, and he is in an absolute frenzy. He thinks that he and everything around him is ablaze, from the living fire that is blown by the One who lives eternally.

↭ LXXIV ↝

The Lord bears me witness that I am not lying: I have
frequently heard one of the brethren crying out when
he was in the intoxication of Christ's love and unable to
contain himself, because of the divine fire burning in his
heart, and the excitement of his heart at the shining forth
of God's glory upon it.

He was crying out: O my God, how your love inflames.
O Lord, how my life is consumed by your love, and I
cannot endure.

Again he cried out: Blessed are they who are intoxicated
by your love many times.

And again: O your unspeakable beauty.

And without knowing himself or anything else he would
cry out time after time without number: Father, my
Father; and other things of an outspoken kind that should
not be passed on in writing, or else I will come under
censure from the Initiated for daring to reveal the un-
written mysteries,‡ while I will be considered by the ‡ *cp. XXIV*
weak to be raving mad.

↭ LXXV ↝

Whoever has tasted the sweetness of Christ will be
diligently occupied in prayer, which, more than any other
labour, brings one near to God; for in prayer the mind
is commingled with God and becomes the image of its
maker, and a recipient of his gifts, and a fountain of his
mysteries.

Through prayer the mind opens the door to the treasur-
ies of God and becomes his treasurer and the divider of
his riches.

Through prayer it is made worthy to behold the Glory
of God and to abide in the Cloud of his majestic light,
within the place of the spirits, in stupefaction and silence,
void of impulses, in ecstasy, and wonderstruck at the
beauty of the many-splendoured rays of light dawning
upon it, stupefying the worlds at their sight, which are
the life and delight of the spiritual beings, stilling their
fiery impulses with their majestic beauty.

᪥ LXXVI ᪥

These are the unspeakable blessings bestowed on those
who are engaged in prayer.

Through it they are called upon to be a dwelling for God,
and he will be their abode and their resting-place, void
of all painful passions. For through it the soul is united
with Christ and thus it sees the glorious splendour of
his majesty, and in his brilliance it sees the loveliness of
its nature and it exults.

Through the travail of prayer there blazes up in the soul
the fire of Christ's love, and the heart becomes frenzied
with longing and sets all the members ablaze; it exults
with love and loses control of itself. The world, together
with its impulses, is obliterated from the heart, and it
awaits departure from it to abide in God and to behold
his face constantly for the delighting of its life.

Through constancy in prayer the mind is made worthy
of ecstasy in God, and ecstasy transports him to the
place of the spirits, which is ineffable light.

᪥ LXXVII ᪥

These precious *pearls* are gathered and stored among
the treasures of his mind by the merchant who is oc-

cupied with prayer. For truly he is swimming in the sea of life and cleansing himself in the mighty floods, to be purified and beautified so as to become a garment of purple for Christ the eternal King.

This is the strenuous diver captivated with desire for the sea that washes him. He would be delighted if he never had to come out of it.

⁓ LXXVIII ⁓

Blessed are you who circle in the waves of light and on the wings of the Holy Spirit, and are enclosed in the all-encompassing deep, whose limit is unsearchable.

Blessed are you who purge your foulness in the un-troubled sea, whose waves are light, and whose floods are flame, consuming the sin of sinners who come to it.

Blessed are you who have disdained the country of your birth and turned to plunge and rise in the lake of the source of all worlds and natures.

Blessed are you who have detested the River Gihon's drinking water,* and always satisfy your soul with living *Nile* waters, the drinkers of which do not die, for they flow from the fount of blessings, which is Christ the splendour of the Father.‡   ‡ *cp. XIII*

Blessed are you whose world is your Maker, whose wealth is your Creator, whose food is the vision of him, and whose drink is the working of his Spirit in your soul.

Blessed are you whose sun does not set and whose soul's eye does not see the night.

Blessed are you whose beauty does not fade, because it shines in the rays of our Saviour's light.

Blessed are you whose joy is in God and will never depart from your soul.

Blessed are you who though on the earth have departed from the earth, and dwell with the spirits in Heaven in the company of your Lord.

Blessed are you with whose soul the sweetness of your God is mingled in intimacy with him, having disdained all victuals that return to corruption.

⁖ LXXIX ⁖

Blessed is the person who has acquired within his soul the treasure of life, that is Christ, who reveals himself in those who love him, for they are all riches of his.

Pen and ink are unable to set forth the wondrous beauties of our Saviour's self-revelation to his seekers. He dawns within them and makes the mirror of the soul bright with his rays and excites it with his glorious majesty; and it cries out involuntarily; he declares to listeners its joy, its exultation, and its ecstasy.

He who has seen the Lord within him and whose soul has been mingled with his light, will find his heart warming with joy at the sight of these lines, which speak of his bliss.

⁖ LXXX ⁖

One of the brethren wrote this for himself and had it constantly set before him, admonishing himself in these words: You have spent your life foolishly, you shameful man, worthy of all evils. However, take care now, on this day that is left over to you from your days gone by, which were devoid of virtues but replete with evils. Do not ask about the world and its organizations, its affairs, and its necessities; nor about individual persons and their condition, and the enumeration of their possessions; do not think about a single one of these things. You have departed mystically from the world and you are accounted dead in Christ; do not live for the world and its own, so that you may anticipate your inner resurrection and be alive in God. Be ready and prepared for reproach, insult, mockery, accusation, and complaint, from everyone; accept them all joyfully as your own, because you truly deserve them. Endure pain and torment, grief and affliction, from the demons whose will you carried out, as you acknowledge. Bear anguish and bitterness, and natural accidents. Persevere in trust in our Lord, and in deprivation of 'absolute necessities' which only turn into dung. Do all this with hope in God, not looking for relief from anywhere else or consolation from anyone else, but cast your anxiety only on the One who blesses. And in all your afflictions find yourself guilty of being the cause of these. Do not blame someone else or one of your troublers for your having eaten of the forbidden tree and contracted various diseases. Joyfully accept bitterness for your purging. For you have left your own soul without judgement, filled though it is with all iniquities, and yet you have judged others in thought and in word. Renounce your foul thinking. Enough, enough of this swinish food that you have had until now. What have you to do with men and women, you impure man? You are not even afraid of intimacy with someone; you have behaved towards your own as one who is not human, and that is it. If you observe all these things with the help of God and take care, you will doubtless be saved. But if not you are going to a dark place to dwell with the demons whose wicked will you have done, to stand shamefaced. See now, I have testified all these things against you. If God justly stirred men up to repay you for the insults and accusations that you have thought and spoken against people, the whole world would be attending to this for a year. Therefore cease now and endure instead everything that comes along.

Every day that brother would admonish himself thus, so that whenever trial or tribulation fell upon him unexpectedly he would not be unable to bear it thankfully, as being to his advantage.

⌇ LXXXI ⌇

One brother said to me: When the memory of paradise had suspended my reason, to ponder on it; and when in a vision it had become like Adam and been enraptured; and moreover, when by the power of the Spirit it had been taken to wonder at the Paradise that is living and life-giving, whose limit is unreachable and whose delight I find within myself; then it was that I was very much amazed at those strenuous labourers in whom is still found, when they meditate on it, an impulse arousing desire for a vision of that paradise of restricted horizons.

⌇ LXXXII ⌇

Happy is he who gazes constantly at you, my Paradise which is seen in me. The tree of life in my heart ever

Christic inflames me with desire for him,* and changes my face by the force of his love, and sets my mind in wonderment at the rays of his beauty. Happy is he who at all times

cp. Jn 7:38 seeks you in himself, for it is from himself that life flows* to him for his delight. Happy is he who at all times carries in his heart the remembrance of you, for it is his own soul which is intoxicated with your sweetness. Happy is he who constantly gazes upon you within himself, for it is his own heart which is enlightened to see secret things. Happy is he who seeks you in his being, for his own heart glows in your fire, and his flesh and bones blaze together in its purifying force.

✥ LXXXIII ✥

Happy is he whose thoughts are silenced by the thought of you, for the Spirit causes rivers of life to well up in him for his own delight, and for those who thirst for a vision of you. Happy is he whose cheeks are burning from the tears of your love, for its drops water the rational lands which once burned with evil fire, so that they produce the fruits of gladness whose eaters do not die. Happy is he who combines thinking of you with his sleeping, for the demons that defile the slothful with fetid fantasies withdraw in terror from him. Happy is he who spreads out his mattress in unceasing admiration of your mysteries and reposes on it in silence and in wonderment over them; from it issues, to rejoice the heart of the diligent, the perfume of life produced by your Holy Spirit, guardian of the purity of his lovers. Happy is he who forgets the company* of the world in conversation *or: affairs* with you, for through you his needs are all fulfilled.

✥ LXXXIV ✥

You are his food and his drink; you are his joy and his exultation; you are his clothing and by your glory his nakedness is covered.* *2 Cor 5:2-4* You are his dwelling and his resting place, and he always enters you for shelter. You are his sun and his day, and it is in your light that he sees hidden things. You are the father who begot him, and like a child he calls you Father.* *Rom 8:15* You have placed the spirit of your son in his heart,* *Rom 5:5* who has given him the confidence* to ask you for everything that is yours, as *1 Jn 5:14* a son to his father. He is in your company all the time, since he knows no father apart from you.

◌ LXXXV ◌

You are united with his soul, you are joined to his members, you shine in his mind, and you capture it to make it amazed at the sight of you. You still the impulses of his soul by the impulse of your love, and you transform the desire of his body by the intensity of your sweetness; he smells your holy scent like a child breathing the scent of his father, and the odour of your grace issues from his body, like the odour of his nurse issuing from a child. At every hour you console him with a vision of yourself; when he eats, he sees you in his food; when he drinks, you are resplendent in his drink; when he weeps, you shine in his tears. Wherever he looks he sees you there, so that everywhere you increase his blessings, and there is no one who does not give him a blessing, except someone who is completely devoid of blessing.

◌ LXXXVI ◌

My Lord and my Life, my mind has been set ablaze by communion with you, there being no companion for me besides you. What shall I do? My soul thirsts for you, my *Ps 63:2*   flesh longs for you.* But ascension to you is found through communion with you, and the sight of your face is given through meditating on you.

◌ LXXXVII ◌

My right hand is incapable of setting your mysteries down *or: images*   in writing.* Like a self-assured sage I apply myself to writ- *or: images*   ing, and the outcome is that these lines* of mine show me up as a feeble person who knows nothing. So it is to you that I will apply myself and thereby find delight, since I have not been able to impart your delight to others through the pen. Who then shall ascend your holy moun- *Ps 24:2*   tain* to look upon your glorious beauty, O Light overflowing with many splendours of wondrous beauty, stunning those who see you, leaving those who know you speechless by your form which has no form, making those marvellers who labour for a vision of you stand motionless? Here are taken away the knowledge of the knowing and the sight of the seeing, through the magnitude of the knowledge and the marvellousness of the true vision.

⁂ LXXXVIII ⁂

And because the eyesight cannot extend to this, being prevented by the dazzling splendours, they say you are Cloud and Darkness, and that bright clouds surround you,* preventing the eyesight of your overeager lovers *cp. Ps 97:2* from gazing inordinately in an attempt to behold your hidden nature. They also call you Sea, as the source of all worlds and the sustainer of all that is, containing and concealing all in your immense abyss, offering facilities for bathers, allowing light people to float in its waves for the purlfying of their beauty. They also designate you Air, Inspiration* of all life, and Breath; they come and go in *Respiration* the midst of you with no obstruction to their progress, though it is not that they are penetrating and passing through you as the air, but that you are extended in them unimpededly, and they move around without hindrance this way and that in your extension within them.

⁂ LXXXIX ⁂

They also compare you to Fire, because it gives without decreasing, it cleans without soiling itself, and although present only partially with everyone everywhere, it is there for everyone in its entirety with the force of its whole nature; one gets from it everything one needs, and if one gives it abundant scope it shows the potency of the operation of its nature* in totality. *or: power*

❧ XC ☙

Thus it is with you in all your lovers, O Good One: you
are present with them in ineffable wonderment, in the
glorious loveliness of your beauty, in the potency of your
nature, in your absolutely supreme knowledge; and with
all your lovers you are present everywhere: in each one
of them you are entirely his, without deficiency, even
though none is capable of possessing you entirely. Glory
to the totality encompassing all totalities without being
limited by them.

❧ XCI ☙

You are also the Father of the rational beings born of
your Spirit. Therefore your Spirit is also styled Genetrix,
feminine gender, in that he has engendered all into this
world so that they may engender children into their
cp. Gen 3:20   world.* But he is Progenitor, in that he shall engender
into his living world rational beings who will engender
cp. Lk 20:35-36   no more.* And just as infants are nourished by their
genetrix and grow up, so those who are born of your
Spirit suck life at your breast in the world without end.

❧ XCII ☙

And just as children resemble their progenitor, so children out of your Spirit are transformed into your likeness, not in nature but in glory; and you make joint heirs
Rom 8:17   with your Son* those who have remained in your inheritance. Glory to you, the Omnipotent, Father of all, who
have made wise our ignorance by the wisdom of your
mysteries, for ever and ever. Amen.

❧ XCIII ☙

What is this wonderful thing that this Unique Singular
One desires to show solely to his lovers, so that they

increase his delight even more? It pleases him well, as I
have learned from him, that those who behold his beauty
should be far removed from the vision of his image, so
that the cleanness of the mirror of their being may be
combined with the clarity of the vision of his face. It is
not for the intelligences that behold God to look upon
his image with desire and not stand in awe of gazing on
him openly, unless they contemplate him presumptu-
ously. It is only obscurely* that holy things may be seen   *1 Cor 13:12*
by the holy, in concord.

⁖XCIV⁖

As for the profane and the disturbed, let them depict
illusions on the outside of the entrance to the mysteries.
For your part, go into your inner room to pray, hidden
from all view, and there you will see your Father hidden,
the reward of your prayer.* From whoever sees your   *Mt 6:5-6*
prayers you receive your recompense; and from him
to whom you manifest your works you will also seek
presents.*   *Mt 6:2, 5*

⁖ XCV ⁖

One thing that pleases the Lord of all is the heart clear
of every spot. And who can achieve this in the company
of many people? The more numerous their number is,
the more things they pour over him which ruffle him,
strip him, and reclothe him in shame; things which are
seductive but defiling; which are beautiful but uglifying.
Happy the hearing that is closed to all those things; happy
the heart that is void of their memory; for in it our sweet
God reveals himself in his glory.

⁖ XCVI ⁖

Lord, who can give to desire the abundance of your
delight unless you are combined with it in the mystery

of union. I am amazed at this mystery. There is no gift like that one for silencing the mind and making it stand motionless under the effect of its sweetness, which goes beyond force. There is also none that lends itself less to being spoken of in figures of speech, and there is none like it for putting the desire of the belly to shame.

ABRAHAM BAR DASHANDAD

⁖ XCVII ⁖

Let the remembrance of your Lord, rather than your breathing, be constantly in your thinking. Keep watch and ward over your soul, lest some perishable thing separates you from the love of Christ. Beware of contact with carnal people, who will cause you to lose your soul as well as your body. Let your psalm-recitation be done with understanding, and your prayer and supplication with discerning feeling. Let everything you have be for Christ; let all your remembrance be of Christ; and let all your thoughts be of Christ. . . .

Take care of your soul, because this world shall pass away and everything in it shall end in destruction. All the sounds and beings in this perishable world shall pass away, and the wicked people and the evil demons shall be put to shame; but the just will rejoice and the holy will be elated. Meditate continually on the new world, and despise the temporal world. . . .

Keep to the way of life that I am teaching you; do not neglect it; do not leave it; and thereby, on thousands of occasions, you will reap the reward of *pearls* and precious stones, from your seed, from your glorious meditation, in virtues, good works, and pure thoughts of wisdom. Be patient of spirit and persist in them, and you will receive the delights of the life that is eternal.

GREGORY BAR HEBRAEUS

∻ XCVIII ∻

From a tender age burning with a love for learning, I was taught the Holy Scriptures with the necessary elucidation, and from an excellent teacher I heard the mysteries contained in the writings of the holy doctors. When I reached the age of twenty years, the Patriarch of the time constrained me to receive the status of bishop. I was then obliged to engage in disputation and discussion with the heads of other confessions, internal and external. And when I had meditated and pondered over this matter for some time, I became convinced that these quarrels of Christians among themselves are not based on facts but merely on words and definitions. For all of them confess Christ our Lord to be wholly divine and wholly human, without mixing, combining, or confusing the natures. This conjoint form is called nature by some, designated substance by others, and named person by others. So I came to regard all Christian peoples, despite their differences, as being in united undiffering agreement. I therefore completely weeded the roots of hatred out of the depths of my heart, and totally abandoned disputation with anyone over doctrine.

∻ XCIX ∻

I then endeavoured to apprehend the force of the wisdom of the Greeks, that is to say: logic, physics and metaphysics [and other sciences]. And because life is short and scholarship is deep and wide, I had to read in every pursuit whatever was most essential. In the course of

my studies in these teachings I resembled someone sink-
ing in the ocean and waving his arms about in all directions in his desire to be rescued. And because in all the
scholarship, internal and external, I did not find what I was
seeking, I almost ended up in complete disintegration.
I do not think it proper to describe the snares and nets
in which I was entangled, because hearing about them
might harm too many weaker persons. To put it briefly:
if the Lord had not sustained my failing faith at that critical time, and if he had not led me to look into the writings of the Initiated, such as Father Evagrios and others,
both western and eastern, and if he had not lifted me
out of the whirlpool of disintegration and destruction,
I would have already despaired of the life of the soul,
though not that of the body.

≺ C ≻

I meditated on these works for a period of seven years,
during which I despised other kinds of knowledge, though
I had to study some of them superficially, not for my
own sake but for the sake of others who wished to be
instructed by me. During this period many stumbling-
blocks laid me low and made me go wrong. Sometimes
I would fall into unbelief and say: How high the sound of
the bell of these monks is, and how lacking in flour their
mill is, meaning that their words contain silly thoughts
which do not come into effect. Sometimes, however, my
mind would admonish me and say: Do not talk nonsense,
and do not think that anything that is not known to you
is therefore not so, since what you do know is much less
than what you do not know.

≺ CI ≻

In this uncertainty of mine I was, so to speak, limping on
both legs, until some of the pure individual light rays
illuminated me, like fleeting lightning, and gradually the

scales covering my eyes fell off, and they were opened, and I could see, though only partly. But I pray without ceasing that I may see the unseen Beloved, no longer dimly but distinctly. And the following few sentences which I arrange here are part of what the lightning flash revealed to me in the night darkness.

↜ CII ↝

The pure soul becomes expert in knowledge not for the sake of the glory that the knowing acquire in the world, but in order that its longing for the face of the Lord of all may be increased and it may be enabled to go into and be hidden in the divine cloud.

↜ CIII ↝

Those who immerse themselves in exoteric and esoteric teachings without caring about purifying the heart, and who think they have reached the stage of perfection, are mistaken. For what profit is there in such a marvellous piece of work as a mirror decorated with *pearls* and gems if it is not cleansed of dross? But one which is cleaned, even if it is of simple workmanship, will work beautifully.

↜ CIV ↝

As hunger is not satisfied by water nor thirst by bread, so too the initiated person who wishes to gaze into the Sinai cloud has little to gain from reading books.

↜ CV ↝

As long as you think you can know God through proofs, signs, and testimonies, you are forging cold iron; faith as *Mt 17:20* a grain of mustard seed is not in you yet.*

ᴗ: CVI :ᴗ

The vision of God comes by shutting off the senses, opening the window of the heart, and removing the veil from the eyes of the mind. As it has been said: close the windows so that the dwelling-place may be lit up.

ᴗ: CVII :ᴗ

Those who penetrate the cloud attain the depth and riches of God's wisdom without the intermediary of complex thought.

ᴗ: CVIII :ᴗ

As the mind necessarily attains elementary knowledge here (such as: the whole is greater than the part, one is half of two), so when it has been admitted into the divine cloud it will likewise of necessity know the hidden and incomprehensible judgements of the Godhead.

ᴗ: CIX :ᴗ

As the senses are unable to apprehend non-material images, so too the mind, when it has not yet loosed the shoes of its body from its feet, is unable to apprehend the images concealed in the cloud, seeing only dimly and backwardly.*   *Ex 33:9-23*

ᴗ: CX :ᴗ

Inside the cloud there is unspeakable delight for the mind in seeing the All-Beauteous. This can also happen outside the cloud, but only as hearing about the beauty of the All-Beauteous, not seeing it.

᭣ CXI ᭤

When the eyes of the mind are opened, in proportion to its aptitude grace is poured out upon it, and it is illuminated by the glorious angelic rays; it becomes familiar with the members of the kingdom, and is ranked among their shining hosts; it rejoices and glorifies with them, becoming a stranger to the world and everything in it.

᭣ CXII ᭤

Anyone who reckons himself among the faithful without having gazed through the doorway of the holy of holies of the cloud is deceiving himself, even if he confesses with his tongue and affirms with his heart.

᭣ CXIII ᭤

A man blind from birth may affirm that colours exist (white, black, green, red), and a deaf man may believe that the sounds of concordant strings and harmonious songs delight the ear, but their belief is nearer to unbelief than to belief.

᭣ CXIV ᭤

Brother, if you do not have revelational faith then do not give sleep to your eyes or slumber to your eyelids until you find the place of the Lord; there you will receive faith and be baptized with fire and spirit, not with water.

᭣ CXV ᭤

Luke 1:78   Revelational faith is found by the prophets and the apostles in the manner of the day-spring from on high,* without labouring or searching; by the solitaries, however, through searching, labouring, exertion, and training. They thus proceed from shadowy faith towards revelational faith.

ᴄ CXVI ᴄ

It is not by bodily labours alone, but by the striving and struggling of a sound mind that perfection is obtained. Accordingly, vary your physical service with spiritual discernment, so that you understand that you work with both mind and body.

ᴄ CXVII ᴄ

When the mind understands that there are words which it is not able to utter, and that there are things such as eye has not seen, nor ear heard, neither have they entered into any heart,* then it ascends above all the stages that are outside the cloud and sets foot on the lowest step inside it.

1 Cor 2:9

ᴄ CXVIII ᴄ

When the mind hears unutterable words which no mouth is able to explain, and when it sees things such as eye has not seen, then it is already resting in the tabernacle of the Lord and is abiding on his holy mountain.

ᴄ CXIX ᴄ

As a mirror is in itself devoid of all images and likenesses, but, in proportion to its purity and cleanness, images of things outside it appear in it, so too the mind is deprived of images, and, in proportion to its purification from the stains of matter, non-material images are reflected in it.

↮ CXX ↬

When the window of your heart is opened you will fly towards the kingdom of God, and there you will see all these things distinctly, and not need to hear them described; and you will no longer be unbelieving but believing.

↮ CXXI ↬

How long will you go on seeking a guide to open up for you in the wall of your heart a window on the Kingdom? Purify the mirror of your mind from stains and then it will show you the images of the two kingdoms and the paths that will lead you to that of heaven, then further to that of God.

↮ CXXII ↬

As long as the thirsty person is incapable of going up to the fountain, the guide has no power to lead him or to carry him; he can merely teach him the nature of his journey and the manner of proceeding on it.

↮ CXXIII ↬

As a ship that has been holed cannot benefit from the wind, even though it is favourable, so a heart in which desires are entrenched cannot benefit from a guide, even if he is of high degree.

↮ CXXIV ↬

A jug whose top is directed towards the earth does not collect water; and the soul whose thinking is directed to earthly things will not have the heavenly gift abiding in it.

↲ CXXV ↳

This is what true life is: suckling at the breasts of supreme
Providence with the perfect. But in the teachers of the
Law and the Scriptures there is nothing of this life save
the description and the name.

↲ CXXVI ↳

Anyone who has not tasted, does not know. Anyone
who has not eaten is not satisfied by talking to someone
who has. Anyone who has not drunk does not have his
thirst quenched by being told about it by someone who
has. Anyone who has not experienced does not benefit
from another's experience.

↲ CXXVII ↳

Some of the teachers who are competently trained in
the Holy Scriptures and their commentaries are not
willing to learn the ways of the kingdom from the initiated, who are not versed in their professional matters.
They do not realize that their knowledge, however
studious they may be, is by hearing, whereas that of the
initiated, however unsophisticated* they may be, is one   *'bald'*
of seeing.

↲ CXXVIII ↳

The initiated possess a special knowledge of their own,
which is acquired by purity of thought, emaciation of the
body, suppression of the senses, and severing of ties.
And when the tabernacle of their heart is illuminated
by it, the kingdom of God is represented in them and
exists within them and is not sought in this mountain or
in Jerusalem.*   *Jn 4:21*

∴ CXXIX ∴

When the sun of the Beloved rises for the lover on the timeless day, and he sees the Solomonic bride in her splendour, revealing herself unveiled to him and taking
Prov 9:1 him into her house with seven pillars,* declaring him to be beloved of all, and taming with him winged and fanged creatures, because they sniff the scent of their Creator on him; for even beings not endowed with senses perceive
God him,* so that demons are subdued and angels minister.

∴ CXXX ∴

These sentences are only profitable to someone experienced in knowledge of divine and human things, who is desirous of seeing by revelation what he has attained by contemplation. Anyone who is without this longing should redouble his meditation on this book, but with intelligent discernment, not by mindless recitation; perhaps his heart will be warmed.

TEXTUAL SOURCES

THE SONG OF THE PEARL

Authorship unknown; a poem of Iranian origin (note the reference to the King of Kings, which is the typical Persian title of royalty; Parthia and Hyrcania as the hero's homeland in the East; pearls and silk as two commodities readily available to the Iranians from the Persian Gulf and China); preserved in a Syriac book recounting the missionary journey of the Apostle Thomas to the Indo-Iranian regions. The poem is put into the mouth of Saint Thomas as a hymn he sings to himself while in a prison in India. The Syriac text is available in T. Jansma, *A Selection from the Acts of Judas Thomas* (Leiden 1952), 35–40. The translation of William Wright (1871) is reprinted with introduction and commentary in A. F. J. Klijn, *The Acts of Thomas* (Leiden 1962). The division of the poem into thirteen stanzas is not in the original.

I(1):	Jansma, 35; Klijn, 120 (1–8)
II(2):	Jansma, 35; Klijn, 120f (9–15)
III(3):	Jansma, 35f; Klijn, 121 (16–22)
IV(4):	Jansma, 36; Klijn, 121 (23–32)
V(5):	Jansma, 36f; Klijn, 122 (33–40)
VI(6):	Jansma, 37; Klijn, 122 (41–48)
VII(7):	Jansma, 37f; Klijn, 122f (49–55)
VIII(8):	Jansma, 38; Klijn, 123 (56–63)
IX(9):	Jansma, 38; Klijn, 123f (64–71)
X(10):	Jansma, 38f; Klijn, 124 (72–78)
XI(11):	Jansma, 39; Klijn, 124 (79–87)
XII(12):	Jansma, 39f; Klijn, 124f (88–95)
XIII(13):	Jansma, 40; Klijn, 125 (96–105)

APHRAHAT THE PERSIAN

Demonstration 6, On the Sons of the Covenant. Syriac text in J. Parisot, *Aphraatis Sapientis Persiae Demonstrationes. Patrologia Syriaca* 1, 2 (Paris

1894, 1907). English translation in J. Gwynn, *A Select Library of Nicene and Post-Nicene Fathers*, Second Series, 13 (Oxford 1898, Grand Rapids 1979).

XIV(14):　　　Parisot, 240–241; Gwynn, 362–363

EPHREM THE SYRIAN

Hymns on the Pearl by Saint Ephraem Syrus, Numbers 81–85 of *Hymns on the Faith*. Syriac text in Edmund Beck, *Des Heiligen Ephraem des Syrers Hymnen de Fide*, in the series *Corpus Scriptorum Christianorum Orientalium*, 154 (Louvain 1955), 248–262.

XV(15):　　　1:1-3, 9-11
XVI(16):　　　2:10-11
XVII(17):　　　5:1-2, 4-8

THE BOOK OF DEGREES

Discourse 12, On the Mystery of the Hidden and the Manifest Church. Syriac text in M. Kmosko, *Liber Graduum, Patrologia Syriaca* 3 (Paris 1926), with Latin translation.

XVIII(18):　　　Kmosko, 301–304

JOHN THE SOLITARY

Three discourses of John the Solitary of Apamea, in reply to a question of Thomasios, On the Mystery of the Dispensation of Christ. Syriac text in Werner Strothmann, *Johannes von Apamea, Patristische Texte und Studien*, Band 11 (Berlin 1972).

XIX(19):　　　Strothmann, 94–96
XX(20):　　　Strothmann, 102
XXI(21):　　　Strothmann, 138–139

John the Visionary, On the Spiritual State of the Soul (in 20 sentences). Syriac text, with English translation, in A. J. Wensinck, *New Data concerning Syriac Mystic Literature* (see item 112 in the reference bibliography below).

XXII(22):　　　Sentence 12

PHILOXENOS OF MABBUG

Discourse 9, On Renunciation of the World. Syriac text in E.A.W. Budge, *The Discourses of Philoxenus* (London 1894), with English translation.

XXIII(23):   Budge, 312, 314, 318

STEPHEN BAR SUDAILI

The Book of the Holy Hierotheos, Syriac text edited by F. S. Marsh (see item **135** in the reference bibliography).

XXIV(24):   Marsh, 1*, 27*, 34*

SAHDONA MARTYRIOS

The Book of Perfection. Syriac text in A. de Halleux, *Martyrius (Sahdona), Oeuvres spirituelles, Corpus Scriptorum Christianorum Orientalium* 200 (Louvain 1960).

XXV(25):   Halleux, 29–30

SIMON TAIBUTHEH

Medico-mystical writings; A. Mingana, *Woodbrooke Studies*, Vol. VII, *Early Christian Mystics* (Cambridge 1934), 281–320.

XXVI(26):   On prayer and on the meaning of communion with God; Mingana, 310 (folio 190b).

XXVII(27):   On the division of the stages; Mingana, 293 (folio 173b)

XXVIII(28):   The rebuke of my soul which loves vain things; Mingana, 319f (folio 200 ab)

XXIX(29):   On the faculties of our inner man and their working; Mingana, 306 (folio 186b–187a)

ISAAC OF NINEVEH

Mystical discourses; P. Bedjan, *Mar Isaacus Ninivita De Perfectione Religiosa* (Paris and Leipzig 1909) offers an edition of the Syriae text. For an English translation see A. J. Wensinck, *MysticTreatises by Isaac of Nineveh* (Amsterdam 1923); also D. Miller (item 156 on the reference bibliography).

XXX(30):	Bedjan, 325; Wensinck, 217
XXXI(31):	Bedjan, 325; Wensinck, 217
XXXII(32):	Bedjan, 325; Wensinck, 217f
XXXIII(33):	Bedjan, 325f; Wensinck, 218
XXXIV(34):	Bedjan, 326; Wensinck, 218
XXXV(35):	Bedjan, 328; Wensinck, 219
XXXVI(36):	Bedjan, 328; Wensinck, 219
XXXVII(37):	Bedjan, 177f; Wensinck, 120
XXXVIII(38):	Bedjan, 179; Wensinck, 121
XXXIX(39):	Bedjan, 179f; Wensinck, 121
XL(40):	Bedjan, 365–7; Wensinck, 245f

DADISHO QATRAYA

On solitude; A. Mingana, *Woodbrooke Studies*, Vol. 7 (Cambridge 1934), 201–247.

XLI(41):	Mingana, 205f (folio 8ab)
XLII(42):	Mingana, 208f (folio 11ab)

JOSEPH THE VISIONARY

Letter on the three stages of the monastic life, British Museum Manuscript Add 14,728, folios 76b–125b. Other manuscripts of the work abridge it and attribute it to Philoxenos of Mabbug, but it is now established that its author was Joseph Hazzaya (the Visionary). The Syriac text of the shorter version was published by Gunnar Olinder, *A Letter of Philoxenus of Mabbug sent to a friend* (Göteborg 1951), with an English translation. A French translation of the complete work was published by F. Graffin, 'La lettre de Philoxène de Mabboug à un supérieur de monastère sur la vie monastique', *L'Orient syrien* 6, 3 (1961), 317–352; 6,4 (1961), 455–486; 7,1 (1962), 77–102.

XLIII(43):	British Museum Ms Add. 14,728, folios 76–77
XLIV(44):	Olinder, 3f
XLV(45):	Olinder, 4f
XLVI(46):	Olinder, 20–22

| XLVII(47): | Olinder, 37f |
| XLVIII(48): | Olinder, 41f |

Book of Questions and Answers, by Abdisho (Joseph) Hazzaya; A. Mingana, *Woodbrooke Studies*, Vol. VII (Cambridge 1934), 274–276.

XLIX(49):	Mingana, 274 (folio 156a)
L(50):	Mingana, 274 (folio 156a)
LI(51):	Mingana, 275 (folio 156b)
LII(52):	Mingana, 275 (folio 156b)
LIII(53):	Mingana, 275 (folio 157a)

On the prayer that comes to the mind in the sphere of serenity; Mingana, 269–272.

| LIV(54): | Mingana, 270 (folio 152a) |
| LV(55): | Mingana, 272 (folio 153b) |

JOHN THE VENERABLE

Discourses of John Saba ('the old man', 'the venerable'), John of Dalyatha; Brian E. Colless, The Mystical Discourses of John Saba (Department of Middle Eastern Studies, University of Melbourne, 1969) (reference bibliography item **193**, Vol. 1).

LVI(56):	Preface; Colless, 1
LVII(57):	Discourse on repentance; Colless, 6
LVIII(58):	Colless, 7
LIX(59):	Discourse on self-custody; Colless, 7
LX(60):	Colless, 7
LXI(61):	Colless, 8
LXII(62):	Colless, 8
LXIII(63):	Colless, 8
LXIV(64):	Colless, 8
LXV(65):	Discourse on flight from the world; Colless, 12
LXVI(66):	Colless, 14
LXVII(67):	Discourse on visitations; Colless, 20
LXVIII(68):	Colless, 21
LXIX(69):	Colless, 21
LXX(70):	Colless, 22f

LXXI(71):   Colless, 38
LXXII(72):   Colless, 38
LXXIII(73):   Discourse on the love of God; Colless, 48
LXXIV(74):   Colless, 48f
LXXV(75):   Discourse on prayer; Colless, 74
LXXVI(76):   Colless, 74f
LXXVII(77):   Colless, 77
LXXVIII(78): Colless, 77
LXXIX(79):   Colless, 78
LXXX(80):   Vatican Syriac Manuscript 124, folios 351b–352b

Letter 51, On the vision of God; Robert Beulay, *La Collection des lettres de Jean de Dalyatha* (Turnhout, Belgique, 1978), 220–231 (*Patrologia Orientalis*, Tome XXXIX, Fascicule 3, No. 180, 472–483), Syriac text with French translation.

LXXXI(81):   Beulay, 220
LXXXII(82):   Beulay, 220
LXXXIII(83):   Beulay, 220, 222
LXXXIV(84):   Beulay, 222
LXXXV(85):   Beulay, 222
LXXXVI(86):   Beulay, 224
LXXXVII(87):   Beulay, 224
LXXXVIII(88):   Beaulay, 224
LXXXIX(89):   Beulay, 224, 226
XC(90):   Beulay, 226
XCI(91):   Beulay, 226
XCII(92):   Beulay, 226
XCIII(93):   Beulay, 226, 228
XCIV(94):   Beulay, 228
XCV(95):   Beulay, 228
XCVI(96):   Beulay, 228, 230

ABRAHAM BAR DASHANDAD

Letter; A. Mingana, *Woodbrooke Studies*, 7, 248–255.

XCVII (97):   Mingana, 253f (folio 65)

GREGORY BAR HEBRAEUS

The Book of the Dove, in P. Bedjan, *Ethicon, seu Moralia, Gregorii Barhebraei* (Paris and Leipzig 1898) to which is appended *Liber Columbae seu directorium monachorum Gregorii Barhebraei*, 521–599; English translation in A. J. Wensinck, *Bar Hebraeus's Book of the Dove together with some chapters from his Ethicon* (Leiden 1919).

XCVIII(98):	Bedjan, 577f; Wensinck, 60
XCIX(99):	Bedjan, 578; Wensinck, 60f
C(100):	Bedjan, 578f; Wensinck, 61
CI(101):	Bedjan, 579; Wensinck, 61f
CII(102):	Sentence 1; Bedjan, 579f; Wensinck, 62
CIII(103):	Sentence 2; Bedjan, 580; Wensinck, 62
CIV(104):	Sentence 7; Bedjan, 581; Wensinck, 63
CV(105):	Sentence 10; Bedjan, 581; Wensinck, 64
CVI(106):	Sentence 11; Bedjan, 581; Wensinck, 64
CVII(107):	Sentence 12; Bedjan, 581; Wensinck, 64
CVIII(108):	Sentence 13; Bedjan, 581f; Wensinck, 64
CIX(109):	Sentence 14; Bedjan, 582; Wensinck, 64
CX(110):	Sentence 15; Bedjan, 582; Wensinck, 64
CXI (111):	Sentence 16; Bedjan, 582; Wensinck, 64f
CXII(112):	Sentence 17; Bedjan, 582; Wensinck, 65
CXIII(113):	Sentence 18; Bedjan, 582f; Wensinck, 65
CXIV(114):	Sentence 19; Bedjan, 583; Wensinck, 65
CXV(115):	Sentence 20; Bedjan, 583; Wensinck, 65
CXVI(116):	Sentence 22; Bedjan, 583; Wensinck, 65
CXVII(117):	Sentence 26; Bedjan, 584; Wensinck, 66
CXVIII(118):	Sentence 27; Bedjan, 584; Wensinck, 66
CXIX(119):	Sentence 36; Bedjan, 586; Wensinck, 67f
CXX(120):	Sentence 41; Bedjan, 587; Wensinck, 68f
CXXI(121):	Sentence 58; Bedjan, 589; Wensinck, 71
CXXII(122):	Sentence 59; Bedjan, 590; Wensinck, 71f
CXXIII(123):	Sentence 60; Bedjan, 590; Wensinck, 72
CXXIV(124):	Sentence 61; Bedjan, 590; Wensinck, 72
CXXV(125):	Sentence 64; Bedjan, 590; Wensinck, 72
CXXVI(126):	Sentence 67; Bedjan, 591; Wensinck, 73
CXXVII(127):	Sentence 68; Bedjan, 591; Wensinck, 73

REFERENCE BIBLIOGRAPHY

MONASTICISM AND MYSTICISM

1. Brock, Sebastian, *The Syriac Fathers on Prayer and the Spiritual Life*. Kalamazoo 1987.

     English translations of extracts from: Aphrahat, Ephrem, Book of Steps, Evagrius, John of Apamea, Philoxenus of Mabbug, Babai, Anonymous I, Anonymous II, Abraham of Nathpar, Martyrius (Sahdona), Isaac of Nineveh, Dadisho, Joseph the Visionary (Abdisho), John the Elder (John of Dalyatha).

2. Mingana, A., *Early Christian Mystics*. Woodbrooke Studies 7. Cambridge 1934.

     Syriac text (reproduction of Mingana ms 601) and English translation of extracts: Simon of Taibutheh, Dadisho Qatraya, Joseph (alias Abdisho) Hazzaya, Abraham bar Dashandad.

3. Baumstark, A., *Geschichte der syrischen Literatur*. Bonn 1922.

     Provides a brief biography and list of writings for each author.

4. Brock, S., 'The Syriac Tradition', in Jones, Cheslyn, Geoffrey Wainwright, Edward Yarnold, *The Study of Spirituality*. London 1986. Pages 199–215.

     Syriac spirituality: brief introduction and bibliography.

5. Brock, S., 'Early Syrian Asceticism', *Numen* 20 (1973) 1–19; reprinted in his *Syriac Perspectives on Late Antiquity*. London 1984.

     Brief survey, including John Chrysostom, Marcion, Tatian, Encratism, the Diaterssaron, the Acts of Thomas, Aphrahat, Ephrem, Simeon the Stylite.

6. Brock, S., 'The consecration of the water in the oldest manuscripts of the Syrian Orthodox Baptismal Liturgy', *Orientalia Christiana Periodica* 37 (1971) 317–332.

     Provides data for relating baptismal formulas to the Song of the Pearl (par. 137 above).

7. Brock, S., 'Clothing metaphors as a means of theological expression in Syriac tradition', **22**, 11–40.

8. Colless, Brian, 'The Place of Syrian Christian Mysticism in Religious History', *Journal of Religious History* 5/1 (1968) 1–15.

     Brief survey of modern study on the subject.

9. Colless, B., 'The Legacy of the Ancient Syrian Church, *Evangelical Quarterly* 40 (1968) 183–196.

10. Colless, B., A Pot-pourri of Eastern Mysticism: Mingana Syriac Ms No. 86', *Milla wa-Milla* 6 (1966) 34–43.

11. Colless, B., Education in the Ancient Syrian Church, *Milla wa-Milla* 7 (1967) 21–30.

    Aspects of education in early Syriac schools and monasteries.

12. Colless, B., 'The Pearl and Grail Quests', *Milla wa-Milla* 15 (1975) 27–35.

    The pearl is a typically eastern symbol and the grail is western, but the East has its grails and the West has its pearls.

13. Ellwood, R. S., *Mysticism and Religion*. Englewood Cliffs, New Jersey 1980.

    A thorough study of the rich variety of human mystical experiences in their religious and social contexts. He has only one Syriac mystic, 'Saint Isaac the Syrian', and he has not studied him at first hand, but through the eyes of Orthodox Christians; he says that Isaac's three stages are 'penitence, purification, and perfection', but see also par. 243 above.

14. Frank, K. S., *Askese und Mönchtum in der alten Kirche*. Darmstadt 1975.

    Collected studies by various scholars.

15. Guillaumont, A., *Aux origines du monachisme chrétien. Pour une phénoménologie du monachisme*. Spiritualité Orientale 30. Begrolles: Abbaye de Bellefontaine 1979.

    Collection of articles in French, mainly on the Egyptian desert monks.

16. Hambye, E. R., 'The symbol of the "coming to the harbour" in the Syriac tradition', *Symposium Syriacum* 1972. Orientalia Christiana Analecta 197 (1974) 401–411.

    Data for elucidating the arrival at the haven in the Song of the Pearl (par. 109–112 above).

17. Hausherr, Irénée, *Hésychasme et prière*. Orientalia Christiana Analecta 176. Rome 1966.

    Collected articles on eastern Christian spirituality.

18. Hausherr, I., *Etudes de spiritualité orientale*. Orientalia Christiana Analecta 183. Rome 1969.

    Collected articles on spiritual authors of the eastern churches.

19. Leroy, J., *Monks and Monasteries of the Near East*. London 1963.

    A sympathetic introduction, translated from French by P. Collin.

20. Murray, R., *Symbols of Church and Kingdom. A Study in Early Syriac Tradition*. Cambridge 1975.

    Detailed study of early titles and symbols applied to Christ and his church.

21. Pena, I., Castellana, P., Fernandez, R., *Les Reclus Syriens. Recherches sur les anciennes formes de vie solitaire en Syrie.* Studium Biblicum Franciscanum, Collectio Minor 23. Milano 1980.

Ancient Syrian recluses, athletes of God; Syrian monasticism; the towers of the recluses; the ascetic life; activities of the recluses. Types of monks: stationary (standing constantly), dendrite (tree-dwelling), akoimete (non-sleeping), grazer (grass-eating), vagrant (idle rover), stylite (pillar-sitter), recluse (enclosed in a confined space), hupaithrian (living under the open sky with no protection from the weather).

22. Schmidt, Margot, *Typus, Symbol, Allegorie bei den östlichen Vätern und ihren Parallelen im Mittelalter.* Eichstätter Beiträge 4. Regensburg 1982.

Includes S. Brock on clothing metaphors; H. Drijvers on the Alexius legend; L. Leloir on the Devil and the Desert Fathers; E. Beck, P. Yousif, and M. Schmidt on Ephrem.

23. Smith, Margaret, *Studies in Early Mysticism in the Near and Middle East.* London 1931.

Chapter 5 deals with Aphraates, Ephraim, John of Lycopolis (John the Seer), Hierotheos, Isaac of Nineveh; Part II covers Islam and Sufism.

24. Underhill, Evelyn, *Mysticism.* London 1911.

Mysticism is a quest for truth and reality, knowledge of ultimate reality without the mediation of the mind or the senses. There are five stages: (1) *Awakening* or conversion, (2) *Purgation* or self-knowledge, through discipline and morality, (3) *Illumination*, radiant ecstasy, but not true union, (4) *Surrender*, or the dark night of the soul, a further purgation of self, (5) *Union* with God, integration with ultimate reality; calm peace, quiet joy.

25. Vööbus, A., *History of Asceticism in the Syrian Orient.* Vol. 1: *The Origin of Asceticism; Early Monasticism in Persia.* Corpus Scriptorum Christianorum Orientalium 184. Louvain 1958.

26. Vööbus, A., *History of Asceticism in the Syrian Orient.* Vol. 2, *Early Monasticism in Mesopotamia and Syria.* Corpus Scriptorum Christianorum Orientalium 197. Louvain 1960.

27. Vööbus, A., *History of Asceticism in the Syrian Orient.* Vol. 3. Corpus Scriptorum Christianorum Orientalium 500 . Louvain 1988.

This volume covers the Syriac mystics.

EUGENIOS OF NISIBIS

28. Vööbus, A., **25**, 138–140, 217–220.

Considers the Eugenios legend to be a fabrication.

TATIAN THE ENCRATITE

29. Vööbus, A., **25**, 31–45.

>   Examines the role of Tatian the 'Assyrian' in the establishing of asceticism in the Syriac world; Encratism and the *Diatessaron*.

30. Quispel, G., Tatian, Enkratismus, **37**, 5–17.

>   Encratism (Hellenistic, abstention from mariage, wine, meat) came from the West to Edessa, before Tatian; it influenced Messallianism (a movement within the church), as found in Pseudo-Makarios and the *Book of Degrees*.

THE ACTS OF THOMAS

31. Wright, W., *Apocryphal Acts of the Apostles*. Vol. 1:171–333. London 1871.

>   Syriac text and English translation of *Acta Thomae*.

32. Klijn, A. F. J., *The Acts of Thomas*. Supplements to Novum Testamentum 5. Leiden 1962.

>   The English translation of William Wright (1871), with introduction, including a survey of the manuscript tradition of the Syriac text and other versions (1–17), and commentary.

33. Jansma, T., *A Selection from the Acts of Judas Thomas*. Leiden 1952.

>   Syriac text, abridged, for student use; includes the Song of the Pearl.

THE SONG OF THE PEARL

34. Bevan, A. A., *The Hymn of the Soul Contained in the Syriac Acts of St Thomas*. Texts and Studies 5, 3. Cambridge 1897.

>   Syriac text and English translation.

35. Poirier, P.-H., *L'Hymne de la Perle des Actes de Thomas*. Homo Religiosus 8. Louvain-la-Neuve 1981.

>   Syriac text, Greek version, and French translation, with bibliography (17–26), comprehensive introduction surveying all previous interpretations of the poem (31–167), and commentary (409–438); also Greek text and French translation of the paraphrase of Niketas of Thessalonika.

36. Colless, B. E., 'The Letter to the Hebrews and the Song of the Pearl', *Abr-Nahrain* 25 (1987) 40–55.

>   An interpretation of the poem as an allegory of the Christian life, in accord with the teachings of the New Testament apostles; an English translation is appended.

37. Quispel, G., *Makarius, das Thomasevangelium, und das Lied von der Perle*. Leiden 1967.

Finds connections between Pseudo-Makarios and the Song of the Pearl (39–64).

THE DESERT ASCETICS

38. Migne, J. P., *Apophthegmata Patrum*. Patrologia Graeca 65 (Paris 1868) 71–440.

Greek text and Latin translation of the alphabetical collection of sayings.

39. Ward, Benedicta, *The Sayings of the Desert Fathers: The Alphabetical Collection*. Oxford-Kalamazoo 1975.

English translation of the Apophthegmata (Migne **38**, 71–440).

40. Budge, E. A. W., *The Wit and Wisdom of the Christian Fathers of Egypt*. Oxford 1934.

English translation of the Syriac version of the *Apophthegmata*.

41. Budge, E. A. W., *The Book of Paradise*, 2 vols. London 1904.

Syriac text and English translation of Ananisho's seventh-century Syriac recension of the *Paradise* (Lausiac History) of Palladios, the *Life of Saint Antony* by Athanasios of Alexandria, the *Asketikon* (the Rule of Pakhomios at Tabenna), *History of the Monks* attributed to Hieronymus (Jerome), *Sayings of the Fathers* (non-alphabetical version).

42. Budge, E. A. W., *The Paradise of the Holy Fathers*, 2 vols. London 1907.

English translation of the *Book of Paradise*.

43. Butler, C., *The Lausiac History of Palladius*. Texts and Studies 6, 1-2. Cambridge 1898 and 1904.

The first volume contains a critical discussion, and the second an edition of the Greek text of the *Paradeisos* of Palladios, also called the *Lausiakon*, because it was written for the prefect Lausos.

43b. Draguet, R., *Les formes syriaques de la matière de l'histoire lausiaque*. Corpus Scriptorum Christianorum Orientalium 389–390, 398–399. Louvain 1978.

44. Draguet, R., *La vie primitive de S. Antoine conservée en syriaque*. Corpus Scriptorum Christianorum Orientalium 417–418. Louvain 1980.

45. Guillaumont, A., 'La conception du désert chez les moines d'Égypte', **15**, 67–87.

The desert is an ambivalent thing: the ideal place for *hesukhia* and union with God, but also the abode of the demons with which the monk must fight and defeat the passions that would turn him aside from his goal.

46. Guillaumont, A., Le dépaysement comme forme d'ascèse dans le monachisme, **15**, 89–116.

The monastic concept of expatriation or voluntary exile (cp. the going forth from home, family, and even homeland in Buddhism) involves becoming a stranger to the world, the concept of *xeniteia*.

47. Guillaumont, A., 'Le travail manuel dans le monachisme ancien: contestation et valorisation', **15**, 117–126.

The question of manual labour as an ascetic exercise; contrasts the perfect in the *Book of Degrees* and the Messallians (who "toil not, neither do they spin") with the Egyptian monks ("anyone who does not work does not eat"), who produced food for their own sustenance and to give away in charity, and also engaged in work to stave off accidie (depression).

48. Guillaumont, A., 'Les visions mystiques dans le monachisme oriental chrétien', **15**, 136–147.

The visionary experiences of Arsenios, Silvanos, Pakhomios, and Evagrios.

EVAGRIOS PONTIKOS

49. Migne, J. P., *Evagrius Ponticus, Opera Omnia*. Patrologia Graeca, 40:1213–1286.
Greek text and Latin translation.

50. Frankenberg, W., *Evagrius Ponticus. Abhandlungen der königlichen Gesellschaft der Wissenschaften zu Göttingen*, 13, 2. Berlin 1912.

Includes the Syriac text of: *Antirrhetikos* (472–544, in eight parts, corresponding to the eight kinds of 'thoughts', *logismoi*, by which the demons arouse the passions), *Gnostikos* (546–553, in 53 'chapters', counsels for the 'gnostic', the initiated monk), Admonition on Prayer (558–562), Epistles (564–634, a collection of 64 letters), the six collections of *Kephalaia Gnostika* (8–421), and an additional group of sixty sentences (422–470).

51. Brock, S., 'Admonition on Prayer', **1**, 64–75.
English translation of this short piece (Frankenberg 558–562).

52. Gressmann, H., *Nonnenspiegel und Mönchsspiegel des Euagrios Pontikos*. Texte und Untersuchungen 39/4:143–165. Leipzig 1913.

Greek text of two sets of metrical sentences, similar to the Biblical *Proverbs*; advice for novices; one set addressed 'to monks living in community', the other 'to a virgin'.

53. Bunge, G., *Evagrios Pontikos, Briefe aus der Wüste*. Trier 1986.
German translation of the letters.

54. Guillaumont, A., *Les six centuries des "Kephalaia gnostica" d'Évagre le Pontique*. Patrologia Orientalis 28, 1. Paris 1958.

Syriac text and French translation of the two Syriac versions of the *Kephalaia Gnostika* ('Chapters of Knowledge'), mystical sentences collected in six 'centuries' (actually groups of ninety sayings). Most of the Greek text has been lost, because the works of Evagrios were banned.

55. Guillaumont, A., *Les 'Kephalaia Gnostica' d'Évagre le Pontique et l'histoire de l'Origénisme chez les grecs et les syriens*. Paris 1962.

Studies the influence of Evagrios on the Syriac churches.

56. Guillaumont, A., 'Un philosophe au désert: Évagre le Pontique', **15**, 185–212.

Concise introduction to Evagrios and his teachings.

57. Guillaumont, A. et C., 'Évagre le Pontique', *Dictionnaire de Spiritualité* 4 (1960) 1731–1744.

Survey of the writings of Evagrios.

58. Guillaumont, A., *Évagre le Pontique. Traité pratique ou le moine*. Sources Chrétiennes 170–171. Paris 1971.

Greek text and French translation of the *Praktikos*.

59. Bamberger, J. E., *Evagrius Ponticus. The Praktikos, and Chapters on Prayer*. Cistercian Studies Series 4. Kalamazoo 1970.

English translation of the *Praktikos* (a work in a hundred brief chapters; the most complete statement of his ascetic teaching), and the Treatise on Prayer (in 153 sayings).

60. Hausherr, I., *Les leçons d'un contemplatif. Le Traité de l'oraison d'Évagre le Pontique*. Paris 1960.

French translation of Treatise on Prayer, with commentary.

61. Muyldermans, J., *Evagriana Syriaca: Textes inédits du British Museum et de la Vaticane*. Louvain 1952.

Survey of Syriac mss containing writings of Evagrios (3–102); Syriac text (104–142) and French translation (143–171) of fifteen pieces attributed to Evagrios by the Syriac scribes (but note that the first of these, The Just and the Perfect, is actually Discourse 14 of *The Book of Degrees*).

ESAIAS OF SKETE

62. Draguet, R., *Les cinq recensions de l'Ascéticon syriaque d'Abba Isaïe*. Corpus Scriptorum Christianorum Orientalium 289–290, 293–294. Louvain 1968.

Syriac text and French translation.

62a. Abba Isaiah of Scetis, *The Ascetic Discourses*. Cistercian Studies series, 150. Translated with an Introduction and Notes by John Chryssavgis and Pachomios (Robert) Penkett. Kalamazoo 2001.

63. Regnault, L., 'Isaïe de Scété ou de Gaza', *Dictionnaire de Spiritualité* 7:2083–2095.

64. Chitty, D. J., 'Abba Isaiah', *Journal of Theological Studies* 22 (1971) 47–72.

MAKARIOS THE GREAT

65. Strothmann, W., *Die syrische Überlieferung der Schriften des Makarios.* Göttinger Orientforschungen, 2 vols. Wiesbaden 1981.

> Syriac text and German translation of the Syriac version of the Makarian writings, much shorter than the Greek corpus, and including a number of non-Makarian pieces; it begins with an abridgement of the Great Letter.

66. Migne, J. P., *Omnia Opera Sancti Macarii.* Patrologia Graeca 34.

> Greek text and Latin translation.

67. Dörries, H., Klostermann, E., Kroeger, M., *Die 50 Geistlichen Homilien des Makarios.* Berlin 1964.

> Greek text of the *Spiritual Homilies*, known as Collection 2.

68a. Mason, A. J., *Fifty Spiritual Homilies of St. Macarius the Egyptian.* London 1921.

> English translation of Collection 2.

68b. Maloney, G. A., *Pseudo-Macarius: The Fifty Spiritual Homilies and the Great Letter.* New York 1992.

> English translation of Collection 2.

69. Klostermann, E., Berthold, H., *Neue Homilien des Makarios/Symeon, I, aus Typus III.* Texte und Untersuchungen 72. Berlin 1961.

> Greek text of Collection 3, except those pieces that already appear in Collection 2.

70. Desprez, V., *Pseudo-Macaire: Œuvres spirituelles, I, Homélies propres à la Collection III.* Sources Chrétiennes 275. Paris 1980.

> Greek text and French translation of the homilies in the Klostermann and Berthold edition of Collection 3, except the eight that also appear in Collection 1.

71. Berthold, H., *Makarios/Symeon. Reden und Briefe, Die Sammlung I des Vaticanus Graecus 694 (B),* 2 vols. Berlin 1973.

> Greek text of Collection 1, the largest, 64 homilies and epistles, beginning with the Great Letter, the longest composition in the entire corpus.

72. Marriott, G., *Macarii Anecdota. Seven Unpublished Homilies of Macarius.* Harvard Theological Studies 5. Cambridge 1918.

> Greek text of 7 homilies appended to 2 mss of Collection 2, some of which also appear in Collection 3.

73. Jaeger, W., 'The Great Letter', in *Two Rediscovered Works of Ancient Christian Literature: Gregory of Nyssa and Macarius.* Leiden 1954.

74. Clarkson, A. P., *Christ and the Christian in the Writings of Pseudo-Macarius: A Study of an Early Christian Spirituality*. Rome 1977.

75. Quispel, G., *Makarius*, **37**, 9–63.

75a. Stewart, Columba, *'Working the Earth of the Heart: The Messalian Controversy in History, Texts, and Language to AD 431*. New York–Oxford 1991.
> A study of Pseudo-Macarius and the *Book of Degrees*, with all the anti-Messalian documents.

DIONYSIOS THE AREOPAGITE

76. Luibheid, Colm, *Pseudo-Dionysius: The Complete Works*. The Classics of Western Spirituality. New York 1987.
> English translation of *The Divine Names, The Mystical Theology, The Celestial Hierarchy, The Ecclesiastical Hierarchy, The Letters*. Greek text in J. P. Migne. Patrologia Graeca 3.

77. Rolt, C. E., *The Divine Names and the Mystical Theology*. London 1920.
> English translation.

78. Sherwood, P., 'Sergius of Resh'ain and the Syriac Versions of the Pseudo-Denis', *Sacris Erudiri* 4 (1952) 174–184.

79. Hornus, J-M., 'Le corpus dionysien en syriaque', *Parole de l'Orient* 1 (1970) 69–94.

APHRAHAT THE PERSIAN

80. Parisot, J., *Aphraatis Sapientis Persiae Demonstrationes*. Patrologia Syriaca 1, 2. Paris 1894, 1907. 1–489.
> Syriac text and Latin translation of the 23 Demonstrations.

81. Gwynn, J., 'Demonstrations of Aphrahat the Persian Sage', A Select Library of Nicene and Post-Nicene Fathers, Second Series, 13: 152–162, 345–412. Oxford 1898; Grand Rapids 1979.
> English translation of Demonstrations 1, 5, 6, 8, 17, 21, 22.

82. Neusner, J., *Aphrahat and Judaism*. Leiden 1971.
> Includes English translation of most of Demonstrations 11–23.

83. Brock, S., Aphrahat, **1**, 1–28.
> English translation of Demonstration 4, On Prayer.

84. Hausherr, I., 'Aphraate', *Dictionnaire de Spiritualité* 11 (Paris 1937) 746–752.

85. Vööbus, A., 'Treatises of Aphrahat', **26**, 173–178, 197–203.
> Discusses their asceticism, and the 'sons and daughters of the covenant'.

EPHREM THE SYRIAN

86. Beck, F., *Des heiligen Ephraem des Syrers Hymnen de Fide*. Corpus Scriptorum Christianorum Orientalium 154–155. Louvain 1955.

>   Syriac text and German translation of the 87 Hymns on Faith, including the 5 Pearl hymns, 81–85.

87. Graffin, F., 'Les Hymnes sur la Perle, de Saint Ephrem', *L'Orient Syrien* 12 (1967) 129–149.

>   French translation of the Hymns on the Pearl.

88. Gwynn, J., *Hymns and Homilies of Ephraim the Syrian*, **81**, 120–151, 165–344.

>   Introduction and English transalation; includes the Pearl Hymns (291–304).

89. McVey, Kathleen, *Ephrem the Syrian: Hymns*. Classics of Western Spirituality 43. New York, 1989.

>   English translation.

90. Brock, S., *Ephrem*, **1**, 30–40.

>   English translation of Hymns on Faith, 20.

91. Lavenant, R., Graffin, F., *Ephrem de Nisibe, Hymnes sur le Paradis*. Sources Chrétiennes 137. Paris 1968.

>   French translation (by Lavenant) of the Hymns on Paradise (introduction by Graffin).

92. Brock, S. P., *The Luminous Eye: The Spiritual World Vision of St Ephrem*. Rome 1985–Kalamazoo 1992.

>   Introduction to Ephrem's spirituality.

93. Vööbus, A., *Ephrem the Syrian*, **26**, 70–110.

>   Outlines Ephrem's asceticism.

94. Leloir, L., 'La pensée monastique d'Éphrem et Martyrius', *Orientalia Christiana Analecta* 197:105–1134. Rome 1974.

JULIAN SABA OF EDESSA

95. Vööbus, A., *Juliana Saba*, **26**, 42–51.

>   The chief sources of information are Ephrem and Theodoret.

THE BOOK OF DEGREES

96. Kmosko, M., *Liber Graduum*. Patrologia Syriaca 3. Paris 1926.

>   Syriac text and Latin translation of the 30 discourses. It is considered to be Messallian.

96a. *The Book of Steps: The Syriac* Liber Graduum. Translated with an Introduction and Notes by Robert A. Kitchen and Maartien F. G. Parmentier, Cistercian Studies Series 196. Kalamazoo 2004.

> Downplays the role of the *Liber Graduum* in the Messallian controversy; it is probably not the missing Asketikon of the Messalians; but it does demonstrate some Messallian tendencies, like the indwelling of demons.

97. Brock, S., The Book of Steps, **1**, 42–61.

> English translation of discourses 12 (On the ministry of the hidden and the manifest church) and 18 (On the tears of prayer).

98. Murray, R., The Church visible, hidden and heavenly in the 'Liber Graduum' and related literature, **20**, 262–271.

> English translation and discussion of discourse 12.

99. Guillaumont, A., 'Liber Graduum', *Dictionnaire de Spiritualité* 9 (1976) 749–754.

100. Guillaumont, A., 'Situation et signification du "Liber Graduum" dans la spiritualité syriaque', *Orientalia Christiana Analecta* 197 (Roma 1974) 311–325.

> The *Book of Degrees* was not composed by a Messallian, but it contains the seeds of Messallianism.

101. Vööbus, A, **25**, 178–197.

> The *Book of Degrees* is not a Messallian work.

102. Adam, A., Rezension von A. Vööbus, *History of Asceticism in the Syrian Orient*, **14**, 230–254.

> The *Book of Degrees* is clearly Messallian (238–244); it has the doctrine of the evil Satanic spirit dwelling in the body; its doctrine of the two grades of Christians (the just and the perfect) is not so much Manichean as Marcionite; it has an exposition of Luke's parable of the lost son, which is to be compared with the Song of the Pearl.

102a. Stewart C., **75a**, 84–92 and passim.

> The *Liber Graduum* is Messallian.

ADELPHIOS OF EDESSA

103. Lavenant, R., **127**, 130–135.

> Philoxenos recounts the story of the monk Adelph to Patriq of Edessa, as a cautionary tale. Syriac text and French translation.

104. Kmosko, M., **96**, CXC–CXCVII.

> Greek text and Latin translation of Theodoret's account of Messallianism (*Ecclesiastical History* 4.10).

105. Vööbus, A., The Messalians, **26**, 127–146.

JOHN THE SOLITARY OF APAMEA

106. Dedering, S., *Johannes von Lykopolis, Ein Dialog über die Seele und die Affekte des Menschen*. Uppsala 1936.
Syriac text of four Dialogues with Eutropios and Eusebios, on the soul.

107. Hausherr, I., *Jean le Solitaire (Pseudo-Jean de Lycopolis), Dialogue sur l'âme et les passions des Hommes*. Orientalia Christiana Analecta 120. Rome 1939.
French translation of the *Dialogues* (Dedering's edition).

108. Rignell, L. G., *Briefe von Johannes dem Einsiedler*. Lund 1941.
Syriac text and German translation of two letters to Eutropios and Eusebios, on the spiritual path, and on the true communion in the new life.
Syriac text and German summary of a letter to Theodoulos, on the mystery of the new life after the resurrection.

109. Rignell, L. G., *Drei Traktate von Johannes dem Einsiedler (Johannes von Apameia)*. Lund 1960.
Syriac text and German translation of (1) Letter on repose (perfection); (2) Discourse on the mystery of baptism; (3) Letter to Theodoulos on baptism.

110. Strothmann, W., *Johannes von Apamea, Sechs Gespräche mit Thomasios, der Briefwechsel zwischen Thomasios und Johannes und drei an Thomasios gerichtete Abhandlungen*. Berlin 1972.
Syriac text and German translation of (1) six dialogues with Thomasios, (2) a letter to Thomasios, (3) three discourses (in response to a letter from Thomasios) on Christ's plan of salvation.
Also contains a survey of the published and unpublished writings of John.

111. Lavenant, R., *Jean d'Apamée, Dialogues et traités. Introduction, traduction et notes*. Sources Chrétiennes 311. Paris 1984.
French translation of Strothmann's Syriac text.

112. Wensinck, A. J., 'New Data concerning Syriac mystic literature', *Mededeelingen der Koninklijke Akademie van Wetenschapen, Afdeeling Letterkunde*, Deel 55, Serie A. Amsterdam 1923.
Syriac text and English translation of twenty sentences on the spiritual station of the soul, by John the Seer.

113. Smith, M., 'John of Lycopolis', **23**, 90–93.
Study of the twenty sentences on the spiritual station.

114. Brock, S., John of Apamea, **1**, 78–100.
English translation of the letter to Hesukhios.

115. Brock, S., 'John the Solitary, On Prayer', *Journal of Theological Studies* 30 (1979) 84–101.

Syriac text and English translation of the discourse on prayer, also attributed to Abraham of Nathpar (see I, 188–196).

116. Bettiolo, P., 'Sulla Preghiera: Filosseno o Giovanni?', *Le Muséon* 94 (1981) 75–89.
Discussion of the discourse on prayer, by Philoxenos or John?

117. Bradley, B., 'Jean le Solitaire (Jean d'Apamée)', *Dictionnaire de Spiritualité* 8 (1974) 764–77.

118. Hausherr, I., 'Aux origines de la mystique syrienne: Grégoire de Chypre ou Jean de Lycopolis?', **17**, 63–86.
The first inkling of the importance of John the Solitary, and his three-stage framework.

119. Hausherr, I., 'Un grand auteur spirituel retrouvé: Jean d'Apamée', **18**, 181–216.
Further clarification on the identity of John the Solitary.

120. Lavenant, R., 'Le problème de Jean d'Apamée', *Orientalia Christiana Periodica* 46 (1980) 367–390.
Returns to the position of Hausherr, there were three monks known as John of Apamea: (1) John the Solitary in the 4th century; (2) John the Egyptian, condemned by Philoxenos and Theodore Bar Koni; (3) the Apamean condemned by Timothy the Patriarch along with Joseph the Visionary and John the Venerable. However, this could be reduced to two personages (3)=(1), or even one (Strothmann).

121. Harb, P., 'Doctrine spirituelle de Jean le Solitaire', *Parole de l'Orient* 2 (1971) 225–260.

122. Halleux, A. de, 'La christologie de Jean le Solitaire', *Le Muséon* 94 (1981) 5–36.

123. Halleux, A. de, 'Le milieu historique de Jean le Solitaire', *Orientalia Christiana Analecta* 221 (1983) 299–305.

PHILOXENOS OF MABBUG

124. Budge, E. A. W., *The Discourses of Philoxenus*, 2 Vols. London 1894.
Syriac text and English translation.

125. Lemoine, E., *Philoxène de Mabboug: Homélies*. Sources Chrétiennes 44. Paris 1956.
French translation of the Discourses.

126. Hausherr, I., Spiritualité syrienne: Philoxène de Mabbug en version française, **18**, 285–299.
Review of Lemoine's translation of the Discourses.

127. Lavenant, R., *La lettre à Patricius de Philoxène de Mabboug*. Patrologia Orientalis 30, 5 (Paris 1963).
Syriac text and French translation.

128. Hausherr, I., Contemplation et sainteté. Une remarquable mise au point par Philoxène de Mabboug, 17, 13–37.

Study of the Greek version of the Letter to Patriq.

129. Tanghe, A., Memra de Philoxène de Mabboug sur l'inhabitation du Saint Esprit, Le Muséon 73 (1960) 39–71.

Syriac text and French translation.

130. Brock, S., Philoxenus of Mabbug, 1, 102–133.

Translation of the discourse on the indwelling of the Holy Spirit.

131. Halleux, A. de, Philoxène de Mabboug, sa vie,ses écrits, sa théologie. Louvain 1963.

132. Graffin, F., 'Philoxène de Mabboug', Dictionnaire de Spiritualité 12, 1392–1297.

133. Grillmeier, A., 'Zur Tauftheologie des Philoxenus von Mabbug und ihre Bedeutung für die christliche Spiritualität', Studies in honour of P. Smulders. Assen 1981. Pages 137–175.

STEPHEN BAR SUDAILI

134. Frothingham, A. L., Stephen Bar Sudaili the Syrian Mystic and the Book of Hierotheos. Leiden 1886.

135. Marsh, F. S., The Book which is called The Book of the Holy Hierotheos, with extracts from the Prolegomena and Commentary of Theodosius of Antioch and from the "Book of Excerpts" and other works of Gregory Bar-Hebraeus. London and Oxford 1927.

Syriac text and English translation.

136. Hausherr, I., 'L'influence du "Livre de Saint Hiérothée"', 18, 23–58.

137. Guillaumont, A., 'Étienne Bar Soudaili', Dictionnaire de la Spiritualité, Tome 4, 1481–1488.

138. Guillaumont, A., 'Étienne Bar Soudaïli', 54, 302–332.

139. Smith, M., 'The Book of the Holy Hierotheos', 23, 94–97.

ABRAHAM OF NATHPAR

140. Penna, A., Abramo di Nathpar, Rivista degli Studi Orientali 32 (1957) 415–431.

In Italian, a survey of the writings attributed to this author in the Syriac manuscripts.

141. Tonneau, R., 'Abraham de Nathpar', L'Orient Syrien 2 (1957) 337–350.

French translation of a biography and extracts from his ascetic tracts.

142. Brock, S., 'Abraham of Nathpar', 1, 64–75, 188–196.
  English translation of two tracts attributed to Abraham (by Evagrios and John the Solitary).

GREGORIOS THE HERMIT

143. Hausherr, I., *Gregorii Monachi Cyprii. De Theoria Sancta*. Orientalia Christiana Analecta 110. Rome 1937.
  Syriac text and Latin translation of the discourse On holy contemplation, by Gregory the Hermit, alias Gregory of Cyprus.
144. Kirchmeyer, J., 'Grégoire de Chypre', *Dictionnaire de Spiritualité* 6 (1967) 920–922.

SAHDONA-MARTYRIOS

145. Halleux, A. de, *Martyrius (Sahdono), Œuvres spirituelles*. Corpus Scriptorum Christianorum Orientalium 200–201 (1960), 214–215 (1961), 252–253 (1965), 254–255 (1965).
  Syriac text and French translation of *The Book of Perfection*, Letters to solitaries, Maxims.
146. Brock, S., Martyrius (Sahdona), 1, 198–239.
  English translation of Book of Perfection 2.8.
147. Halleux, A. de, 'Un nouveau fragment du manuscrit sinaïtique de Martyrius-Sahdona', *Le Muséon* 73 (1960) 33–38.
148. Brock, S. P., 'A further fragment of the Sinai Sahdona manuscript', *Le Muséon* 81 (1968) 139–154.
149. Halleux, A. de, Un chapitre retrouvé du Livre de la perfection de Martyrius, *Le Muséon* 88 (1975), 253–295.
150. Leloir, L., 'Martyrius', *Dictionnaire de Spiritualité* 10 (1980) 737–742.
151. Leloir, L., 'Martyrius', **94**, 124–131.

SIMON TAIBUTHEH

152. Mingana, A., Medico-Mystical Work, by Simon of Taibutheh, **2**, 1–69, 281–320.
  Syriac text (folios 163a–200b) and English translation.

ISAAC OF NINEVEH

153. Bedjan, P., *Mar Isaacus Ninivita de Perfectione Religiosa*. Paris 1909.

Syriac text (in East Syrian script) of 82 discourses, and an appendix of other works attributed to Isaac (but in one case actually by Dadisho, 601–628), including a treatise on contemplation of the mysteries of the cross (589–600).

154. Ploeg, J. van der, 'Un traité nestorien du culte de la croix', *Le Muséon* 56 (1943) 115–127.

Latin translation of the treatise on the cross (Bedjan 589–600).

155. Wensinck, A. J., *Mystic Treatises by Isaac of Nineveh* (Amsterdam 1923; Wiesbaden 1969).

English translation (inelegant) of the 82 discourses published by Bedjan (153); it has Bedjan's page numbers in the margin, for ease of reference to the Syriac original.

156. Miller, D., *The Ascetical Homilies of Saint Isaac the Syrian*. Boston: Holy Transfiguration Monastery, 1984.

English translation of the Greek version (but with reference to the Syriac original), with table of correspondences of the Greek and Syriac numbering of the discourses. Also excerpts from *The Book of Grace*, attributed rightly or wrongly to Isaac.

Note that Letter 4 of the printed Greek version is the Letter to Patriq of Philoxenos of Mabbug, while 2, 7, 43, and 80 are by John of Dalyatha (John the Venerable).

157. Touraille, J., *Isaac le Syrien: Œuvres spirituelles*. Paris 1981.

French translation of the Greek version of 'the 85 ascetic discourses and the letters'.

158. Kadloubovsky, E., Palmer, G. E. H., *Early Fathers from the Philokalia*. London 1954. Pages 183–280.

English translation of the excerpts from Isaac's discourses in the Russian *Philokalia*, under the heading Directions on spiritual training.

159. Bettiolo, P., Gallo, M., *Isacco di Ninive: Discorsi ascetici*, vol. 1. Rome 1984.

Italian translation of the first six discourses in Bedjan's edition (153,1–99).

160. Bettiolo, P., *Isacco di Ninive: Discorsi spirituali*. Magnano 1985.

Italian translation of the four Centuries (see 161).

161. Brock, S., 'Isaac of Nineveh: some newly-discovered works', *Sobornost* 8:1 (1986) 28–33.

An introduction to the projected publication of Oxford Bodleian ms syr. e. 7, containing Part 2 of Isaac's works: four Centuries of Chapters on Knowledge, and numerous discourses, including two repeated from

Part I (54 and 55 in Bedjan's edition, **153**), and the one on contemplation of the cross (Bedjan,**153**, 589–600).

161a. Brock, S., *Isaac of Nineveh (Isaac the Syrian), The Second Part, Chapters IV–XLI.* Corpus Scriptorum Christianorum Orientalium 554–555 (Scriptores Syri 224–225). Louvain 1995.

Text and translation of the manuscript mentioned in **161**, except I–III, which include the four sets ('centuries') of sentences on spiritual knowledge.

162. Brock, S., 'St Isaac of Nineveh and Syriac spirituality', *Sobornost* 7:2 (1975) 79–89.

Concise introduction to Isaac's mysticism.

163. Bunge, G., 'Mar Isaak von Nineveh und sein "Buch der Gnade"', *Ostkirkliche Studien* 34 (1985) 3–22.

Accepts the *Book of Grace* (a collection of seven centuries of sayings) as a late work of Isaac, but D. Miller (**156**, lxxxi–lxxxv) thinks they belong to Simon Taibutheh.

164. Khalifé-Hachem, É., Isaac de Ninive', *Dictionnaire de Spiritualité*, 7 (1971) 2041–2054.

Introduction and detailed bibliography.

165. Khalifé-Hachem, É., La prière pure et la prière spirituelle selon Isaac de Ninive', in *Mémorial Mgr Gabriel Khouri-Sarkis*. Louvain 1969. Pages 157–173.

Discussion of Isaac's paradox that at the very height of prayer, prayer is no more.

166. Khalifé-Hachem, É., L'âme et les passions des hommes d'après un texte d'Isaac de Ninive', *Parole de l'Orient* 12 (1984–1985) 201–218.

French translation and analysis of Discourse 3 (Bedjan, **153**, 20–31), detecting influences of Evagrios and John the Solitary.

167. Smith, M., Isaac of Nineveh, **23**, 97–102.

168. Chabot, J. B., *De S. Isaaci Ninivitae Vita, Scriptis et Doctrina*. Paris 1892.

DADISHO OF QATAR

169. Mingana, A., *A Treatise on Solitude*, by Dadisho Katraya, **2**, 70–143, 201–247.

Syriac text (photo-reproduction, 201–247, folios 3b–55b) and English translation.

170. Brock, S., Dadisho, **1**, 303–312.

English translation of a section (on pure prayer) from the *Discourse on Solitude*.

171. Guillaumont, A., Albert, M., 'Lettre de Dadisho Qatraya à Abkosh, sur l'hesychia', *Mémorial A.-J. Festugière*. Geneva 1984. Pages 235–245.

172. Draguet, R., *Commentaire du livre d'Abba Isaïe par Dadisho Qatraya*. Corpus Scriptorum Christianorum Orientalium 326–327. Louvain 1972.

   Syriac text and French translation of his Commentary on the *Asketikon* of Esaias of Sketis.

173. Guillaumont, A., 'Dadisho Qatraya', *Dictionnaire de Spiritualité* 2 (Paris 1957) 22–23.

JOSEPH THE VISIONARY

174. Mingana, A., Mystical treatise by Joseph Hazzaya, **2**, 177–184, 256–261.

   Syriac text (256–261, folios 85b–90a) and English translation of 'the fifth letter of Rabban Joseph' on the shortest path that brings us to God, through 'pure prayer'.

175. Mingana, A., Mystical treatises by Abdisho Hazzaya, **2**, 145–175, 262–281.

   Syriac text (262–281, folios 143b–162b) and English translation of 5 pieces, by Joseph Hazzaya, published under the name of his brother Abdisho. The last of these, on the operations of grace, is also found at the end of the Epistles of John the Venerable (Beulay's edition, Letter 49).

176. Brock, S., Joseph the Visionary (Abdisho), **1**, 313–325.

   English translation of two short pieces from Mingana Syriac Ms 601: On spiritual prayer (248b–249a) and On the stirrings of the mind during prayer (both published and translated by Mingana, 2, 272–274, 163–164).

177. Brock, S., Anonymous II, **1**, 179–185.

   In this short discourse on prayer as a ladder leading up to God, Brock sees a similarity of style with John of Apamea; nevertheless, the presence of 'the five contemplations' of Evagrios indicates that this cannot be a composition of John, since he apparently never refers to them; the mention of the fragrance of the contemplative vision imparting sweetness to the mind's palette (183, 184) suggests Joseph Hazzaya (cp. Mingana, **2**, 149, 164, and Olinder **179**, 41–42); also the ladder metaphor (cp. Mingana, **2**, 161, 179, 184).

178. Bunge, G., *Rabban Jausep Hazzaya: Briefe über das geistliche Leben und verwandte Schriften, Ostsyrische Mystik des 8. Jahrhunderts*. Trier 1982.

   German translation of a selection of writings: the letter on the 3 degrees (77–211), letter on the various operations of grace (213–221), letter on the operation of grace (223–238), the fifth letter (239–261), discourse on spiritual contemplation (263–268), 3 discourses on prayer (269–287, 289–294, 295–298), excerpts from the chapters of knowledge

(299–324), extracts from the book of questions and answers (325–355), 3 prayers (357–367).

179. Olinder, G., *A Letter of Philoxenos of Mabbug sent to a Friend. Göteborg's Högskola's Årsskrift* 56. Göteborg 1950.

Syriac text and English translation of the abridged version of Joseph Hazzaya's letter on the three degrees, wrongly attributed to Philoxenos.

180. Graffin, F., 'La lettre de Philoxène de Mabboug à un supérieur de monastère sur la vie monastique', *L'Orient Syrien* 6 (1961) 317–352, 455–486, 7 (1962) 77–102.

French translation of the complete version of the letter on the three degrees.

181. Harb, P., 'Faut-il restituer à Joseph Hazzaya la *Lettre sur les trois degrés de la vie monastique* attribuée à Philoxène de Mabbug?', *Melto* 4 (1968) 13–36.

Convincing demonstration of Joseph's authorship.

181a. Jausep Hazzaya, *Lettre sur les trois étapes de la vie monastique*, ed. Paul Harb, François Graffin, Micheline Albert, Patrologia Orientalis t. 45, fasc. 2 = no 202. Turnhout 1992.

Text and French translation of the discourse mentioned in **178–181**.

182. Draguet, R., *Commentaire anonyme du Livre d'abba Isaïe (fragments)*. Corpus Scriptorum Christianorum Orientalium 336–337. Louvain 1973.

Syriac text and French translation of nine substantial fragments of a commentary on the *Asketikon* of Esaias of Skete, which may well be Joseph's commentary on the Book of the Merchant (thought to be the Isaiah *Asketikon*). Draguet rejects Joseph as the author of these fagments, but they bear his characteristic marks; they are certainly later than Isaac of Nineveh, who is quoted as the teacher of the writer.

183. Graffin, F., 'Un inédit de l'abbé Isaïe sur les étapes de la vie monastique', *Orientalia Christiana Periodica* 29 (1963) 449–454.

Syriac text and French translation of the eighth fragment of the anonymous commentary edited by Draguet.

184. Beulay, R., 'Des Centuries de Joseph Hazzaya retrouvées?', *Parole de l'Orient* 3 (1972) 5–44.

Some of Joseph's chapters on knowledge have been included among the works of John the Venerable (John Saba of Dalyatha).

185. Beulay, R., 'Joseph Hazzaya', *Dictionnaire de Spiritualité* 8 (1974) 1341–1349.

Summary of Joseph's life, writings, and teachings.

186. Guillaumont, A., 'Sources de la doctrine de Joseph Hazzaya', *L'Orient Syrien* 3 (1958) 3–24.

Evagrios and Makarios as important sources of Joseph's doctrine.

187. Scher, A., 'Joseph Hazzaya, écrivain syriaque du VIIIᵉ siècle', *Rivista degli Studi Orientali* 3 (1910) 45–63.

Surveys the biographies and manuscripts.

188. Sherry, E. J., 'The Life and Works of Joseph Hazzaya', *The Seed of Wisdom. Essays in Honour of T. J. Meek*. London 1964. Pages 78–91.

An introduction to Joseph and his mysticism.

189. Sims-Williams, 'Syro-Sogdica I: An Anonymous Homily on the Three Periods of the Solitary Life', *Orientalia Christiana Periodica* 47 (1981) 441–446.

English translation of an incomplete Sogdian text found in Turkestan, presumed to be translated from Syriac; the author notes that it is comparable to works of John the Solitary, Isaac of Nineveh, and Joseph Hazzaya. Joseph is a likely candidate (there are comparisons with his Letter on the Three Degrees, 122–124, such as the 'sweetness' mingled with the monk's solitary service in the middle stage, after a struggle with passions, and the thoughts becoming collected; also the ladder, as in **177**).

JOHN THE VENERABLE

190. Beulay, R., *La Collection des Lettres de Jean de Dalyatha. Patrologia Orientalis* 39, 3. Turnhout 1978.

Syriac text and French translation of the epistles of John Saba ('the venerable') of Dalyatha.

191. Beulay, R., 'Jean de Dalyatha et sa lettre XV', *Parole de l'Orient* 2 (1971) 261–279.

French translation and detailed study of one of the epistles.

192. Brock, S., John the Elder, 1, 327–338, 362–364.

English translation of Letters 5 and 12 (Beulay's edition) and two prayers (from Letters 15 and 42).

193. Colless, B. E., 'The Mysticism of John Saba. Vol 1, The Mystical Discourses of John Saba. Vol. 2, John Saba and the Legacy of Syrian Christian Mysticism'. Thesis: University of Melbourne, 1969.

Syriac text and English translation of most of the discourses.

194. Sherwood, P., 'Jean de Dalyata: Sur la fuite du monde', *L'Orient Syrien* 1 (1956) 305–312.

French translation of one of the discourses, on withdrawal from the world.

195. Beulay, R., 'L'enseignement spirituel de Jean de Dalyatha'. Thèse de 3ᵉ cycle, déposée à l'École Pratique des Hautes Études, 5ᵉ Section. Paris 1974.

Exhaustive analysis of the works of John Saba.

195a. Beulay, Robert, *L'enseignement spirituel de Jean de Dalyatha, mystique syro-oriental du VIIIe siècle*, Collection 'Théologie historique' 83. Paris 1990.
This and the following volume constitute the published version of his thesis.

195b. Beulay, Robert, *La Lumière sans forme. Introduction à l'étude de la mystique chrétienne syro-orientale*, Collection 'L'Esprit et le Feu'. Chevetogne 1987.
A masterly survey of Syriac Christian mysticism, concentrating on the Nestorian mystics of the 7th and 8th century and the influence exerted on them by Evagrios, Pseudo-Makarios, John the Solitary, Pseudo-Dionysios, Gregory of Nyssa, and the Doctors of the Nestorian Church; also includes four writers who do not appear in this book, namely Henanisho of Beit Qôqa, John Bar Penkayé, Nestorius of Nuhadra, and Berikhisho.

196. Beulay, R., 'Jean de Dalyatha', *Dictionnaire de Spiritualité* 8 (Paris 1974) 449–452.
Brief introduction to his life and works.

197. Colless, B. E., 'The Mysticism of John Saba', *Orientalia Christiana Periodica* 39 (1973) 83–102.
Survey of some of the sources of his teaching, which must be read in the light of Beulay's publications on the subject.

198. Colless, B. E., 'Le mystère de Jean Saba', *L'Orient Syrien* 12 (1967) 515–523.
Problems in identifying John Saba: John bar Penkayé or John of Dalyatha?

199. Colless, B. E., 'The Biographies of John Saba', *Parole de l'Orient* 3 (1972) 45–63.
Conflicting traditions about the identity of John Saba.

200. Beulay, R., 'Précisions touchant l'identité et la biographie de Jean Saba de Dalyatha', *Parole de l'Orient* 8 (1977–1988) 87–116.
John of Dalyatha (the mystic) is John Saba and quite distinct from John bar Penkayé (the scholastic).

201. Munitiz, J., 'A Greek 'Anima Christi' Prayer', *Eastern Churches Review* 6 (1974) 170–180.
The 'Anima Christi' may have been influenced by John of Dalyatha's prayer in the discourse on flight from the world (see Sherwood, **194** above, and extract LXVI in the anthology).

ABRAHAM BAR DASHANDAD

202. Mingana, A., 'Mystical treatise by Abraham bar Dashandad', **2**, 185–197, 248–255.
Syriac text and English translation of a letter on the solitary life.

203. Jansen, H. L., 'The Mysticism of Abraham bar Dashandad', *Numen*, 4 (1957) 114–126.

> Analysis of the piece published by Mingana (**202**).

GREGORY BAR HEBRAEUS

204. Bedjan, P., *Liber Ethikon seu Moralia Gregorii Barhebraei*. Paris 1898.

> Syriac text of the *Ethikon* and *Book of the Dove*.

205. Wensinck, A. J., *Bar Hebraeus's Book of the Dove together with some chapters from his Ethikon*. Leiden 1919.

> English translation with detailed introduction to the *Book of Ethics* and *Book of the Dove*.

206. Colless, B. E., 'The Mysticism of Bar Hebraeus', *Orientalia Christiana Periodica* 54 (1988) 153–173.

> Sources of his mysticism, notably Joseph Hazzaya and John of Dalyatha.

207. Teule, Herman G. B., ed., *Gregory Barhebraeus, Ethicon, Memra I*, Corpus Scriptorum Christianorum Orientalium 534–535 [Scriptores Syri 218–219]. Louvain 1993.

> Syriac text and English translation of the first section of the Book of Ethics (**204**).

Scriptural References

Arabic numerals refer to paragraphs in the introduction.
Roman numerals refer to excerpts in the anthology.

Genesis		Judges	
1:2	141	5:24-27	232
2:7	185		
2:24	132	2 Samuel	
3:20	XCI	19:8	56
6–9	284		
14:17-20	29	Psalms	
18:27	93 L	4:6	XVIII
		22:6	93 L
Exodus		24:2	LXXXVII
2:23	23	45:7	28
10:21-23	104	63:2	LXXXVI
12:29-30	23	97:2	LXXXVIII
13:3	23	107:23	109
13:21	109	107:26	237
16:3	32	107:30	109
24:10	71	132:4	XXIX
32:1-6	32		
33:9-23	CIX	Proverbs	
33:22	XXXVII	6:6-8	XXIV
		9:1	CXXIX
Leviticus		Ecclesiastes	
14:4	58	1:14	XXXVII
Numbers		Isaiah	
6:26	XVIII	6:3	LV
19:6	58	8:18	29
		22:13	7
Deuteronomy		33:17	134
8:12-14	32	61:8-10	22
32:18	33	61:10	106

GLOSSARY AND INDEX

Arabic numerals refer to paragraphs in the introduction.
Roman numerals refer to excerpts in the anthology.
Bold Arabic numerals refer to items in the reference bibliography.

Aaron, brother of Moses, and the first High Priest of Israel: 146
abbot, abbacy, head of monastery: 252
Abdisho (see also: Joseph the Visionary): 253
abode, dwelling (see also: indwelling): of God LXXVI; for God XXVII LXXVI;
   Christ as soul's abode LXXXIV
Abraamios, Abramios, 9th-century monk of Saint Sabas monastery: 241
Abraham, Hebrew patriarch: 53 93 94
Abraham bar Dashandad, 8th-century East Syrian mystic: 267–279 XCVII
   195b 202–203
Abraham of Nathpar, 6th-century East Syrian mystic: 226–227 **140–142 195b**
abyss: of God LXXXVIII; of evil LXVI
acedia, accidie, Greek *akedia*, listlessness, one of the 8 passions of Evagrios:
   214 (torpor) 229 (depression) 249 (dejectedness)
Acts of the Apostles: 9 XLVI
Acts of (the Apostle Judas) Thomas: 9 10 11 38 113 164 **31–33**
Adam: 7 50 104 185 187 LXXXI
adamant, diamond or other hard substance: 20 I XI
Adelphios of Edessa, 4th–5th century Syrian mystic: 171–191 213–220 **103–105**
Adiabene, region south of Mosul and east of the Tigris river: 226
admonition (in Song of the Pearl): 30
adoption: by God 137 LV
adoration: with bowed head XIII
advent: second coming of Christ 141 XIV
afterlife: Egypt 4; Babylonia 5–6; 159–160 (see also: world to come)
agate, a hard precious stone: I XI
air, atmosphere: LXXXVIII
Albertus Magnus, Saint Albert of Cologne, 13th-century scientist and theologian:
   128
Alexandria, city of Egypt, ancient centre of Greek science and theology: 219
Al-Ghazali (d. 1111), Muslim theologian and Sufi mystic: 281
all: all in all 222 224 X XC

earth: XXII CXXIV; on earth but departed from the earth LXXVIII
east: 17 274 I III IV V VI VIII
Ecclesiastical Hierarchy, by Pseudo-Dionysios: 119 122
ecstasy, rapture: 64 65 243 246 266 XXXXLVI LXVII LXX LXXII LXXVI LXXIX
   (see also: wonderment)
Edessa, Urhai (now Urfa in Turkey), ancient Syrian city: 8 144 145 149 171 209
   213 219; Persian school of Edessa 209
Egypt, Nile river valley and its desert: 3 4 29 63 259; symbolizing the material
   world 12 18 22 23 24 28 29 32 47 108 113 148 194 195 237 254 272–276
   II–VIII
election, chosen by God, predestination: 14 195; the elect 165 166
Elijah, Eliyahu, Elias, prophet of ancient Israel: 27 88 146
emerald, green precious stone: XXV
Encratism, early ascetic movement, connected with Tatian: 7 146 **29–30**
Enkidu, companion of Gilgamesh: 5
enlightenment: see illumination
Ephrem, Aprem, Saint Ephraim of Nisibis and Edessa, 4th-century Syriac poet
   and theologian: 12 45 58 110 136 143 144–151 152 181 251 XV–XVI **86–94**
Epistles, letters of the Apostles: XLVI
Erigena, Eriugena, Johannes Scotus, 9th-century Irish philosopher-theologian: 128
eschatology, eschatological, concerning the last things: 221–222
Esaias of Sketis, Abba Isaiah, 5th-century monk in Egypt: 73–78 129 237 251
   253 **62–64 195b**
essence: the luminous Essence 224 LXVIII
Essenes, sect of Judaism: 165 (see **15**, 13–23)
ethereality: experiences 255; sounds LIII LIV LV
ethics, morals, morality: 232 281
Ethikon, Book of Ethics, by Gregory Bar Hebraeus: 125 281 **204–206**
Eucharist: 58 148 149 178 181 261
Eugenios of Nisibis, Mar Awgin, legendary founder of Syriac monasticism: 3 4 145
   228 **28**
Eukhites (praying people): 186; (see also: Messallians)
Euphrates, the western river of Mesopotamia: 5
Evagrios Pontikos, Evagrius Ponticus, 4th-century mystic-monk in Egypt: 44 46
   65 66 67–72 83 84 123 129 169 170 176 192 214 221 227 229 231 236 242
   251 253 254 256 265 281 XCIX; Evagrianism 221 242 **49–61 195b**
Eve: daughters of Eve 140
evil, wickedness: 217 222 254 XX XXVIII LI LIX LXIX LXXX XCVII;
   good and evil eventually united in God 222
exodus: of Israel from Egypt 23 32 108 109 113 237 254
exorcism, expulsion of demons: 10 88 177
experience: CXXVI (see also: ethereality, mysticism)
eye, eyes, eyesight: 188 XLVI LII LXXXVII LXXXVIII; of mind LII LV CVI CXI
   CXVIII; of heart 188; of soul XLVI LXXVIII

John, Saint, Apostle, Evangelist: 45

John the Baptizer, John the Baptist: ascetic model 9 146; baptism of Christ 146 200

John Bar Penkayé, John of Penek, author of a history of the world, and the Book of the Merchant, a work of mystical theology, of which two 'centuries' survive: 259 **195b 199 200**

John of Damascus, Johannes Damascenus, Saint, doctor of the church, 8th-century monk of Mar Saba monastery (see: Sabas): 127 177 188

John the Egyptian (John the Solitary of Apamea?): 213 219 **118–120**

John the Monk (John the Solitary?): 170

John the Solitary of Apamea, 5th-century Syrian mystic: 192–208 227 229 234 242 243 253 254 265 XIX–XXII **106–123 195b**

John the Venerable, John Saba, John of Dalyatha, 8th-century East Syrian mystic: 1 10 17 18 19 69 77 86 91 98 125 126 169 175 176 253 258–266 267 283 284 LVI–XCVI **190–201**

John the Visionary (John the Solitary of Apamea?): 90 110, 112

Joseph the Visionary, Yausep Hazzaya, alias ÔAbdisho, 8th-century East Syrian mystic: 1 44 70 71 77 84 85 89 93 95 96 97 128 169 175 176 188 210 252–257 258 265 267 283 XLIII–LV **174–189 195b**

joy, gladness, bliss, delight: 107 108 110 198 227 235 244 245 246 262 277 XIII XIV XIX XXXVII XLIV XLVI XLVII XLVIII LIII LVI LX LXI LXII LXIX LXXI LXXVIII LXXIX LXXXIII LXXXIV LXXXVII CX CXI

Judaism, the religion of the Jewish people: 165

judgement: of God 207 208 XLIV; contemplation of 215 LIII (see also: contemplation)

jug: CXXIV

Julian Saba, 4th-century monk of Edessa: 8 145 150 170 171

justification, being accounted righteous: 217

Justin Martyr, Saint, 2nd-century Christian apologist, teacher of Tatian: 7

Kellia ('Cells'), one of the desert monastic sites in Egypt: 63 (see **15**, 151–167)

Kephalaia Gnostika, Chapters of Knowledge, esoteric sayings of Evagrios: 67 70 176 **54**

kindness: 96 107 LI

king, King of kings: I V VI VII XI XIII; Jesus Christ 156 LXXVII; God 11 17 50 53 56 76 107 114 134 142 234 275

kingdom: I II V VI XIII; of God 14 16 30 53 107 148 171 195 197 221 234 275 276 XIV XV XIX CXI CXX CXXVI; within 211 LXIII CXXVIII

kiss, embrace of love: 44 96 162 VII LI

kneeling, genuflexion, bending the knees, going down on the knees: 245 XXXVII XLVI LXIX

knowledge: XII XXIII C CXXVII; spiritual, divine, knowledge of God 44 46 47 50 51 121 125 137 138 149 150 156 202 217 224 235 236 239 243 244 278

relaxation: XXXVII

renunciation: of family, property, the world, and withdrawal from society 75 85 88 89 100 154 161 164 183 199 212 217 231 233 256 263 XLIV XLV XLIX LXV LXXIII XCVII; of self and reason 121

repentance, returning to God: 37 131 200 233 262 269 XLIV; personified LVII–LVIII

rest, repose: as gift of God 76 137 234 284 LXXI

resurrection: of the dead 7 106 111 132 202 204 244 245 XLVI; of Christ 7 31 106 196 XIV; mystical 224 XIV LXXX

retreat, in monk's cell: 248

revelation: of Christ 100 197 211 LXXIX; divine revelations 126 235 239 245 256 281 284 XXVII XLII LIII LIV LV LIX LXI LXVII LXVIII LXX CXXX

reward: 271 274 277 XXI XLI XLVI LX XCIV XCVII

righteous, upright: 256 XLIV XLVIII L XCVII 152 153 154 155 177 217

righteousness: way of 217; works of 284; hunger for XIV

river: rivers of life LXXXIII

robe, robes: shining 22 27 46 47 50 51 52 57 59 106 107 111 138 141 142 150 195 198 234 244 277 278 II VI X–XIII; of incorruptibility 137 138 178

rock: of revelation (Mount Sinai) XXXVII; of shipwreck XXXVI

ruby, red precious stone: I XI XXV

Sabas, Saint Sabas, Mar Saba (d. 532), founder of a monastery in Palestine: 219 259

Sabbas, 4th-century Syrian monk (Messallian): 186 190

sacraments: inefficacy? (Messallians) 174 178 182

sacrifice, offerings: 149 (fasting) 191 (prayer) 224 (mystical) 235 (prayers) XXVII (spiritual)

sadness, one of the 8 passions of Evagrios: 214

Sahdona, alias Martyrios, 7th-century East Syrian mystic: 191 230–235 260 XXV **145–151 195b**

saints: abode of XIV; celestial LIII; as model LXIX

salt: of truth XIV

salvation, being saved: 137 (deposit) 160 197 245 272 LXXX

sanctification: of soul XLVI LXVII LXX; saying Holy, holy, holy LV

sapphire, transparent blue precious stone: XI; reference to Exodus 24:10 71 242 LII

Sarbug, Greek *laburinthos*, unidentified place in Mesopotamia (see **35**, 255–260): place of demons in The Song of the Pearl III VII

sardonyx: onyx with layers of white sard: XI

Satan, the Devil, the adversary, the enemy, the evil one: 24 26 29 33 107 136 139 147 157 171 172 177 188 197 232 XVIII XXIV LVII LXVI LXIX LXX; fall from heaven XXIV (see also: dragon, serpent)

saviour: XVIII XX XLVI LXXVIII; saved saviour 13

scarlet: 58 I (see also: toga)